# A PRACTICAL GUIDE TO CULTIVATING
## THERAPEUTIC PRESENCE

# A PRACTICAL GUIDE TO CULTIVATING
## THERAPEUTIC PRESENCE

## Shari M. Geller

Foreword by Daniel J. Siegel

American Psychological Association • Washington, DC

Published by
American Psychological Association
750 First Street, NE
Washington, DC 20002
www.apa.org

To order
APA Order Department
P.O. Box 92984
Washington, DC 20090-2984
Tel: (800) 374-2721; Direct: (202) 336-5510
Fax: (202) 336-5502; TDD/TTY: (202) 336-6123
Online: www.apa.org/pubs/books
E-mail: order@apa.org

In the U.K., Europe, Africa, and the Middle East, copies may be ordered from
American Psychological Association
3 Henrietta Street
Covent Garden, London
WC2E 8LU England

Typeset in Goudy by Circle Graphics, Inc., Columbia, MD

Printer: Sheridan Books, Chelsea, MI
Cover Designer: Mercury Publishing Services, Inc., Rockville, MD
Cover Art: *Expanding Into the Moment*, 2010, by Shari M. Geller

The opinions and statements published are the responsibility of the authors, and such opinions and statements do not necessarily represent the policies of the American Psychological Association.

**Library of Congress Cataloging-in-Publication Data**

Names: Geller, Shari M., author. | American Psychological Association
Title: A practical guide to cultivating therapeutic presence / Shari M. Geller.
Description: Washington, DC : American Psychological Association, [2017] |
  Includes bibliographical references and index.
Identifiers: LCCN 2016041088 | ISBN 9781433827167 | ISBN 1433827166
Subjects: | MESH: Psychotherapy | Mindfulness | Interpersonal Relations
Classification: LCC RC480.5 | NLM WM 420 | DDC 616.89/14—dc23 LC record available
  at https://lccn.loc.gov/2016041088

**British Library Cataloguing-in-Publication Data**
A CIP record is available from the British Library.

*Printed in the United States of America*
*First Edition*

http://dx.doi.org/10.1037/0000025-000

To my mother—even though your physical presence is missed, your wit of words and spiritual intrigue have formed who I am today. I am thankful for the love I feel that grows each and every day.

# CONTENTS

# FOREWORD

DANIEL J. SIEGEL

Being present as a psychotherapist is the fundamental state of mind that is the gateway to creating effective psychotherapy. In this masterful practical summary of a life's work, Shari M. Geller powerfully guides us through the art and science of developing the capacity to be present as clinicians so that our clients, our patients, and even our individual selves will benefit. In your hands rests an exquisite compendium of wisdom, research-based concepts, and useful practices that can help you enhance your clinical impact by developing therapeutic presence.

Psychotherapy is the practice of helping the mind, "psyche" having the synonyms of soul, spirit, intellect, and mind. Yet all too often the term *mind* is not defined in the practical fields of mental health and education or in the academic fields of psychology, psychiatry, neuroscience, or even philosophy. Naturally, we use the term *mind* to refer to our feelings, thoughts, and behaviors; we evoke mind with the subjective experience of consciousness; and we often state that the "mind is what the brain does." Mind includes each of these, and even the information processing that goes beneath consciousness. Yet the mind may be more than simply brain activity, and perhaps even more than our private feelings and thoughts.

In the field of interpersonal neurobiology, we view mind as the emergent, self-organizing, embodied *and* relational process that regulates energy and information flow both within us and between us. Optimal self-organization naturally arises with a process of linking differentiated parts to one another—a fundamental drive of complex systems that can be termed *integration*. With integration, a system achieves a FACES flow of being flexible, adaptive, coherent, energized, and stable. These are the components of harmony, the outcome of integration, and what can be proposed as the essence of health. When not integrated, systems tend to move toward chaos, rigidity, or both. A reinterpretation of mental distress revealed in the symptoms of the various syndromes of mental disorder is that these each can be viewed as an example of chaos or rigidity. In this perspective, helping those with mental suffering is carried out through the process of cultivating integration.

How can we achieve this? We cultivate well-being and integration through our relationships that are filled with therapeutic presence. Presence is the portal for integration to arise.

When presence is blocked, integration may be impaired. As Shari Geller magnificently reveals in this guide, cultivating presence promotes healing. Without presence, effective therapy is compromised; with presence, the natural capacity for healing is released within the attuned and resonating relationship that cultivates trust and unleashes the innate drive for integration.

As I read these pages, I was filled with a deep sense of gratitude, and awe, for how Geller's fabulous guide seamlessly weaves the science of presence with practical steps for how presence can be cultivated more fully in our clinical work. Filled with stories of actual therapeutic sessions, including the inner workings of the clinician's own mind, along with cutting-edge research findings from clinical investigations as well as neuroscientific studies, *A Practical Guide to Cultivating Therapeutic Presence* can serve as a foundational work for all therapists. Whether you are new to our wonderful profession or are a seasoned clinician, this guide can help you develop the "therapeutic relational presence" that not only is key to effective psychotherapy but will also enhance your own mental and medical well-being. A wide array of research has suggested that when we cultivate the integration that presence facilitates, we develop physiological and psychological well-being, and those directly communicating with us will sense the connection and resonance that presence permits and will be moved toward integrative health. With our deep interconnections, even the larger world around us will benefit as well. It's a win-win-win situation. The question is, are you ready to begin? There's no better place to start, or continue your practice of presence, than right now and right here. Enjoy the journey of being that lays ahead in these powerful and inspiring pages!

# PREFACE

When someone deeply listens to you—it is like holding out a dented cup
you've had since childhood—and watching it fill up with cold, fresh water.
When it balances on top of the brim, you are understood.
When it overflows and touches your skin, you are loved.

—John Fox (1995, p. 153)

My first experience with therapeutic presence was a personal one. Not long after my mother died in my late teens, I had several severe abdominal symptoms that despite numerous tests were not clearly diagnosed. Eventually one doctor told me that my gut-wrenching pain likely was emotional at its core, even though clear physical pain sent me to the emergency department frequently. At that time irritable bowel syndrome was barely understood, yet its psychophysiological nature seemed to fit given the stress and grief I was "swallowing" inside.

I began psychoanalysis, seeing Dr. W two to three mornings a week. I tried to share my grief and early family difficulties, and I watched him scratch on his pad with a glazed look in his eyes. A few times I caught him nodding off as his eyes became heavy. I also once noticed that there were doodles in the margins of his pad (and not very good ones!). He would offer me irrelevant theories on my issues. When I shared with him that I did not feel heard, he analyzed this in terms of my early background with tumultuous parental relationships and the complicated loss of my mother—no acknowledgment that he was distant or nodding off. I felt alone in that relationship. In spirit of my tenacity to learn, I stayed with the therapy hoping I would learn what *not* to do when I became a therapist, but increasingly I felt lonely and frustrated.

Eventually I found a new therapist, Beverley, who approached our sessions with what I now understand to be therapeutic presence. She was fully attuned with my experience and made me feel understood, safe, and deeply held. I felt connected with her as she read my experience, even when I did not know what I was feeling. I was able to engage in therapeutic work that was challenging, yet felt possible in the safe arms of her presence. To this day I am grateful for her approach with me, as it allowed me to feel accepting of my pain, grief, and anxiety, while remaining able to challenge my inner world. I recognize that the only way I could engage in the painful work of therapy was when I felt safe and connected.

This experience led to my interest in the humanistic–experiential tradition under the supervision of my mentor, coauthor, and dear friend, Dr. Leslie Greenberg. My research in therapeutic presence began as a dissertation with his mentorship and has evolved over the past couple of decades of research, writing, training, and being a psychologist. My clinical therapy practice affirmed that when I was present, I could feel my clients suffering with my body, with calm and compassion, and I would hear responses in myself that facilitated their growth. I recall one client looking up at me as a tear streamed down her face, sharing "I feel heard for the first time in my life. It makes me want to break down this wall inside, and stop feeling so alone." My eyes welled up as I could feel something profound shift in her and in our relationship.

I believe in personal practice and the embodiment of presence. My understanding of therapeutic presence is also informed by a 26-year personal practice of mindfulness meditation and group drumming. My training, research, personal practice, and years of clinical experience have taught me some essential principles and practices for cultivating presence in life and in the therapy room that I intend to share here with you. I hope they are helpful for you and, in turn, in your relationships with clients and in everyday life.

I feel incredibly grateful for the many people and influences that have contributed to the evolution of this book. I have experienced a number of life changes in this time of writing, and there are so many people, places, and moments of inspiration that have been a part of bringing this vision to fruition. I wish to extend my gratitude to each and every one, although I may not have the space to acknowledge all here.

I want to thank my mentor and dear friend Leslie Greenberg, who has taught me how to unfold such an ineffable experience in a way that is clinically meaningful. I am grateful to have practiced and studied with mindfulness and psychotherapy masters, including neuroscience researchers and theorists Daniel Siegel and Stephen Porges, who have led the path in clarifying the power of presence and safety in relationship. I also wish to thank my clients, who have taught me about the value of being in the moment and the impact of when I am not there.

I am thankful for the unconditional love and playfulness of my therapy dog Zen and for the countless hours we spent at Scenic Sounds immersed in writing. Also for my writing moments that extended to Prague, Israel, and Bucerias, Mexico—places of calm and beauty from which my writing could flow with ease.

I am grateful to my dear friend Lee Freedman for her mindful way of evoking an experience of presence with photography and the generous offer to include her images in this book. I am also thankful for the invaluable editing and feedback from medical student Rebecca Lauwers, whose presence will certainly benefit her future patients. I value the feedback on the manuscript I received from Lee Freedman, Michele Chaban, and Camilla Graziani. I am thankful for the support and feedback I received from Susan Reynolds, David Becker, Liz Brace, Caroline Barnes, and the good design sense of Ron Teeter at the American Psychological Association.

There are many others, such as my friends and colleagues who have supported me in this journey as I hid away to immerse myself in this writing process (you know who you are!). Gratitude to Shelley, Monty, and the incredible team at our Centre for MindBody Health; the amazing group of therapists at my associate practice in Grey/Bruce; and (in no particular order) Lee, Michele, Yifaht, Serine, Rhonda, Andrew S., Andrew B., Angie, Solomon, Ian, Natty G., Jonni, Hilary, Gayle, Marni, and their beautiful children. I am appreciative to my yoga buddies and Dr. Cathy Hornby, whom I would visit each time I was immersing into a writing period so my mind could slow down and my body could come into alignment and integration.

I am thankful for my family and their unconditional love, their grounding support, and most of all their humor, including my Dad, Wendy, Stuart, Susan, and Debbie. A special thanks to my treasured nieces and nephew, Jessica, Samantha, and Zachary, who always invite me to step out of busyness and into the moment to have fun, laugh, and find balance and joy in being together (that is when they are not traveling the world!).

Of course last and most I offer my deepest gratitude to my Beshert and beloved partner, Camilla. Her constant presence, unconditional love, and unbounded support taught me what it means to truly feel held in the safe and loving arms of another. Her profound ability to attune has allowed me to expand into life and love, and be the best of myself. I would not have been able to complete this book, amidst a leg break and a busy life, without her grounding and love. I am so grateful. I am also thankful for and inspired by her children—Rachel, with her kindness, empathy, and zest for life, and Sarah, with her curiosity, humor, and passion.

I could not be more blessed to truly experience how love, connection, and presence serve as the foundation to a life that thrives and can serve others. Thank you all.

# A PRACTICAL GUIDE TO CULTIVATING
## THERAPEUTIC PRESENCE

©2016 M. Lee Freedman.

# INTRODUCTION

I've learned that people will forget what you said, people will forget what
you did, but people will never forget how you made them feel.
—Maya Angelou (as quoted in Booth & Hachiya, 2004, p. 14)

Thank you for joining me in this dialogue about deepening your therapeutic presence. Together we will explore this positive way of relating for the
benefit of others and our own well-being. Over 20 years of reflecting, training,
and writing on therapeutic presence have crystallized for me that how we are
with clients is more essential than what we do to promote their growth. This
is supported by psychotherapy research that has consistently affirmed the
relationship as the most consistent predictor of change (Allison & Rossouw,
2013; Norcross, 2011). Yet what contributes to the relationship has been
more ethereal. This is changing. A nascent body of research is clarifying that
*therapeutic presence* is a necessary and preliminary step to creating safety in
our clients and facilitating a strong therapeutic alliance and effective therapy
(Dunn, Callahan, Swift, & Ivanovic, 2013; Geller & Greenberg, 2002, 2012;
Geller, Greenberg, & Watson, 2010; Hayes & Vinca, 2011; Pos, Geller, &
Oghene, 2011). As Maya Angelou eloquently wrote, how we make others
feel leaves the most lasting impression.

http://dx.doi.org/10.1037/0000025-001
*A Practical Guide to Cultivating Therapeutic Presence*, by S. M. Geller
Copyright © 2017 by the American Psychological Association. All rights reserved.

## WHAT IS THERAPEUTIC PRESENCE?

Therapeutic presence is a way of being with your clients that optimizes the doing of therapy. It involves bringing all of yourself to the encounter and being present on multiple levels: physically, emotionally, cognitively, spiritually, and relationally. The in-body experience of therapeutic presence includes (a) being grounded and centered in yourself, while (b) feeling deeply immersed in the moment, with (c) a larger sense of expansion or spaciousness. The first three qualities could reflect presence in daily life, such as when you are engrossed in a conversation or watching a sunset. The next quality is what makes it therapeutic: that your presence is with the intention of (d) being compassionately with and for your client, in service of their well-being. Therapeutic presence involves attuning to your clients' experience, and to your personal experience of being with them, moment to moment. It entails an intimacy with others that is highly absorptive and a connection within yourself that is grounded and centered.

Therapeutic presence goes beyond a state of being to evoke a relational process. When you are present with your clients, they can experience feeling met, felt, and understood. This activates a neurophysiological experience of safety, which strengthens the therapeutic relationship and allows for optimal engagement in the work of therapy. There is a reciprocal relationship between your extending yourself with your clients and their feeling your presence, as you both develop greater presence within and between you. A portal opens up to an I–Thou encounter that is larger than each individual (Buber, 1958), also known as therapeutic relational presence (Geller, 2013a; Geller & Greenberg, 2012). Relational presence evokes a sense of connection, and of being seen and seeing, as no other human experience does. It is ultimately this shared presence that leads to therapeutic change.

## WHY A BOOK ON CULTIVATING THERAPEUTIC PRESENCE?

Although the value of presence and the therapeutic relationship is not new for us, guidance on how to cultivate and sustain this experience is virtually absent from psychotherapy literature and training. There are many therapy approaches; some are instructional in nature, with steps on what to do with your client. These steps can be difficult to apply clinically without a moment-to-moment attunement to our client. Our clients (like ourselves) are complex human beings with different manners of expression, personalities, issues, and varying needs. Without a foundation on how to be with and relate to our clients moment to moment, with sensitivity to who they are and their unique experience, prescriptive steps will be less effective. Alternatively, building relationships that are deeply immersed in the present facilitates your clients' natural growth and supports the precise timing of your responses and interventions to align with their readiness.

My hope is that this book will serve as a practical guide to strengthen your therapeutic presence. Together we will explore the skills of presence in the therapy room. Ways of listening, relating, and responding will be illuminated. You will also learn specific breathing, postures, and vocalizations that promote greater calm and connection for both you and your clients. These practices are grounded in neuroscience, particularly Stephen Porges's (2011) polyvagal theory, which teaches us how our prosody (rhythm) of voice, open posture, and breathing patterns can evoke safety in our own body and in others we are with. These phrases (prosody, open posture, breathing patterns—among others) come up repeatedly throughout the book because of how important the physical expressions of presence are to conjuring a sense of safety in your clients and, thus, their openness and engagement in the work of therapy. I will also offer suggestions to create the conditions for presence in your own life, as cultivating presence requires us to care for our personal relationships and our overall well-being.

## CULTIVATING PRESENCE IN THE MIND, BODY, AND BRAIN

The perspective offered in this book honors the integrated nature of body, mind, brain, and relationships and the vital role they play in our therapeutic process. This view reflects a fusion of humanistic–experiential principles, Eastern perspectives, and neuroscience. In humanistic–experiential perspectives, we first need to be in touch with our emotions and ongoing flow of experience as felt in the body (Gendlin, 1978; Greenberg, 2007, 2010; Greenberg, Rice, & Elliott, 1993; Perls, 1970; Rogers, 1980). In this way, the mind and emotions are embodied: Emotions involve bodily changes that have a strong effect on our thoughts and behaviors (Damasio, 1999, 2005; Greenberg, 2010; Niedenthal, 2007). Current perspectives in psychology are beginning to recognize the concept of embodiment that is central to this view, that the body has a major influence on the mind and psychological processes (Glenberg, 2010; Siegel, 2010, 2011; Tschacher & Bergomi, 2011). This is aligned with Eastern perspectives such as traditional Chinese medicine, where mind and the brain are viewed as living in the heart (Yu,

2009). Neuroscience is providing emerging support for the interconnection of mind, body, and relationships (Porges, 2011; Schore, 2009, 2012; Siegel, 2010, 2011).

Presence is an embodied experience, and we need to access presence in the body if we wish to influence our mental states. A lot of the practices are therefore designed to increase connection with your body, so that you can take the necessary steps to regain presence when needed. For example, noticing when we are slumped or when our body or facial muscles are tense can inform us that we may be emotionally reactive or shut down. By taking deep exhalations and relaxing our body posture, we can be aware of our disconnection, calm ourselves, and reconnect with the present moment.

This perspective also holds that we are relational. We are interconnected with others, and therefore we are constantly influencing each other through our mental and emotional states. This can be intentional in a positive direction. If I am calm and grounded, my clients' nervous system can entrain with mine, and they too become calmed. The opposite is also true—my agitation or distraction can cause my client to shut down. With awareness, we can shift our bodily state so we are less thrown by our clients' emotional states. For example, I can ground myself in the present while sensing my clients' emotional world, to keep myself steady and to evoke a relational environment for my clients so they can be calm. Presence can therefore be evoked through harmony in the body, as well as in harmonious and safe relationships. This book holds the view that body, brain, and relationships are intertwined, with the body being a portal through which we can access and express our presence.

## WHY INCLUDE NEUROSCIENCE IN A PSYCHOTHERAPY BOOK?

This book draws on current neuroscience research to illuminate how the practices offered can enhance therapeutic presence. Current neuroscience is validating what humanistic perspectives and Eastern philosophies have said for many years, providing a glimpse of the profound impact we have on others at the levels of brain and body (Geller & Porges, 2014; Porges, 2011; Schore, 2009, 2012; Siegel, 2010, 2011). Understanding the neurophysiological process of presence in ourselves, with clients and in relationships, helps us fine-tune our therapy and relational skills so that we can activate states of safety, growth, and healing. It assists us as we look after our own physiology as therapists. It also supports our creative and flexible use of the appropriate technique in response to what is alive in the moment.

You may intuitively know how to adjust your vocal tone with a client when she or he is in distress or convey a message with your body that you are harmless. Grounding your technique in neuroscience theory can help you link new concepts and familiar experiences in a way that binds your approach into a more cohesive whole, from which a deeper understanding can emerge. For example, I am more inclined to breathe in rhythm with my client's breath (a process I refer to later in this book as *entrainment breathing*) when I understand how it invites a greater read of my client's experience and invites her or his body to settle in connection with mine. It also motivates me to practice (both in life and in session) so I can become more adept at cultivating and using my presence to evoke safety and connection. We fuel our commitment to practice when we understand what is happening when we are present and the potential for good that comes with it.

The new insights that come from creating dialogue across different perspectives speak to the importance of an interdisciplinary approach. If we view presence from only one perspective, we limit our access to its richness. Engaging dialogue across perspectives helps to maintain a broad focus and understanding of the process of change.

This book includes some basics on the brain as they relate to psychotherapy that will also help keep you current. It is possible that your clients are reading popular sources that reference the brain, so grounding the therapeutic process in neuroscience can provide you with a language to talk to your clients about the fullness of their experience. It can also help them engage more deeply in their own growth process. The science lends legitimacy to interventions some clients may otherwise dismiss. The recent spark in mindfulness research and practice is a testament to this.

Although I find neuroscience exciting, I recognize that not everyone may see the value in knowing what is happening at the neuronal level during the therapy process, and that sometimes encountering new ways of conceptualizing experiences can be uncomfortable. However, I believe that this information is essential to the optimal practice of therapeutic presence. Know that it takes time and repetition to really absorb content that is of a different realm than we may be used to. I have gone into detail in Chapter 3 to provide a primer on the brain in relation to presence. In later chapters I then link some of the material back to the brain to invite an understanding of how certain practices can activate processes in the brain and body. This purposeful repetition occurs so you can connect experiential and conceptual perspectives during practical application. It also provides you with more exposure to the most important material, to help you encode the information in long-term memory. With practice, you may discover that these techniques feel as organic to the healing process as I believe them to be.

## A PARADIGM SHIFT: FROM DOING TO BEING

To really cultivate the quality of relating that I am proposing, we need to become comfortable with slowing down to be present within ourselves and in our relationships. We are a society that reveres being busy, achieving through following particular steps, and being independent. This view can infiltrate the therapy setting through prescriptive approaches that over-emphasize stepwise efficiency, filling time with tasks, and being independently masterful at technique. Rather than measuring effectiveness as how much we do and how quickly we do it, and rigidly adhering to a series of steps, we need to focus on our interdependent nature and the value of flexibly discovering what is not yet known through opening to the moment. This requires a value shift from prioritizing doing to focusing on being, to bring greater presence and a different kind of attention to what we do. This aligns with the habits of highly effective people who emphasize slowing down, setting limits, living a balanced life, being flexible, and working with others instead of alone (Covey, 2004).

Another misconception from society that may subtly impact therapists is that to be effective with others we need to learn to influence them. In fact, presence is often misconstrued as charisma. Although our urge to help may reflect our wanting our clients to feel better, be happier, and live more meaningful lives, it can also reflect our own desire to feel masterful in bringing about these outcomes. Overvaluing influence undermines the goals of therapy. Relating effectively requires us to see ourselves as a facilitator and partner with our clients in their growth, rather than as an authority on their lives. My students in training have viewed this shift in perspective as a relief. To put aside the pressure to be an authority on their client, rather than respond to this basic human need to be heard, as only when clients feel felt and understood can change even be possible.

Focusing on presence also means shifting from traditional ways of knowing (thinking and analysis) to knowing through sensing and feeling, then allowing our cognition to emerge from that place of subjectively and relationally being in the moment. To do this, we must know our inner world intimately, as we are interconnected with others. This requires building capacity and competency in being with and knowing your subjective world and in being relationally present, while being able to shift back and forth between what we have objectively learned as professionals and what we are subjectively sensing in the moment.

This paradigm shift also invites us to see being efficient and effective as encompassing taking care of ourselves, working together in communities, and nourishing our personal relationships. It asks us to listen deeply to what we need to feel healthy and whole. This might mean taking time to work through the issues that keep us from being more connected in our relationships and to reflect on how to better align our values with our actions.

Relating with presence is very difficult in a world where we are flooded with distractions, all vying for our attention. Technology and e-mail demands, along with pressure to produce outcomes quickly, have compromised our basic ability to slow down and have a healthy relationship with others and ourselves. Yet we can slow down, with conscious attention and practice. And the paradox is that in slowing down we can often become more productive and efficient than when we are living by the rules of a fast-paced, achievement-focused world, because we are less burnt out, are more joyful, and feel healthier and more supported.

This book is therefore not as much about what we do, as how we do it. It is about approaching our clients in a state that is open and ready to receive, clear of an agenda, so we are able to relate intimately and engage fully with their inner world. It is a shift from a paradigm of independence to one of interdependence, from prescriptive practice to collaboration, and from care of others to including care for ourselves.

## VISION FOR PSYCHOTHERAPY TRAINING

Part of this paradigm shift invites psychotherapy training across traditions to include foundational training in cultivating therapeutic presence and promoting positive therapeutic relationships. Currently, most training programs guide students in intervention and techniques, with little guidance on how to be when offering these tasks. They may talk about the importance of presence and therapeutic relationships, yet without a focus on cultivating these skills. I am not minimizing the value of interventions. I am suggesting that an inclusion of cultivating presence and personal and relational growth should be of equal importance. This book can serve as a resource and manual, and in the final chapter I provide some further suggestions for training.

Presence is trainable, as evidenced by several years of workshops in which I have seen people shift from rigid ways of relating to responding with fluidity and flexibility in the moment. Their ability to engage with presence improved with sustained commitment to practice. The brain itself changes to a healthier state when people are present in relationship (Schore, 2009,

2012; Siegel, 2011). Practice in presence enhances brain, body, and relational integration (Hanson & Mendius, 2010; Siegel, 2010), which means you can develop greater access to the presence experience in session.

In the chapters to follow, we learn a lot more about how the mind, brain, and body contribute to the experience of presence, but here's a taste: Mindfulness training, which is a fundamental practice in cultivating therapeutic presence, helps to balance the nervous system and can foster the ability to feel or take in the depth of the client's pain with greater intimacy and less reactivity (Baldini, Parker, Nelson, & Siegel, 2014; Escuriex & Labbé, 2011; Hanson & Mendius, 2009). I propose that training also needs to include relational practices (e.g., group drumming, relational mindfulness) to explore how we can be open and intimate in relating with our clients, while remaining in contact with our own experience. This simultaneous connection to self and others is the foundation for relating with presence.

If the relationship is the foundation of good therapy, and presence the foundation of a good relationship, we must teach future clinicians the art of being present within and with others. It is essential to balance the doing mode of therapy with the being mode, for greatest efficacy in our client's healing. This book will equip therapists with the tools to provide a more complete therapeutic experience and optimal conditions for their clients' growth.

## OVERVIEW OF THE BOOK

This book picks up where my previous book coauthored with Leslie Greenberg leaves off. Our previous book, *Therapeutic Presence: A Mindful Approach to Effective Therapy*, focused mostly on the theory of therapeutic presence (with some practices woven in), to help understand the richness of the therapeutic presence model from a knowledge-based perspective (Geller & Greenberg, 2012). The current book moves from theory to practice to evoke an experiential and neurophysiological understanding of presence, both in relationship with clients in session and in your life. I have written in a conversational style so that you and I can explore the practices and skills of presence, not just as distant concepts but also as direct experiences. I have also incorporated vignettes[1] to illuminate the concepts in examples that are relatable.

---

[1]Any references to clients in the vignettes or any other clinical material in this book have been disguised to protect client confidentiality.

Part I does infuse this personal approach with theory so that you can obtain some grounding in therapeutic presence even if you have not read the first book. Chapter 1 focuses on an introduction to the concept of presence in therapy, including discerning it from other therapeutic concepts such as mindfulness, listening, and countertransference. Chapter 2 provides a background on how experiences akin to presence have been viewed in different theoretical approaches over time. Chapter 3 provides current neuroscience understanding and background of therapeutic presence, as it is the platform on which many of the practices and skills are built.

The focus of Part II is more directly clinical, helping you develop the skill of presence in session. Chapter 4 provides guidance on creating the conditions for therapeutic presence before a session, so you arrive at the encounter with a sense of presence in yourself, clear of agenda and preconceptions. Chapters 5 and 6 are both focused on presence in session itself. Chapter 5 explores how to receive your client from that place of openness you have fostered, including reading the moment-to-moment experience of your client and attuning to how this is experienced within yourself. Chapter 6 teaches how to skillfully respond to your client from the information you have received. This includes promoting contact non-verbally with your client to foster safety, using neurophysiological practices and principles such as entrainment and resonance. Chapter 7 discusses the challenges you might face in being therapeutically present, with some suggestions for overcoming them.

Once you have a sense of the clinical importance of presence and how to skillfully facilitate therapy with presence, we focus on strengthening your personal presence in your daily life. Being adept in therapeutic presence goes beyond what you do in the therapy encounter to how you live day to day.

Part III is brimming with in-life practices. The chapters are designed around an empirically validated model of therapeutic presence (Geller & Greenberg, 2002). Many practices are described in detail, so you can follow them easily and also use them to facilitate the cultivation of presence in others (e.g., students, trainees). Practices for daily life are first described in Chapter 8 with mindfulness and experiential exercises. Chapter 9 explores practices you can engage in your life to boost particular aspects of the process of therapeutic presence, such as receptivity, inward attuning, and extending and contact. Chapter 10 invites you to foster the in-body qualities of the experience of presence: grounding, immersion, expansion, and being with and for the other.

Part IV is focused on the integration of in-life presence with therapeutic presence to reach an even deeper relational connection. Chapter 11 provides a glimpse at therapeutic relational presence, which is a larger and more expansive experience of connection reflecting the spiritual domain as viewed through the relationship. Finally, Chapter 12 pulls together the learning from this book as well as suggest future directions.

Appendix A provides you with resources, tools, and smartphone applications to help cultivate presence in your life and relationships. Appendices B and C include markers for therapists' presence and clients' safety. Appendix D offers you a model for optimizing your therapy session with therapeutic presence.

## How To Use This Book

This book is ideal if you are an experienced therapist looking for a renewal of your therapy practice and your life. It can also be a valuable resource for novice therapists and/or as a practical guide if you are a trainer, so that you can guide your students in cultivating this foundational approach as a part of your training program.

I encourage you to explore the practices offered throughout this book directly so that you can get a feel for the process of and challenges to cultivating this in-the-moment state of being. Practicing presence involves both informal practice in your daily life and formal intentional practices. I recommend you set aside a time each day (20–30 minutes) for intentional presence practice and self-care. To embody presence requires time to immerse yourself in the sensory experiences of the moment. To support this I further recommend going on a retreat or taking a workshop that is focused on cultivating presence, such as through individually or relationally based mindfulness (see Chapter 12 and Appendix A for suggestions). To support the value of self-care and a renewed sense of well-being, you will be encouraged to attend to stress, unresolved issues, and any personal challenges to experiencing the type of intimacy that presence entails.

Throughout the book I offer different practices to evoke various aspects of therapeutic presence. However, the benefits of some are overlapping. The different styles of practices offered are an invitation for you to notice what you personally may gravitate to, as I believe it is more likely you will put into place that which you are naturally inclined toward. Explore them all to see what is the right fit for you.

I encourage you to take several pauses throughout this book, to allow the concepts and practices to infuse into your body and experience. To support this, each chapter begins with an image and a quote. The majority of the images were created by mindfulness-based psychiatrist M. Lee Freedman[2] through a practice of presence, where one uses the camera as an opportunity to fully sense the experience in the moment, including the relationship with

---

[2]Where noted, photographs are used with permission from M. Lee Freedman. Copyright ©2016 by M. Lee Freedman.

the subject. These images are designed to evoke a feeling of the subject of the chapter before you immerse yourself in descriptive words.

I encourage you to linger with the photo and quote before absorbing the chapter content, to activate a felt experience of the topic. Read the quote while taking a few full breaths, sensing the feeling of the words in your body. Then allow yourself to sense the image just as you experience it, noticing the feeling evoked in your body as you zoom in on an aspect of the image and then widen your focus to take in the whole. Attention to your sensory world using the image and quote can help to activate a right-brain felt experience processing of information. This will complement your left-brain rational understanding so that over time these different ways of processing can come together and you can experience the material from a more integrated internal state. This is also true of the practices within the chapters.

**Transition Practices**

To further support the absorption of material and to open more fully to the moment, each chapter closes with an opportunity to pause for a brief breath awareness practice. Pausing with a compassionate awareness is the hallmark of presence. It allows us to notice what we are experiencing, to clear ourselves inside of the remains of where we have just been, and to enter into the next moment with a more open and present stance. This helps us to fully experience what comes next without the overload or distraction of what came before. Practicing mindful transitions is especially important when transitioning between sessions to help you release any emotional residue following a session and to enter into the next one feeling clear, open, and present. The practices are of course optional, so choose what you feel curious about engaging in, knowing they are here for you if you choose to strengthen your experience of presence.

There is no better time to start cultivating presence than now. Enjoy this brief mindful breathing practice as a way of pausing and beginning to explore your breath as an anchor to the present moment. It is designed to help you be in touch with the here and now of your body and to use your breath as an anchor into the moment, which are central components of cultivating presence.

### TRANSITION PRACTICE: FEELING THE RHYTHM OF YOUR BREATH

- Pause and invite your awareness into this moment by bringing your attention to your breath.

- Rest your hand on your belly to physically connect to your inhale and exhale.
- Feel the rise and fall of your hand on your belly in rhythm with your inhale and exhale.
- Take a few full breaths while noticing the sensations of your breathing.
- When you are ready, return your attention to reading or to the next phase of your day.

# I
# THEORY

©2016 M. Lee Freedman.

# 1

# THERAPEUTIC PRESENCE: THE FOUNDATION FOR EFFECTIVE THERAPY

What opportunities of understanding we let pass by because at a single decisive moment we were, with all our knowledge, lacking in the simple virtue of a full human presence.

—Karl Jaspers (as quoted in May, 1983, p. 157)

Think of a difficult time when someone was there for you. Perhaps it was a special family member or friend who really helped you through a trying moment. How did it make you feel? What was it like to be seen, heard, and enveloped with compassion and presence? Will you ever forget that person or time? Likely not. Even fleeting moments with someone who was compassionate and present with us are moments we will never forget.

Now contrast it with a memory of when someone was not present. How did that feel? Or an experience of when you were absent for someone, and it caused immeasurable distress. It could be a loved one or a client. You will likely not forget that one either. As Karl Jaspers illuminated, when we are not present we create misunderstandings; even more detrimental, we can cause others to emotionally shut down and disappear from us.

My experiences with a highly absent therapist and a highly present therapist, as shared in the Preface, fueled my intrigue to discover further

http://dx.doi.org/10.1037/0000025-002
*A Practical Guide to Cultivating Therapeutic Presence*, by S. M. Geller

the healing impact of therapists' presence. Now, decades later, I hope my understanding through research and clinical practice helps solidify why and how therapeutic presence can be the most valuable way we can be with our clients.

## THERAPEUTIC PRESENCE: AN ESSENTIAL WAY OF BEING

Therapeutic presence is the foundation for a positive therapeutic relationship and effective therapy. It is a way we can receptively attune with our clients, within ourselves, and with the moment-to-moment unfolding of therapy. Approaching clients in this present state, without agenda or preconception, invites a way of listening that is finely tuned to the moment. When we receive and attune with our clients in the moment, they feel safe, heard, and understood, which is the essence of promoting positive change. When we feel and read our clients' experience, responses and interventions emerge that are in resonance with what is most helpful. Relating with a calming presence also invites our clients' nervous system to calm, and they feel safer and regulated through our interpersonal connection (Geller & Porges, 2014).

An empirically validated model of therapeutic presence serves as the framework for this book (Geller & Greenberg, 2002, 2012). This model illuminates three overarching categories by which therapeutic presence can be understood: *preparing* the ground for presence to emerge, the *process* of presence itself, and the in-body *experience*. I have taken the qualities from the model and transported them into the clinical encounter to further your understanding of therapeutic presence in action.

## THERAPEUTIC PRESENCE UNPACKED

Therapeutic presence is a way of preparing for therapy. Our intention for self-care and to cultivate presence in our own lives, and in our personal relationships, allows presence to be experienced with greater ease in the therapeutic session. Taking the time to become present before a session can improve therapy outcome. For example, research has shown that just 5 minutes of centering prior to a session improves session outcome and reduces clients' psychological distress (Dunn, Callahan, Swift, & Ivanovic, 2013). Preparing for presence can clear the emotional residue from a previous therapy session so you can begin each session feeling open, energized, and refreshed.

Therapeutic presence is a process or way of doing therapy. As defined in the model (Geller & Greenberg, 2002), you are first (a) open and *receptive* to clients' experience, attuning to their verbal and nonverbal expressions. You then (b) *attune inwardly* to your resonance with clients' in-the-moment experience, which serves as a guide to (c) *extend and promote contact*. With therapeutic presence you can monitor your own experience in therapy (Geller, 2013a). Your inner sensory system tells you how your client is receiving your responses and interventions and what is occurring moment to moment in the relationship. This helps you to recognize the optimal moments for particular responses or interventions so they are offered with the greatest impact and precision, and in resonance with what is emerging in the now.

Therapeutic presence is an internal experience. When you are deeply present to an experience or person, the body qualities are palpable. This experience includes feeling (a) *grounded*, centered, and in contact with yourself, while being (b) *immersed* with your clients' pain and suffering. There is a simultaneous experience of (c) *expansion*, in which a larger perspective and spaciousness emerges amidst the detailed attention to the moment. Therapeutic presence is infused with compassion, as you are (d) *with and for* the other, in service of your client's healing process. These qualities are combined to create the whole experience, yet focusing on aspects helps to determine which aspect you may need to grow or strengthen.

Therapeutic presence is also a relational experience. When clients perceive us as present with them, they are invited to become more present to themselves and in the relationship. A larger state of shared presence begins to emerge. With relational presence, therapists and clients are in synchronicity, which is felt as vitality, flow, and connection. This supports an intersubjective consciousness or sharing of the same emotional landscape (Geller & Greenberg, 2012; Stern, 2004). In these moments, we are in synch in a way that optimizes therapeutic movement.

Therapeutic presence is growth promoting for therapists, clients, and the therapeutic relationship. When we are present we feel energized, balanced, effective, and less burdened by the difficult emotional work of psychotherapy. Clients feel heard, understood, and safe, which is experienced on a neurophysiological level and even outside of conscious awareness (Geller & Porges, 2014; Porges & Carter, 2014). This sense of safety softens their defenses, allowing them to become open to their own experience and to us, and to engage in the work of therapy.

Therapeutic presence is a way of communicating to your client a feeling of safety and understanding. Presence is conveyed through body posture, gestures, and entrainment of breath and prosody (vocal tone) in rhythm with clients (Geller & Porges, 2014). We are responding to what is unspoken using nonverbal means, and our clients are receiving this and feeling heard, felt, seen, and accepted.

## Nonpresence or Absence

One way to understand presence is to explore what it means to be absent or distracted. For example, busyness before a session can prevent presence from emerging, as can the inability to manage our emotions in session. The following are examples of nonpresence prior to the session:

- staying busy, moving from one session right into the next without pause;
- ignoring bodily needs, such as hunger, thirst, and bathroom needs;
- squeezing in e-mail checking, and calls, without a moment's pause; and
- feeling stressed or overwhelmed by one's own unresolved or ongoing issues.

The following are examples of nonpresence during the session:

- continuously checking the time;
- having a predetermined idea of what is needed or what is "right" for the client;
- keeping too far of an emotional distance from the client;
- being too enmeshed with a client and losing a sense of self;
- feeling overwhelmed by the client's emotional response;
- making self-judgments at own responses or misunderstandings;
- feeling bored, tired, or sleepy;
- being preoccupied with events or needs prior to or after a session; and
- not hearing what client is communicating (i.e., missing words or whole sentences as well as not noticing nonverbal expressions).

And finally, the following are examples of nonpresence following the session:

- lack of vitality,
- fatigue,
- self-criticism,
- relief that session is over,
- agitation,
- inner tension, and
- lack of clarity or focus.

Some of these experiences can be informational. For example, boredom or tiredness could be your resonance with your clients' current state (i.e., sensing they are shutting down emotionally) or a countertransference response (you are feeling shut down emotionally). Stay tuned for how to discern and work with these cues in Chapters 5 through 7.

## Paradoxes

The experience of therapeutic presence has many paradoxes and thus requires that we have a dual level of consciousness. We are asked to balance both the subjective and the objective. For example, we must constantly shift our awareness between the internal and external (self and others) and from being deeply connected yet separate and reflective. We need to be absorbed and in contact with our clients' suffering, yet remain grounded and unshaken. This steady yet immersed awareness allows us to listen deeply and respond effectively. Examples of how being present requires this dual level of awareness and experience are illustrated in the categories below.

In your experience of being with your clients and in the relationship:

- being intimately engaged and resonant with your client's emotions yet remaining spacious, calm, and centered;
- accepting your client in the totality of his or her experience, yet offering new possibilities or an environment in which to make novel discoveries;
- being spontaneous but only as it directly relates to or benefits your client;
- allowing your personal self to be with the client but letting go of personal concerns/issues;
- allowing your own emotions and wounds to be accessed and communicated if helpful but not losing a sense of center or making your own healing the focus;
- feeling connected to and joined with your client, yet maintaining a separate sense of self;
- feeling the depth of your client's experience, yet being cognizant of that experience as separate from your own feelings and sense of self;
- keeping your boundaries open and permeable, yet maintaining contact with yourself as separate; and
- maintaining a sense of openness, wonder, and intrigue toward your client and his or her experience, yet being a trained and learned professional with expertise.

In your focus and immersion in the moment:

- feeling flexible and responsive with what arises, yet maintaining a consistent focus;

- letting go of your beliefs and theoretical knowledge yet allowing these to interact with what is live in the moment and to inform your responses; and
- being with the known (of theory, your client) and the unknown (of experience, what is to emerge).

In your responses and interventions:

- letting go of preconceptions, yet offering the client helpful responses and interventions that align with his or her current state in the moment; and
- letting go of a laid-out plan for the session, yet allowing your direction or interventions to follow and attend to your client's safety and readiness.

These paradoxes illuminate the challenge of holding within you different and opposing states all at once. Having this dual level of awareness is central to skillfulness in therapeutic presence. This may begin as a conscious process and emerge with greater ease over time. We give much focus to working with these paradoxes in the proceeding chapters through increasing the fluidity and flexibility of our attention, both cognitively and experientially.

## BACKGROUND RESEARCH ON PRESENCE AND IMPLICATIONS FOR THERAPY

Presence in general promotes positive health in our mind, bodies, and relationships (Siegel, 2007, 2013). Presence can affect us on a microscopic level, altering epigenetics (the expression of genes) and improving health and well-being (Parker, Nelson, Epel, & Siegel, 2015; Siegel, 2013). For example, practicing presence has been shown to lengthen telomeres, the protective caps at the end of chromosomes that relate to healthy aging (Epel, Daubenmier, Moskowitz, Folkman, & Blackburn, 2009). Experiencing connection with another empathically attuned and present individual can actually enhance immune functioning. For example, patients who perceived their doctor to be empathic and present had fewer cold symptoms and recovered 1 day sooner than patients whose doctor was perceived as distant (Rakel et al., 2009).

Therapeutic presence as a foundational approach has been studied across different disciplines. In osteopathy, presence has been shown to influence the technique (palpation) of the osteopath and to strengthen the relationship between therapist and patient (Durrer & Rohrbach, 2013; Rozière, 2016). For art therapists, presence is understood as individual and relational and can assist therapists to be more attuned to their client, strengthening the therapeutic relationship (Schwarz, Snir, & Regev, 2016).

In psychotherapy, research on therapeutic presence is growing and has suggested how essential and valuable it is. Presence is the first step to developing a therapeutic alliance and promoting successful therapy. Research has suggested that presence is a necessary precondition to being empathic and fostering the positive therapeutic relationship we know underlies effective therapy (Geller, Greenberg, & Watson, 2010; Hayes & Vinca, 2011; Pos, Geller, & Oghene, 2011).

Across therapy traditions, the greatest opportunities for growth and healing emerge in the fertile ground of the present moment (Geller & Greenberg, 2012; Stern, 2004). Therapists' presence has the potential to improve outcome regardless of approach, as therapeutic presence is transtheoretical or a common factor (Geller et al., 2010; Geller & Greenberg, 2012; Geller, Pos, & Colosimo, 2012; Hayes & Vinca, 2011). This is supported by research suggesting that therapeutic presence predicts greater outcome across both technical (i.e., cognitive behavioral) and relational (emotion-focused and person-centered) therapies (Geller et al., 2010).

Research has also suggested that clients need to experience their therapist as present to have a positive therapeutic relationship and a successful session outcome (Geller et al., 2010). It is not enough to evaluate ourselves as present; we must also be skillful in communicating presence to our clients. This can be enhanced through our attunement to self, which is the basis for attuning to others (Siegel, 2007, 2011).

How can you express your presence nonverbally? In Chapter 3 we explore the neurophysiological basis for this, and in Chapters 5 and 6 we discover the skills for doing so, as presence is conveyed through body posture, gestures, and entrainment of breath and prosody (vocal tone) in rhythm with clients (Geller & Porges, 2014). Throughout the book there are suggestions for using specific breath, posture, and vocalizations to engage and exercise specific neural pathways that promote inner calm and receptivity, which are reflective of the therapeutic presence experience (Porges & Carter, 2014).

## HOW DOES THERAPEUTIC PRESENCE PROMOTE EFFECTIVE THERAPY?

We know that therapeutic presence is healing in and of itself, yet how that happens is less clear. The following is a brief explanation of how this occurs, with the promise of an elaboration of the neurophysiological principles to follow in Chapter 3.

First, (a) we become present by attuning to ourselves, which then (b) allows us to attune with our clients, and as a result (c) our clients begin to feel safe from a neurological, physiological, and emotional perspective (Allison & Rossouw, 2013; Cozolino, 2006; Geller & Porges, 2014; Porges, 2009, 2011; Schore, 2003, 2012; Siegel, 2007, 2011). This process has three important effects:

1. Our clients' defenses drop away, and an optimal portal opens up to allow engagement in the work of therapy (Geller & Porges, 2014; Porges, 1995, 1998, 2011).
2. Our clients' nervous systems begin to calm in resonance with our calm and grounded presence, and they develop presence and acceptance within themselves, feeling more connected in the therapeutic relationship (Geller & Porges, 2014; Siegel, 2007).
3. Our responses and interventions are offered in attunement to what is poignant in the moment for our clients, including their readiness to receive.

Through repeated experiences of safety, our clients can develop a greater sense of safety in other relationships. Feeling in positive connection with others is central for well-being, growth, and health (Cozolino, 2006; Porges, 2003; Siegel, 2007, 2010, 2011).

## THERAPEUTIC PRESENCE: A FOUNDATIONAL YET DISTINCT THERAPEUTIC SKILL

Therapeutic presence is related to, yet distinct from, other important therapeutic concepts and processes, such as the therapeutic alliance, listening, attention, empathy, countertransference, and mindfulness. The discernment and relationship between therapeutic presence and other therapeutic processes is complex, as there are many overlapping elements. Yet some basic distinctions are explained next.

### The Groundwork for a Positive Therapeutic Alliance

According to Bordin (1979), the therapeutic alliance consists of having (a) a *bond* with the client, (b) a shared understanding of the client's *goals*, and (c) an agreement on the *tasks* or interventions that will effectively help to achieve these goals. The relational bond is most reflective of Rogers's (1957) therapeutic relationship, which includes therapists being empathic, authentic, and positively regarding. We know from decades of research that the therapeutic alliance is a consistent predictor of clients' change (Norcross, 2011).

Therapeutic presence helps you to forge a bond with your client and attend to the shared goal-setting process, but it is a more fundamental stance that cannot be encompassed by these elements of the alliance alone. Therapeutic presence is a binding force that influences whether and how the bond is forged, and how and when shared goal setting and interventions occur.

Therapeutic presence begins internally in the therapist, and therefore many aspects of it precede the alliance formation. Presence expands to a relational state in the encounter as clients feel safe to open up, and a deeper connection between both ensues. The bond is formed when a foundation of safety and security is established through therapeutic presence. This experience invites the client to become present in himself or herself and open to the relationship, and it creates the bidirectional flow of shared presence that deepens the therapeutic bond. Therapeutic presence also precedes the empathy that is so central to Rogers's conception of the therapeutic relationship (see section on empathy just ahead), but is distinct from this construct too.

Therapeutic presence allows you to attune to what is most central for your client. Goals are formed conjointly between you and your client as you listen deeply to the client's experience, offering ways of viewing her or his issues as directly resonant to what the client is expressing and you are receiving. Within the session, presence allows you to read what is happening for the client and then respond or offer an intervention (akin to the task aspect of the alliance). This allows your interventions to be in a direct relationship with your client's therapy goals, as you are holding all of her or his experience in the multiple levels of awareness that presence entails. Therapeutic presence is therefore distinct from, but a prerequisite to, developing a strong therapeutic alliance.

## Therapeutic Presence: Is It Listening and Paying Attention?

We are trained and skilled in paying attention and listening to our clients, yet these important therapeutic processes are not the same as therapeutic presence. The latter is a more fundamental core stance that allows for attuned listening. Being receptive and open to our clients' experience, the precursor to the therapeutic presence process, allows us to sense the nuances and subtleties of the client's experience in the moment. This sensing is also more than attentiveness to our clients' words and phrases. We use our bodies to read their state and feel their immediate nonverbal experience to access primary feelings and needs and to respond in a way that is attuned to the moment. We are tracking our clients' bodies to listen to the emotions, images, and physical sensations. We are also listening to the clinical wisdom, techniques, and historical client information that emerge in the moment in response to the client's expressed need and experience. The following clinical example illustrates this point.

When Susan shared her pain around the loss of her mom, I could see her eyes glance down and a quick shudder through her shoulders. I felt a resonance of fear in my body experienced as tightness in my chest. I paused to feel more deeply what this tightness was about and noticed this was not something I typically feel. I heard the word *fear* in my mind and knew this was an emotional resonance with Susan's experience. When I reflected this sense of fear to her, Susan's eyes softened, and she opened up further about her terror of being alone. We were then able to do some deeper work to help her both express the grief and manage the fear she was experiencing.

Therapeutic presence includes a readiness to be in contact with one's self, with the client and his or her in-the-moment experience, and what is emerging in the therapeutic relationship. Thus, it precedes and supports deep listening, both to what is spoken and unspoken. And although listening deeply is also an essential part of being therapeutically present, it alone doesn't encompass the full experience of presence.

### Therapeutic Presence and Empathy: Different or the Same?

Therapeutic presence is not the same as empathy, yet it is a prerequisite for empathic communication. Empathy is an active process of (a) understanding your client's experience as if it were your own and (b) translating or reflecting the meaningful parts of the experience back to your client (Barrett-Lennard, 1981). Empathy has both an affective and cognitive component, as we need to understand our clients' experience both emotionally and through their perceptual awareness to fully get the complexity of their experience and communicate it back (Watson, 2007). To enter into the experience of the other on these different levels, we need first to be clear, open, and present inside of ourselves.

Being present allows you to generate a calm and receptive openness so you can tune in to your client's expressed and felt experience in an untainted form. Once in that state, you can hear, feel, and understand what the client is saying and experiencing, and reflect it back to the client in a way he or she can receive it. Presence is therefore not the same as empathy; it is the precursor to empathy. You can be present without being empathic; however, you cannot be empathic without first evoking presence.

### Therapeutic Presence and Countertransference

Countertransference occurs when our personal conflicts and issues are triggered in the session and shape our perspective and responses (Hayes, Gelso, & Hummel, 2011). With therapeutic presence we may pick up certain emotions or bodily experiences that are resonant with the client. These experiences are therapeutically useful in understanding our client as resonant of a bidirectional attunement between us and can help shape our responses. Yet they are different from countertransference. With countertransference, our experience of reading the moment is muddled by our own triggers or unresolved difficulties. Training in therapeutic presence can help to discern these.

Being skillful in presence helps us quickly recognize the different sensations that arise when our bodily resonance is clinically informative and when our perception of the client's reality is being tainted by our own emotional reactions. Therapeutic presence demands a high level of self-awareness, which helps us to either put aside our own interfering experience if countertransference is felt or to respond effectively and stay in contact with the client if our sensing is informational. In this way, therapeutic presence and its associated practices are safeguards against inappropriate management of countertransference reactions (Hayes et al., 2011). Also, the more grounded we are (by building our capacity for presence), the more steady we will be in the face of material that could otherwise trigger countertransference reactions.

### Therapeutic Presence and Mindfulness

Mindfulness is all the rave these days, as both a concept and a program to reduce stress and improve health. As a meditator of 25 years who was often teased by my family for going off to a quiet room and turning down the lights, I am pleased yet at times cautious about mindfulness becoming a new household word. I hear people on the street saying "be mindful of that car" or "be mindful and turn your cell phone off in the office." The colloquial use of the term seems to conflate mindfulness with just generally being aware.

Jon Kabat-Zinn (1990), the originator of mindfulness-based stress reduction (MBSR), defined mindfulness as a way of being aware in the present moment, without judgment and with acceptance. Mindfulness in the psychotherapy world is generally an approach offered through programs such as MBSR or mindfulness-based cognitive therapy (Kabat-Zinn, 1990; Segal, Williams, & Teasdale, 2002). Mindfulness-based therapies teach clients mindfulness skills like meditation, awareness, mindful speaking and listening, and mindful movement practices.

It important to distinguish mindfulness from presence, as they are interrelated yet distinct. I find it helpful to see mindfulness as a practice and presence as part of the experience that mindfulness cultivates (particularly an experience of being present). Therapeutic presence includes more than awareness of the present, as it is a larger experience of being grounded, spacious, immersed, and in contact with one's self while being in a compassionate relationship with others. It is also a process and way that we attune with ourselves and our clients in therapy—being receptive and responding from this place of internal and intrapersonal attunement. Therapeutic presence then goes beyond mindful awareness in its overarching goal of facilitating deep healing through relationship.

In this book we discuss mindfulness as a practice for therapists that can help to cultivate their presence, not as a practice to teach clients to be mindful. Mindfulness practice is a fundamental way that therapists can cultivate being fully in the moment with a client, regardless of therapeutic approach or technique. It helps therapists fine-tune their moment-to-moment awareness, an essential component of presence. Mindful practice helps us to bring our attention back from feeling distracted, overwhelmed, or shut down so that we can (a) open more fully to the moment within ourselves and with others, (b) deepen the therapeutic relationship, and (c) read and respond to the moment in an effective and meaningful way.

## THERAPEUTIC PRESENCE AS TRANSTHEORETICAL

Therapeutic presence promotes safety and a positive working alliance that creates the conditions for clients' growth and change across different approaches. Although it is central to humanistic and relational treatments, it is also important in manual-based therapies, where the combination of the therapeutic relationship and technique support the best outcomes.

In relationally based therapies, therapeutic presence communicates to the client "I am here for you," "I understand you," and "I accept you." It allows clients to feel respected and heard, which deepens the therapeutic relationship and their engagement in the therapy. In technical approaches, such as cognitive or behavioral interventions, presence can improve the impact of the delivery of the intervention (Freidberg, Tabbarah, & Poggesi, 2013; Gelso, 2011; Goldfried & Davila, 2005; Holtforth & Castonguay, 2005; Leahy, 2003). When therapists provide interventions to clients that are purely technical and detached from a person-to-person encounter, the impact will be limited. Offering an intervention with therapeutic presence also creates a feeling of resonance for both the therapist and the client that strengthens the relational bond.

Therapeutic presence offers an approach to listening effectively to the whole experience of clients. However, therapists from different modalities may use a particular focus as a portal to understanding their clients. As a cognitive therapist, the words are essential to attend to; as a narrative therapist, the story is important. As an emotion-focused therapist, listening for core pain and adaptive and maladaptive primary and secondary emotions is a central focus. A behavior therapist may be interested in how people are acting in the world and want to know about changes in their behavior. Yet across all therapies, attuning to the present moment of the client's experience can provide therapists with (a) cues for poignancy based on how something is expressed by their clients and (b) links and new connections that can inform the response or intervention needed to facilitate effective therapy. It can also help therapists to (c) read clients' readiness for interventions by assessing their sense of safety and (d) track clients' experience to indicate how responses and interventions are being received. The attunement and contact with self also help therapists to understand and respond to clients as well as recognize and remove inner distractions and triggers.

Therapeutic presence supports therapists in assessing their own needs and energy level so that there is a careful balance between giving and receiving, which is vital across therapy modalities. This in turn helps therapists to sustain their own energy and mitigate burnout. To support your self-care, I invite you to pause now, as you prepare to end this chapter, to feel your breath.

## TRANSITION PRACTICE: PAUSE, NOTICE, AND RETURN

- Pause and invite three deep breaths.
- Notice any physical or emotional sensations in your body in this moment, with acceptance and nonjudgment.
- Now return to the sensation of just breathing.
- When you are ready, transition to the next chapter of this book or the next moment in your day.

# 2

# HISTORY OF
# THERAPEUTIC PRESENCE

All real life is meeting.

—Martin Buber (1958, p. 11)

The roots of presence in the therapeutic relationship go back to the early days of psychotherapy. Aspects of presence were highlighted across different therapeutic approaches, such as Freud's evenly suspended attention (M. Epstein, 2007) and Perls's (1970) contact, and help inform our current understanding. Therapeutic presence as understood currently reflects the entirety of the different aspects of presence: the embodied and relational qualities of being fully in the moment, within the therapist, with the client and in the relationship between them. The emotional, physiological, neurological, and interpersonal entrainment that occurs when the relationship between therapists and clients deepens into the moment provides the safe connection from which growth and healing occur. This brief historical account of various conceptions of presence will aid your understanding of the whole experience.

http://dx.doi.org/10.1037/0000025-003
*A Practical Guide to Cultivating Therapeutic Presence*, by S. M. Geller

## PSYCHOANALYSIS: EVENLY SUSPENDED ATTENTION

The original voice of presence stems from psychoanalysis and Sigmund Freud. As I understand it, the analyst was to have an impartial awareness of all that occurs in the field of perception, without judgment. The therapist evenly applies attention to all that is expressed in the therapy encounter, similar to qualities of therapeutic presence but with an important distinction. Freud's evenly suspended attention seems to reflect analysts' calm but traditionally detached mental state. With therapeutic presence, therapists are grounded and steady yet also deeply and authentically engaged in relationship with the client.

Aspects of therapeutic presence were reflected in the work of analyst Theodore Reik (1948), who described "listening with the third ear." Reik saw attention as reflecting a revolving searchlight, allowing for an openness and attentiveness to all that is relevant. This allows analysts to have effective timing and content for interpretations, and to make intuitive leaps rather than purely cognitive analytical interpretations (M. Epstein, 2007).

In the opening pages of *Civilization and Its Discontents*, Freud (1930) wrote about a concept akin to spaciousness. He expanded on French dramatist and literary expert Romain Rolland's "oceanic feeling," having been encouraged by Rolland to explore meditation and religion from a psychoanalytic tradition (M. Epstein, 2007). However, Freud minimized the oceanic feeling's original conception as a boundless sense of connection to something larger, attributing it instead to a longing for parental protection stemming from an ego ideal.

Postanalytic theories such as object relations theory do incorporate more emphasis on the therapeutic relationship (i.e., Fairbairn, 1952; Winnicott, 1969). Rather than seeing individuals purely in Freudian pleasure-seeking terms, object relations theory sees individuals in terms of their impulse to relate to others (Bacal & Newman, 1990). Experiences in infancy are thought to create internal templates that individuals carry with them into adulthood, shaping their expectations of others ("objects") and themselves ("subject"). Although Melanie Klein's initial formulation of a complete object relations theory focused on the therapeutic relationship as a vehicle for transference and countertransference, her followers took a less restrictive view of the role of the relationship in the therapy encounter (Nuttall, 2000). The therapeutic relationship is viewed as personal and real, and a "holding environment" in which the client can heal early relationship traumas (Watts, Cockcroft, & Duncan, 2009; Winnicott, 1960). This occurs in part by encountering the empathy and steadfastness of the therapist and ultimately internalizing the therapist as a "good object" (Nuttall, 2000). Today the interpersonal connection in psychodynamic therapies appears to be of equal value, if not greater, than facilitating insight.

Akin to theories of therapeutic presence, modern psychodynamic approaches highlight the present moment in the therapeutic relationship (Mitchell, 2000; Stern, 2004). The lived experience of each moment in the relationship is seen as valuable, and therapists are invited to be open and changed by this moment-to-moment encounter. The influence of neuroscience has influenced psychodynamic theories to recognize the bidirectional attunement that is inherent in therapeutic relationships, including the value of therapists' reading the embodied expression of emotions and traumatic memories (Hopenwasser, 2008). Stern (2004) described three different present-moment experiences:

- regular present moments—time in which we live and experience in the moment,
- now present moments—a charged experience that pops up in the moment that requires us to respond or act in a certain way, and
- moments of meeting—two people become aware and live each other's experiences in a present-centered moment of intersubjective connection.

In summary, traditional psychoanalysis and more modern psychodynamic approaches have contributed to aspects of therapeutic presence such as

- evenly suspended attention (Freud);
- oceanic feeling (akin to spaciousness; Freud and Rolland);
- listening with the third ear (Reik);
- therapists' steadiness and the therapeutic relationship as healing (Fairbairn, Winnicott); and
- present-moment attention in the therapeutic relationship (Stern).

## CLIENT-CENTERED THERAPY: PRESENCE AS AN UNDERLYING CONDITION FOR GROWTH AND CHANGE

A belief in a fundamental tendency toward growth is the essence of the person-centered approach. Carl Rogers's (1957, 1980) humanistic therapy was founded on his belief in providing the conditions for growth and change. According to Rogers, being empathic, unconditionally accepting, and genuine was necessary and sufficient to create a positive environment to stimulate clients' natural tendency toward growth and change.

Current thinking and research has suggested that presence is more primary than empathy, acceptance, and authenticity (Geller, 2013a; Geller et al., 2010; Schmid, 2001; Segrera, 2000; Wyatt, 2000). To understand a client and to be accepting and authentic, the therapist has to first be present: grounded, open, and receptive to whatever experiences the client wishes to bring. At the end of his life, Rogers started to rethink his position and began to see that this primary quality of being present promotes healing. He was quoted posthumously about this:

> I am inclined to think that in my writing I have stressed too much the three basic conditions (congruence, unconditional positive regard, and empathic understanding). Perhaps it is something around the edges of those conditions that is really the most important element of therapy—when my self is very clearly, obviously present. (as cited in Baldwin, 2000, p. 30)

One of the most profound discoveries of our research was that a *relational presence* emerges as therapist and client become present to each other (Geller, 2013a, 2013b; Geller & Greenberg, 2012). In this copresence, therapist and client are coexperiencing the moment (Cooper, 2005; Schmid, 2002). The shared reality allows the therapist to sense, feel, and know the client's experience so that the presence and responses are attuned to what is most facilitative of healing.

Presence is grounded in humanistic traditions, particularly in person-centered therapy:

- presence is the primary condition for growth and change;
- to be empathic, the therapist must first be present; and
- presence with the client can develop into a shared or relational presence that allows for the therapist to feel and share in the client's experience.

## GESTALT, DIALOGICAL, AND BUBER—PRESENCE IN THE BETWEEN

Here-and-now awareness through the senses, emotions, and cognitions and in the relationship is the cornerstone of gestalt therapy (Perls, 1970; Yontef, 2005). The immersion aspect of presence reflects the gestalt technique of "letting the world fill you" through direct contact in the moment (Perls, 1970). Sensory experiments are a gestalt technique to heighten awareness and include such practices as exaggerating movements in the body. Although these aid the client's overall awareness and sense of being in flow with the moment, genuine encounter in the relationship can only occur if the therapist approaches the client with a receptive presence (Friedman, 1996).

*Contact*, a gestalt term, is an essential element in the process of therapeutic presence. Being in direct and immediate contact with the client is key in gestalt therapies (Perls, 1970). Yontef (2005) described how the therapeutic relationship facilitates the healing process and stated that "change happens through the contact between the therapist and patient. The emphasis is on 'meeting' the patient, on contact without aiming" (p. 95).

Gestalt therapy adopted Buber's I–Thou relationship as one of its pillars (Perls, 1969). The I–Thou encounter is participatory—a meeting of the pure and whole existence of the other, without attempt to objectify the other (Buber, 1958). A dialogical form of gestalt therapy, integrating the basic principles of gestalt therapy and Buber's I–Thou, has also brought the notion of presence, along with meeting and encounter, into the foreground (Hycner & Jacobs, 1995; Watson, Greenberg, & Lietaer, 1998; Yontef, 2005). Therapists' openness and authenticity allows for this contact, encounter, and meeting. Presence here is reflected in a turning and offering of one's whole self to the client (Hycner, 1993). To meet the other, one first has to be in contact with the self. Yet to truly experience and see the other with clarity, one must also empty or bracket one's own knowledge, judgments, preconceptions, and self-experience. Emptying the self prepares the therapist to receive from the client.

Meeting the other with presence allows for a deeper meeting in the *between* as the therapist and client then become present with each other. The between is something larger than each individual, and according to Buber (1958), taps into the numinous and spiritual dimensions. Healing occurs from the meeting between people as they become present with each other.

The fourth quality of the experience of therapeutic presence, being with and for the other, is grounded in gestalt principles yet also stems from Buber. It reflects the notion of the dialogical between I–It (distance and objectivity) and I–Thou (connection occurring as two people become present with each other). Buber's I–Thou relationship allows for immediacy in contact and in dialogue, supporting healing through connection (Hill et al., 2008). Both are important in a therapeutic encounter, as being separate (I–It) helps in understanding the other through objectivity, and being in direct contact and immersion (I–Thou) allows for deep connection and healing. Awareness of self and the other reflects the *inclusion* concept in presence. Inclusion is another part of the I–Thou encounter and is closely linked to presence, as it entails direct and immediate contact with another, without losing contact with one's self (Friedman, 1985, 1996; Purcell-Lee, 1999; Rotenstreich, 1967).

Hence therapeutic presence qualities that are grounded in gestalt therapy include

- here-and-now awareness—presence through the senses,
- authenticity to deepen the therapeutic relationship,
- receptivity and letting in—emptying one's self to allow the other in,
- bracketing preconceptions and judgment,

- contact—being in direct connection and meeting your client fully in the moment,
- inclusion—being centered and separate in one's self while being in contact with the client, and
- healing through meeting—shared presence through connection is healing and larger then than the sum of individuals.

## LÉVINAS AND THE PRIMACY OF THE OTHER: THE FACE-TO-FACE ENCOUNTER OF PRESENCE

Gestalt therapy and Buber's I–Thou relationship are grounded in the notion of healing through meeting. Healing emerges for both therapist and client as they encounter each other with presence. Taking it to another level, Lévinas (1985) described the *face* as where the presence of the other is expressed. The face demands the barriers to drop and for each person to encounter the other's vulnerability and strength. This built-in "ought" conjures a sense of obligation to behave toward the other with compassion. Both humanness and justice are therefore revealed for Lévinas in the relationship.

Faces, then, are information centers where we can convey to clients that we are fully with them, while also reading their emotions and experiences. Through the fine attunement of our attention and sensing, we can read the personality, feelings, and soul of the other. Whereas Buber conceived of this form of relating as a "symmetrical co-presence," Lévinas's face-to-face encounter is focused on the asymmetrical nature of this contact: a feeling of responsibility for the care of the other is conjured without knowing if it will be reciprocated. This is the type of relationship created by presence in a therapy relationship. As a therapist, I am being there for the other without knowing how the other will respond (Geller & Greenberg, 2012).

Lévinas (1985) extended Buber's (1958) I–Thou relationship by attending to

- face-to-face encounters to express and feel presence in the relationship, and
- a direct and profound encounter through the face that reveals both humanness and a response to care with and for the other.

## EXISTENTIAL THERAPY—PRESENCE AS HEALING

Therapists' presence is one of the primary healing conditions in existential therapy (Schneider, 1994; Schneider & Krug, 2009). Presence needs to be cultivated by the therapist, rather than conceptually learned. Particularly because the therapist's presence can invite a sense of vulnerability and pain to the surface for clients, therapists must also know how to convey comfort and understanding with their presence. Three aspects of presence, according to Bugental (1978, 1983, 1987), are

- availability and openness to all aspects of the client's experience,
- openness to one's own experience in being with the client, and
- the capacity to respond to the client from a synthesis of one's own experience and one's perception of the client's experience.

There is an emphasis in existentialism on presence. Rollo May (1983) expanded on what is meant by presence when he stated that

> the relationship between the therapist and client is taken as a real one, the therapist being not just a shadowy reflector, but an alive human being who happens, at that hour, to be concerned not with his own problems but with understanding and experiencing as far as possible the being of the patient. (p. 156)

Existentialists focus on learning all that one can about therapy but then letting it go at the moment of meeting the client. Rollo May (1958) described the therapist as an artist who spends many years in disciplined study learning technique, yet knowing that if focused on technique alone, the creative vision will be lost. Therapeutic techniques and interventions are offered from what is poignant in the shared moment, rather than being preplanned prior to the session. Without presence, techniques can fall flat and even be at a disservice to the client.

Key aspects of therapeutic presence have emerged from existentialism, such as

- presence as basis for healing;
- presence including availability to the client, openness to the self, and the capacity to respond from presence; and
- technique informed by being present with the client.

## EXPERIENTIAL APPROACHES: PRESENCE IN THE BODY

A focus on bodily felt emotions is central in experiential approaches such as emotion-focused therapy (EFT; Greenberg, 2007, 2010; Greenberg, Rice, & Elliott, 1993) and focusing (Gendlin, 1978). In these approaches, the therapeutic relationship is key to helping clients access their primary bodily felt emotions. The relationship is characterized by therapists' presence, which serves to help their attunement to affect and to communicate empathy, acceptance, and unconditional regard (Geller & Greenberg, 2012;

Greenberg, 2007). To establish a positive therapeutic relationship, therapists must first be present (Greenberg, 2007). Therapists' presence is what helps clients to feel safe and received, so they can access their emotional experience. It also provides therapists a way to emotionally attune so that interventions are precise and helpful.

Gendlin's (1978, 1996) focusing technique helps clients access their bodily felt experience to gain awareness and facilitate growth. Therapists' skill in focusing themselves is required, which includes presence with their own bodily felt experience. The radical acceptance of everything is central to presence, to illuminate how all experience, pleasant and unpleasant, needs to be respected and heard in the wider expanse of presence. Deep listening on the part of the therapist is necessary and only possible through presence, holding an attitude of not knowing, curiosity, openness, and interest (Jordan, 2008). Unconditional presence is required, which Welwood (2000) described as "the capacity to meet experience fully and directly, without filtering it through any conceptual or strategic agenda" (p. 116).

EFT and focusing approaches inform our understanding of how therapeutic presence

- is a primary condition for a positive therapeutic relationship;
- invites safety for client to engage in effective therapeutic work;
- involves being authentic and aware of one's own emotional world;
- includes acceptance, not knowing, curiosity, and openness; and
- provides capacity to meet experience directly without filter and agenda.

## COGNITIVE BEHAVIORAL APPROACHES: PRESENCE OF MIND

Cognitive behavioral therapy (CBT) does not traditionally emphasize presence or the therapeutic relationship. There has been more recent interest in the possible role that these may play in effective therapy (Gelso, 2011; Goldfried & Davila, 2005; Holtforth & Castonguay, 2005; Leahy, 2003; Lejuez, Hopko, Levine, Gholkar, & Collins, 2005; Waddington, 2002); however, there is more focus on collaboration than on bond or the relationship in and of itself (Gelso, 2011). What contributes to a positive alliance, however, is not clearly defined or trained in CBT (Goldfried & Davila, 2005).

Some CBT therapists have recognized that increasing their present focus on both problems as they occur in the therapeutic relationship and the therapy process would improve outcomes in CBT (Kanter et al., 2009). Studies have suggested that presence can be a significant clinical resource in

CBT, as presence and attunement to the client in the moment can optimize the timing and effectiveness of therapeutic techniques (Geller et al., 2010; Kanter et al., 2009). With presence, therapists still lead the intervention but with flexibility and responsiveness to the moment.

Traditional behavioral therapies do not emphasize the relationship, focusing primarily on symptom relief through changing behavior. However, there are some innovative and effective interventions that recognize the role of the relationship in behavior change. For example, dialectical behavior therapy (DBT; Linehan, 1993a, 1993b; McKay, Brantley, & Wood, 2007) recognizes the quality of attention of the therapist as well as the clients. DBT emphasizes a blend of acceptance and behavior change. It is through the relationship that acceptance is conveyed, in the context of helping the client make behavioral changes. This treatment is rooted in both behaviorism and Zen philosophy. DBT was initially designed for borderline personality disorder and people with strong suicidal ideation; however, it is currently used with other emotional challenges, particularly to aid in emotional regulation.

Modern cognitive therapies along with DBT share the values of

- personal practice of acceptance and present-moment awareness as important for therapists,
- present-moment attention of both problems and of the therapy process as providing the foundation for effective use of cognitive interventions, and
- change needing to be first grounded in acceptance of what is true in this moment.

## MINDFULNESS-BASED THERAPIES: A PRACTICE FOR PRESENCE

The revival of the ancient practice of mindfulness has provided a practice to generate presence in clinicians and clients. Mindfulness is a way of paying attention on purpose to the present moment, with acceptance and nonjudgment (Kabat-Zinn, 1990). It involves "clear seeing yet with undiminished compassion" (Salzberg, 1999, p. 7). Mindfulness requires a willingness to come close to our pain and discomfort without judgment, striving, manipulation, or pretense (Salzberg, 1999; Santorelli, 1999; Welwood, 1996). Several approaches use mindfulness as a meditation or practice to cultivate presence and reduce suffering.

Mindfulness-based stress reduction, birthed by Jon Kabat-Zinn (1990), incorporates these principles of acceptance and nonjudgment to help clients with chronic pain reduce their suffering. Since its early days, this approach has expanded to help people with numerous conditions as well as to aid in living everyday life to the fullest.

Other modalities have incorporated mindfulness principles into their approach. A blend of CBT and mindfulness has become popular as an approach to reduce depression and anxiety. Mindfulness-based cognitive therapy (Segal, Williams, & Teasdale, 2002) was designed to prevent relapse from depression. Initially the focus was on teaching clients mindfulness skills without a requirement for therapists to have a commitment to a personal mindfulness practice. Segal et al. (2002) later included therapists' mindful practice as essential, including the cultivation of present-centered attention and an attitude of acceptance. This both encourages a level of self-understanding of the highlights and pitfalls of facing one's own experience with acceptance and helps to better respond to clients' experiences (Geller & Greenberg, 2012).

Mindfulness programs have also been designed for specific conditions, such as addiction (mindfulness-based relapse prevention; Marlatt, Bowen, Chawla, & Witkiewitz, 2008), eating disorders (mindfulness-based eating awareness training by Jean Kristeller; Kristeller & Quillian-Wolever, 2011), and attention-deficit/hyperactivity disorder (Zylowska, 2012). Mindfulness approaches emphasize that the facilitator or therapist must have a personal mindfulness practice to gain awareness, self-development, experiential skill, and sensitivity to the client's experience.

Mindfulness is a wonderful practice to cultivate present-moment awareness and related qualities of therapeutic presence. By focusing on the breath as an anchor, and noticing the experiences that arise without judgment and with a spacious awareness, mindfulness practice helps to develop an open and accepting relationship with one's own present-moment experience. This strengthens the ability to be present and allowing of the client's experience, without shutting down or becoming overwhelmed. Mindful practice heightens therapeutic presence qualities such as attention, awareness, warmth, and compassion that can help to deepen the therapeutic relationship (Shapiro & Carlson, 2009).

The following are four ways that mindfulness can help cultivate therapeutic presence:

- Practicing mindfulness and presence with oneself helps to build the capacity to sustain attention while being present with clients.
- Mindfulness heightens self-compassion and acceptance of one's own experience, which is the foundation to being compassionate and accepting of clients' experience.
- Mindfulness reduces stress and enhances well-being and self-care, which prevents burnout and increases capacity for sustained presence with clients.

- Mindfulness supports openness, receptivity, and grounding, so therapists can be with clients' experience without becoming overwhelmed or shutting down.

## NEUROSCIENCE: PRESENCE AS A GATEWAY FOR INTEGRATION IN BRAIN AND BODY AND IN RELATIONSHIP

Breakthroughs in brain imaging techniques and the popularization of neuroscience perspectives have exponentially increased our understanding of therapeutic presence as both a healthy state and a safe container for clients and the therapeutic relationship. New perspectives such as Daniel Siegel's (2007, 2010, 2011) interpersonal neurobiology and Stephen Porges's (2003, 2009, 2011) polyvagal theory offer us a way of understanding what happens in the brain and body when in presence in the relationship. The next chapter explores the neuroscience of therapeutic presence, including how this way of relating evokes a sense of safety in the therapeutic encounter, providing optimal conditions for growth and healing. As you complete your reading of this chapter, pause if you wish for a brief transition practice to support grounding into this moment.

## TRANSITION PRACTICE: GROUNDING INTO THE MOMENT

- Pause and invite your awareness to your feet as they rest on the ground.
- Be aware of the force of gravity, as has existed for billions of years, keeping your feet steady and solid on the ground.
- Feel the contact place between feet and ground as you take three full breaths.
- Return your attention to reading or the next phase of your day.

©2016 M. Lee Freedman.

# 3

# NEUROPHYSIOLOGY OF THERAPEUTIC PRESENCE

> One of the key practical lessons of modern neuroscience is that the power
> to direct our attention has within it the power to shape our brain's firing
> patterns, as well as the power to shape the architecture of the brain itself.
> —Daniel J. Siegel (2011, p. 39)

We are at an exciting time when the union of psychotherapy and neuroscience is teaching us how the interconnections between mind, body, and brain can help us grow. If we can change our experience, we can change our brains. This speaks to the value of intentionally inviting presence in life and in relationships: The more we experience presence, the stronger the neural pathways for presence become (Hanson & Mendius, 2009; Siegel, 2010). Practices that cultivate the qualities of therapeutic presence leave a memory or imprint in the brain and the body. So repeated practices of presence allow this state to be accessed more easily over time.

We intuitively recognize that we impact each other in relationship. Neuroscience confirms this, by revealing mechanisms in the brain and the body that leave us changed by our interactions with others. When we are intentional about the way we relate, we increase the possibility that others receive and feel our calm and attuned presence. The changing nature of the

http://dx.doi.org/10.1037/0000025-004
*A Practical Guide to Cultivating Therapeutic Presence*, by S. M. Geller

brain means that in these encounters, the brains and bodies of those we aim to touch are being altered too.

This chapter incorporates neuroscience theory to support (a) how practice can deepen presence and (b) how presence in therapeutic relationships can create the conditions for safety that effective therapy needs. A deeper understanding of how we impact our clients, not just through conventional psychotherapeutic techniques but also neurophysiologically helps us to be intentional in our own bodily state, using nonverbal means to attune with our clients in a way that facilitates healing. This understanding supports our self-development as therapists, as we identify areas requiring more attention in our personal and professional lives. We can build the neural pathways that support presence and, with ongoing practice, turn present-centered relating into a characteristic or trait rather than just a momentary experience.

## A PRIMER ON THE BRAIN

*Neuroaxis* is the term used to describe the direction of the brain's evolution over time: from bottom to top, and inside to out (Hanson & Mendius, 2009). Tracing the brain's development along the neuroaxis is a useful way to understand its diverse regions and their complementary functions. At the most basic level, the brain can be divided into three evolutionary layers constituting what we call the *triune brain*: the brainstem, limbic regions, and cortex (Siegel, 2011).

### The Triune Brain

The lowest and deepest regions of our brains hold the primitive but essential structures we associate with survival (Siegel, 2010, 2011). The brainstem, for example, automatically regulates heartbeat, breathing, and sleep, among other functions. It is also responsible for such reflexes as orienting to a sudden movement across the room (Isa & Sasaki, 2002).

Above the brainstem is the thalamus, which receives and relays basic sensory information to higher cortical regions (Hanson & Mendius, 2009). A nearby structure, the hypothalamus, regulates basic physiological and emotional drives (e.g., hunger, thirst, sex, intense fear and anger) by directing the pituitary gland. The adrenal rush you feel at the starting line of a race has been brought to you by the hypothalamus and pituitary gland, which neurochemically nudge your adrenal glands to send you a surge of required energy and activation. The adrenals can also be directed to release stress hormones, such as cortisol, which is critical to maintain the body's homeostasis but can also interfere with our well-being if chronically elevated (Siegel, 2011).

Moving forward in time and along the neuroaxis, the limbic system houses the amygdala, hippocampus, and basal ganglia. In a broad way, the amygdala is most commonly associated with the fear response; the hippocampus with consolidating multiple pieces of sensory, linguistic, and factual information into memories; and the basal ganglia with direct intentional movement and reward and stimulation seeking (Hanson & Mendius, 2009; Siegel, 2011). The limbic system is in constant conversation with the most evolved part of the human brain and the focus of many of our presence practices: the cortex.

The cortex has four lobes in each hemisphere, which, like the hemispheres, specialize while being interconnected: the frontal, parietal (perception), temporal (language and memory), and occipital (vision) lobes (Siegel, 2011). Sensory and motor strips span the cortex.

The prefrontal cortex, cingulate, and insula are together responsible for the functions that make us most recognizable as humans: the capacities to reason abstractly, plan, self-monitor, inhibit impulses, have intuitions, and connect with others (Hanson & Mendius, 2009).

### Vertical Integration

The prefrontal cortex is often represented as the conductor of the orchestra, the regulatory counterpart to the "primitive" lower brain regions that require its direction. There is something to be said for this. When I talk about changing your brain to change your life, what I really mean is learning to harness the cortex's power to be discerning in its responses to the lower regions. Their relatively fixed and automatic circuits energize us and perform vital functions, but balanced life requires the gentle guiding hand of the cortex. When we practice presence, mindfulness, focused attention, patience, and empathy, we are building connections from the cortex to the regions of the brain that want to orient to every change in the environment and defend aggressively against any perceived threat. The bond formed between the highest and lowest regions of our brain (or *integration*, as we will call it), makes each better than it would be alone and transforms limbic reactivity altogether (Hanson & Mendius, 2009; Siegel, 2011).

### Horizontal Integration

To make matters a bit more complex, the cortex can also be divided into two halves or hemispheres, and each hemisphere has its own set of lobes. The lobes of the right and left hemisphere are connected by a thick band of fibers called the corpus callosum. The corpus callosum lets the hemispheres communicate with each other to integrate the distinct types of information and processing styles that they each bring to the table.

The "right brain/left brain" distinction fell into disrepute for a number of years as being an overly simplistic way of thinking about the complexity of the brain (McGilchrist, 2010). The argument was that both hemispheres process the same input (e.g., sounds, sights) and so they really aren't different after all. But when we consider *how* each hemisphere processes input, the differences are clear: They focus on specific elements, each essential. McGilchrist (2010) offered this illustration: The left hemisphere's ability to narrowly focus visual attention is what allows a bird to spot pellets of food on the ground against the backdrop of pebbles and sand. The right hemisphere's visual attention is also active, but in scanning the wider environment for predators nearby. Lateralization is key to survival.

So each hemisphere is a specialist of sorts. The left hemisphere attends to details, labels and makes lists, is analytical and logical, and uses language (Siegel, 2011). The right hemisphere, which develops earlier, has more direct connections to subcortical regions, making it the expert in emotions, bodily-felt sensations, and social communication (Siegel, 2011). The right is non-verbal and highly image oriented and metaphorical in its conceptualizations. It also integrates information in a holistic way, putting together the details the left loves to note. The popular statements "Artists are right-brain dominant" and "I'm good at math so I'm left brain" sound simplistic, but there is actually some truth to the distinction. Of these asymmetrical hemispheres, individuals tend to have one that dominates their processing style. Horizontal integration gives us the best of both worlds.

When well regulated and in balance, the symphony that emerges—a product of the efforts of the left and right hemispheres, subcortical and cortical regions—underlies our capacity to feel the thrill of laughter in a relationship or grieve deeply after a loss, to think logically even when distressed, to identify justified anger from a disproportionate response, and the list goes on. Equilibrium in the brain (or not) changes so much of what it feels like to be alive. The good news is that we can change the structure and function of our brains according to how we use them. When we can reconcile left, right, subcortical, and bodily input to respond with intentionality, these effects are felt throughout our lives and relationships.

## NEUROPLASTICITY

The picture I am painting about the malleability of the brain contrasts with the limited notion we had not so long ago that that the wiring of the brain was fixed. We now know that there is fluidity in brain structure and circuitry. The ability of the brain to change and adapt as a result of experience is known as *neuroplasticity*. Doidge (2007) broke the word down into its component parts: *neuron*, referring to the cells of the nervous system, and *plastic*, meaning "changeable, malleable, modifiable" (p. xix). Neuroplasticity encompasses the growth of new nerve cells, the proliferation of connections between cells, and the deepening of these connective circuits over time (Siegel, 2011). We can see evidence of neuroplasticity from technological advances in brain imaging. We also see it in the way people become adept at new things: taking up another language in midlife, learning how to rollerblade, becoming more patient and loving.

Doidge's (2007) fascinating book and video, *The Brain That Changes Itself*, document individuals' breakthroughs in recovering lost functionality through targeted exercises of nonfunctional or adjacent areas of the brain. For example, the brains of those with visual impairments can learn to sense vision by drawing on other regions. What could this mean for those who haven't had traumatic brain injuries per se but do have entrenched patterns of perceiving, experiencing, and interacting with the world? Can psychotherapists similarly capitalize on the power of neuroplasticity in the service of clients' healing? And what about us, as therapists: Could working with our own neuroplasticity make us better at what we do?

## Practice Makes Presence

It is remarkable how experience affects our brain, literally changing neurological structure in lasting ways and, in turn, changing the way we relate to our experiences (Begley, 2008; Doidge, 2007; Hanson & Mendius, 2009). This has profound implications for the cultivation of presence. Each time we practice presence in our personal life and relationships, there is more cellular activity and a neurological imprinting in the regions associated with that experience. The circuits of the brain that conjure the experience of presence are deepened and strengthened through repetitive use, like walking a fresh trail through the forest so many times that a defined path emerges. Over time the experience of presence will become more accessible and familiar.

A Native American teaching story that I often share speaks powerfully to the value of practice:

> A Native American grandfather was talking to his grandson about how he felt. He said, "I feel as if I have two wolves fighting in my heart. One wolf is the vengeful, angry, violent one. The other wolf is the loving, compassionate one." The grandson asked him, "Which wolf will win the fight in your heart?" The grandfather answered: "The one I feed." (Forsyth & Eifert, 2007, p. 72)

# PRESENCE IN THE BODY AND BRAIN

Before delving into the implications of neuroplasticity and the power of the relationship in psychotherapy, let's consider how therapeutic presence is experienced in the body and brain of the therapist. What is going on when presence is occurring and when it is enhanced?

## Mindfulness and Meditation

Numerous studies show that when we practice a form of being present, the brain grows more integrative fibers and creates new pathways in the associated regions (Farb, Segal, & Anderson, 2013; K. C. R. Fox et al., 2014; Hölzel et al., 2011; Lazar et al., 2005; Yang et al., 2016). These practices may be a formal mindfulness or meditation regime, experiential exercises, or simply "being there" more fully in relationships and in everyday life. Depending on the specific requirement of each practice, differing parts of the brain will be involved. The close relationship between mindfulness and meditative states, and presence, makes mindfulness and meditation literature a good place to start in understanding the neural correlates of presence. These diverse practices are commonly categorized as either "focused attention" or "open monitoring" (e.g., see Lutz, Slagter, Dunne, & Davidson, 2008). The regions and networks recruited have both differences and similarities, and some research has suggested that the level of expertise of practitioners can play a role too (K. C. R. Fox et al., 2016; Lutz, Jha, Dunne, & Saron, 2015).

Focused-attention techniques (e.g., transcendental meditation) cultivate the ability to hold an object of meditation in one's mind, whether it be a mantra, image, or visible object. When meditating, practitioners show activity in regions associated with directing and sustaining attention (Lutz et al., 2015). If we think of the therapy setting, the client could be considered the therapist's "object" of meditation, enhancing a state of focused attention in vivo.

In open-monitoring techniques, such as mindfulness meditation, which comprise the majority of the practices in this book, the aim is to maintain a spaciousness of mind, letting thoughts and feelings rise and recede without attachment or judgment. The "focus" is paradoxically remaining "unfocused" on any one piece of mental fodder—*letting go* of fixation and using the breath as an anchor. As a result, these practices tend to recruit regions associated with monitoring and meta-awareness, and over time there is less and less internal interpretation of, or elaboration on, thoughts that arise (one of the ways we otherwise get internally stuck; K. C. R. Fox et al., 2016; Lutz et al., 2015). In the therapy setting, the skills fostered by open-monitoring meditation let the therapist notice internal bodily cues and emotions and observe insights and judgments, without fixating. This spaciousness of mind also lets the therapist shift between monitoring oneself, client, and the space between, without getting figuratively stuck.

We can also differentiate the brain-level changes of meditators by *structure* (i.e., anatomical differences), and *function* (i.e., the circuitry and firing patterns). Meta-analyses show change in both (Cahn & Polich, 2006; K. C. R. Fox et al., 2014, 2016). Mindfulness meditation, for example, adds billions of synaptic connections and a measurable thickening of brain tissue in areas related to attention and sensory awareness (Lazar et al., 2005).

A recent meta-analysis attempted to track the patterns of neuroanatomical activation and deactivation across four meditative styles and found clear differences (K. C. R. Fox et al., 2016). One region of the brain, however, showed up in every style: the insular cortex, which plays a major role in monitoring of body states, empathy, and metacognition. The findings of this study speak to the importance of having a diverse set of practices with which to cultivate presence. The tasks involved in therapeutic presence draw on the skills of multiple forms of meditation: For example, to focus fully on the client and encounter, you must inhibit distractions like self-concerns or judgments, and to stay fully in the moment-to-moment unfolding, you must receive and let go, receive and let go, over and over again.

Mindfulness and meditation research supports that after extensive practice, sustaining attention requires less effort (Davidson & Lutz, 2008). Meditation also improves learning, memory, emotion regulation, and perspective taking (Hölzel et al., 2011). Regular meditation practice creates a more balanced autonomic nervous system (and therefore state of calm) and strengthens our adeptness at returning to balance if our equilibrium is disrupted by stress or emotional reactivity (Collard, 2007, p. 173). In the therapeutic encounter, this means that when we feel pulled out of the moment (distracted or emotionally overwhelmed), with practice we can more rapidly notice, name the experience, and return our attention to our client.

## Zeroing in on the Prefrontal Cortex

The prefrontal cortex, what we have called the conductor of the orchestra, is a major player in our ability to be present. Let's look more closely at this center of connection at the front of the brain, heralded as housing the "higher order" functions and differentiating human beings from other mammals.

Siegel (2007) described nine particular functions associated with activity of the middle areas of the prefrontal cortex that reflect a whole-brain integration: body regulation, attuned communication, emotional balance, response flexibility, empathy, insight, fear modulation, intuition, and morality. These functions are also the requisite parts of therapeutic presence.

As therapists, our work draws on every one of these functions: the ability to balance our bodily and emotional states, attune to ourselves and others, flexibly respond on the basis of what is happening in the moment, be empathic, access insight and intuition, moderate our fear, and respond (morally) in a way that is with and for the client, and not driven by self-interest. I speculate that the experience of therapeutic *presence*, which underlies our ability to do therapy work, draws on each of these functions too. If, as this work suggests, the middle prefrontal cortex is so central to the experience of therapeutic presence, practices geared toward enhancing our functionality in these realms will also enhance our presence as therapists.

## The Nervous System in Presence

When one is in a state of presence, it is suggested that the autonomic nervous system is both activated and balanced, with a slight stimulation in the sympathetic nervous system (arousal) and a heightening of the parasympathetic nervous system (calm; Siegel, 2013). The (ideal) experience is one of calm alertness. The breath is long and slow, the body relaxed yet open and alert, the heart rate regulated, and the attention keenly focused.

Anxiety and states of distress that signal a dysregulated nervous system have a powerful influence on our ability to use our cognitive resources (Eysenck, Derakshan, Santos, & Calvo, 2007), including those of the middle prefrontal cortex. So a major theme throughout this book is working with the nervous system—both our clients' and our own.

How can you conjure this state of calm alertness? That is part of the journey of the rest of this book. But to start, diaphragmatic breathing, relaxation practices, yoga, music, mindfulness practices, grounding or centering exercises, and deep listening are some examples. Every time we balance the autonomic nervous system by stimulating the parasympathetic nervous system and down-regulating the sympathetic nervous system, we are leaning our body and mind toward greater calm and well-being. Balancing the nervous system on a regular basis can also help therapists to develop qualities of presence such as grounding, centering, and equanimity. These qualities of presence help people to confront painful or difficult events (e.g., clients' suffering or personal hardship) with less reactivity.

## The First Building Block of Practice: Pausing

Pausing is one of the building blocks of therapeutic presence practice. However, you may find that being asked to pause sets off impatience and a desire to ignore this section. The current pace of life has been so wired into us that slowing down can feel uncomfortable and create resistance. Yet the cost of not slowing down is significant, causing a disconnection within by not listening to our inner world, and a disconnection from others through not taking time to connect.

If there were only one way you were able to cultivate presence, I would suggest that you pause regularly. In pausing, the parasympathetic nervous system is stimulated, generating greater calm and attentiveness (Siegel, 2013). Frequent pauses throughout the day, accompanied by intentional and conscious breathing, can help to slow down our internal busyness and create a deeper awareness of our in-the-moment experience.

### Presence Pause: Breathe Out and Take It All In!

Given that there is so much information flowing in these pages, I invite you to slow down for a moment to pause and integrate what we have discussed, before moving on to the next section.

- Pause in this moment and notice the rhythm of your breath without changing it.
- Count to three on the in-breath and four on the out-breath.
- Lengthen the time of the inhalation and exhalation. For example, inhale for 5 seconds, pause briefly, and exhale for 8 seconds.
- Take a moment to reflect on how you feel after pausing to be conscious of your breath.
- When you are ready, bring your attention back to the page and read on.

*Reflection*

Conscious breathing, which is a foundational presence practice, helps to support presence. This practice involves taking longer and slower breaths, which allows for a strengthening in heart-rate variability, helps to decrease heart rate, and activates the parasympathetic nervous system, creating an inner sense of calm and safety. This is the first step toward heightening awareness of our experience in the moment.

## COREGULATION: CREATING SAFETY THROUGH PRESENCE IN RELATIONSHIPS

Not only can personal presence and presence-based practices change your brain, but experiencing the attuned presence of another person can too. The nervous systems of individuals are in constant communication, and so our bodies, brains, and ultimately our functioning can be changed through relationship. One formal definition of *coregulation* is the bidirectional linkage of oscillating emotions between different partners, contributing to the emotional stability of both (Butler & Randall, 2013). So in clinical terms, if I calm myself, then my client will calm in resonance with my grounded presence, as our emotions, bodies, and brains are bidirectionally linked. Alternatively, if I am not grounded and present, then I can be thrown off or dysregulated by my clients, becoming emotionally overwhelmed. The polyvagal theory helps us understand how this comes about, and its insights have direct application to the clinical setting.

## Polyvagal Theory

Polyvagal theory describes the evolution of the mammalian nervous system to include a third wing beyond the fundamental fight/flight and immobilization responses, called the social engagement system (Porges, 1995, 1998, 2003, 2011). The fight/flight portion of the autonomic nervous system depends on sympathetic activation. Immobilization and social engagement are parasympathetic responses, but their divergent outcomes depend in part on the portions of vagus nerve they activate. The *vagus* is a "wandering" cranial nerve that connects the brain to organs like the heart, lungs, and intestines. The portion of the vagus that underlies social communication and engagement, the *ventral vagus*, is myelinated—meaning it transmits signals very rapidly and can override the unmyelinated *dorsal vagus* (immobilization response).

As mammals, you and I are equipped with this social engagement system. The ventral (or "smart vagus") supports face-to-face communication and helps us to inhibit sympathetic excitation (which triggers fight/flight behavior) so that emotions are well regulated. It is thus a big part of our ability to function in social interactions.

Polyvagal theory further explains that potent cues of safety or danger outside of our conscious awareness are detected by cortical areas and shift our physiological states (Geller & Porges, 2014; Porges, 2011). Our shifting physiological states are communicated from visceral organs to the brain via the vagus. These cues are also communicated from the regions to which the vagus nerve has projections—such as the striated muscles of the face and head. Because of these connections to the face running all the way down to the subdiaphragmatic region, the way that people use their faces, voices, breath, and bodies can say a lot about how calm or activated they are feeling in a given moment. When vocal prosody (pitch, rhythm, and timbre of voice) is rich, the body is open, and the face is at ease, a general state of calmness is being experienced, and this supports spontaneous social engagement behaviors (Geller &

Porges, 2014; Porges, 2011). The ventral vagus provides us with an integrated "face-to-heart" connection.

There is not only a bidirectional communication between brain (i.e., central nervous system) and body but also a bidirectional communication between the nervous systems of people who are in relationship with each other (Cozolino, 2006; Porges, 2011; Schore, 2012; Siegel, 2007, 2010). This communication is not necessarily in conscious awareness; it is more of a "gut" (visceral) sense that informs us of how we are feeling in an interaction. In this way, safety and unsafety are experienced and mediated by physiological states (e.g., bodily felt agitation when unsafe, internal sense of ease when feeling safe). This process of automatic evaluation of safety or risk in relationship has been labeled *neuroception* (Porges, 2003). Neuroception most likely involves areas of the prefrontal and temporal cortices with projections to the amygdala and the periaqueductal gray (Porges, 2003).

## Lack of Attunement and Emotional Dysregulation

We know that trauma and early lack of attunement (i.e., a caregiver who is indifferent to the needs of the child) can cause lasting emotional dysregulation (Schore, 2003; Van der Kolk, 2014). Lack of attachment to a primary caregiver leaves a child feeling chronically in danger. A person with a trauma background may have an autonomic nervous system that chronically overreacts to any indication of danger, responding defensively or shutting down even when there is no risk (Siegel, 2010). For example, a therapist looking the wrong way or raising an arm to adjust the window blinds could be perceived by a client as rejection (in the case of looking away) or preparation to strike (in the case of raising an arm) if the client is primed toward sensing unsafety. This chronic sense of endangerment can create a negative feedback loop: From it springs a tendency to avoid or react strongly to others, which inhibits the formation of positive social interactions that could help to counter this feeling.

## Regulating in Relationship

The regulators of emotions and physiology are embedded in relationship (Cozolino, 2006; Geller & Porges, 2014; Porges, 2011; Schore, 2009, 2012). Although the brain can change in response to trauma or misattuned relationships, the brain can also change when in positive and safe relationships, such as with a person who is present, caring, and in synch with us. The bidirectional nature of the social engagement system means that positive interactions between ourselves and our clients can influence their vagal function to dampen stress-related physiological states and support growth and restoration.

### Right Brain to Right Brain Communication

Attuned right brain to right brain communication is a pathway to regulation in relationship (Quillman, 2012; Schore, 2009, 2012; Siegel, 2010). In a given exchange, there are the words that are communicated (which is primarily a left-brain activity), yet there is an additional nonverbal way we express emotions and experiences as human beings. *Right brain to right brain* refers to these nonverbal ways, including body posture, vocal expressions, facial expressions, and gestures.

From the perspective of right brain to right brain communication, we listen with our body and senses (our right brain) to what is expressed via the body of our clients (their right brain's communication). This is the essence of presence: listening beyond the words from our clients. We do this while communicating with our own bodies that we are listening, attuning, hearing, feeling, and understanding them (i.e., using our nonverbal communication to respond).

Right brain to right brain communication involves (a) recognizing that our right brain is receiving information from a client's right brain (i.e., sensing the look on a person's face or body posture) and (b) when they are in that mode, using nonverbal ways to communicate back rather than just words. For example, if we sense unsafety through tension in the face or shallow breathing, we can promote safety by leaning forward and breathing with them with a caring look.

## FEELING SAFE AND PROMOTING GROWTH IN THE THERAPEUTIC RELATIONSHIP

Creating safety is the most powerful effect of therapeutic presence and is the foundation of a positive therapeutic alliance, supporting the tough work of psychotherapy. Being attuned, receptive, accepting, calm, and engaged with our clients allows them to feel heard, felt, and calmed. When a client feels safe with their present therapist, the client's physiological state lets him or her open up and explore vulnerabilities, as well as engage in other effective therapeutic work. This sense of safety strengthens the therapeutic relationship so that therapy can efficiently progress.

The polyvagal theory proposes that cues of safety or danger are communicated interpersonally from the upper part of the face and through eye contact, prosody of voice, and body posture. The therapeutic relationship is infused with nonverbal messages that are outside the realm of our aware-ness yet are being interpreted by clients in a physiological or gut sense way. The neuroception of safety is detectable by physiological markers (e.g., open posture, soft facial features, breathing). Through the therapist's warmth and prosody of voice, soft eye contact, open body posture, and receptive and accepting stance, the client experiences a calm and safe therapist and further opens in the therapy encounter. The work of therapy is profoundly enhanced. Therapeutic presence also allows the therapist to attune to and recognize (i.e., in the facial expression of the client) when the client is (a) feeling open and ready for an intervention or (b) not feeling safe and to repair or slow down the intervention. It also helps to recognize and regulate our own reactivity so we can maintain authentic connection with our clients.

Attending to clients' cues and inducing calm through our own recep-tive presence are two significant ways to promote regulation in a client's ner-vous system. This activates a neurophysiological experience of safety in our clients and the positive engagement that flows from that experience. From a physiological standpoint, the client's nervous system detects features of safety that we communicate with our body, face, voice, and breath; her or his defenses lower and spontaneous social engagement behaviors occur (Geller & Porges, 2014).

Repeated experiences of presence, both in the therapist and in the cli-ent in relationship with a present-centered therapist, also exercise the neu-ral muscles for safety in relationships outside of therapy. This allows clients to eventually feel safe in their interpersonal relationships and feel a greater sense of well-being and connection. Research has suggested that a safe thera-peutic environment facilitates the development of new neural pathways for clients, which in turn contributes to the repair of attachment injuries and provides the positive social interactions that are essential for clients' health and growth (Allison & Rossouw, 2013).

So when clients feel us being present, open, and centered and will-ing to hear, feel, and hold their pain with our caring and grounded pres-ence, it can actually deactivate the trauma response and over time give their brain an experience of safety that eventually extends to other rela-tionships. This is powerful and hopeful. Our presence can both reduce distress and provide a soothing comfort that changes the structure of the brain to feel safe, grow, and restore healthy functioning. Our presence also invites our clients into feeling more present and accepting within themselves, which activates a state of brain and body integration. This intrapersonal integration has been shown to increase well-being, increase immune functioning, and create greater happiness and fulfillment (Siegel, 2007, 2010).

# PRESENCE AND INTEGRATION

The ultimate goal of practicing presence ourselves, using presence in therapy, and helping clients to become more present to their own experiences is to foster *integration*—both intra- and interpersonally. Integration involves being differentiated (separate) yet linked (interconnected; Siegel, 2010). Presence invites this integrated state of being separate from, yet deeply connected to, our clients, while attending to fluctuating aspects of our own experience and identity. This integration is experienced as a sense of harmony and well-being, where we feel joined with others and with ourselves: "the essence of presence."

One way to think of this all-encompassing and layered state of integration is as one that can occur in a series of steps: By fostering personal integration, we can then resonate more fully with others. Personal integration requires an ability to sense our internal states (called *interoception*); to balance subcortical input with cortical control; and to bring together reason and emotion, detail and holism, language, and feeling through horizontal integration. When we are more personally integrated, our capacity for integrating with others also grows.

## Personal Integration

Being aware of our experience, as we are during mindfulness practice, facilitates a knowing of ourselves that is both subjective and objective. We learn to sense our inner body and to recognize and be with our feelings and experiences without judgment or reactivity. This attunement with ourselves fosters interconnections between the hemispheres, the levels of the triune brain, and the body. Such a state of integration contrasts with living a life divorced from one's body or from either rational or emotional states. Self-attunement is the basis for personal and therefore relational integration (Hanson & Mendius, 2009; Siegel, 2007).

## Interoception

Attuning to one's own experience is key to reading others. *Interoception* is the inner sensory capacity of the body, which works through both physiological feedback and through our perception of that feedback (Wiens, 2005). Inner sensations refer to communication not just from our visceral organs but also from receptors on body surfaces found on the inside, like the tongue and gums (Blakeslee & Blakeslee, 2007). Through interoception we sense and interpret our internal body states to self-regulate or maintain homeostasis. Interoception is also a fundamental part of our ability to become present in general by attuning to ourselves, and also to others.

What underlies interoception, and how can we enhance our own, to then connect better with others? Our brains hold representations of the landscape of our bodies in what have been called *body maps* (Blakeslee & Blakeslee, 2007). Body maps can be found throughout the whole cortex, and we have sets for both internal sensations and for externally oriented sensory perception. Touch your index finger to the tip of your nose. How did you know how to do that? Your body maps tell you about where each part of your body is in space, what it feels like to be there, and exactly how to move your body to align your finger where you intend for it to go. Signals from receptors all over your body funnel upwards to the sensory maps in your cortex and then back downwards from your motor maps to direct action. Body maps are also a part of how you registered the sensations you felt in your finger and the tip of your nose when you brought them together. And when you pay close attention to the sensations you feel, you enhance the level of perceptible detail in the map of your index finger and the tip of your nose in your brain.

What does this mean for building interoceptive awareness? When we attend to internal body sensations, we likewise enhance cortical representations of our visceral body in our minds (Critchley, Wiens, Rotshtein, Öhman, & Dolan, 2004; Farb et al., 2013). The more we notice sensations, the more acute and discerning our perception of these sensations becomes. As a therapist, your body is your primary tool for registering what is happening inside yourself, inside your client, and between you and the client in session. By building your ability to sense your interior, you will become more adept at sensing what is happening in the present moment with yourself and with your clients too. Internal sensations are registered and integrated primarily in regions of the brain's *insula* (Farb et al., 2013; Flynn, 1999). It is no coincidence that the insula is also majorly implicated in the experience of empathy (Leigh et al., 2013; Mutschler, Reinbold, Wankerl, Seifritz, & Ball, 2013). So both being aware of your experience and being able to sense inwardly (the aim of the presence practices) activate a state of brain and body integration and provide a foundation for integrating in relationship.

**Relational Integration**

Interpersonal integration occurs through the linkages we forge in relationship and is an essential part of our overall state of integration and felt sense of balance and well-being. From a basis of self-attunement, we can resonate with others through a synchrony that occurs at the level of bodily movements all the way down to the microscopic level of cells (Hasson, Ghazanfar, Galantucci, Garrod, & Keysers, 2012; Praszkier, 2016). It is our nature as embodied and relational beings to enter into these patterns of connection with others. So we can help our clients heal by guiding them to become more present in the body and in relationship, and doing the same within ourselves.

### Brain-to-Brain Coupling, Resonance Circuitry, and Mirror Neurons

Siegel (2011) outlined a sequence of brain regions involved in the experience of attunement (and empathy) that he called the *resonance circuitry*. This circuit includes a mirror neuron system, identified by other researchers for its relation to empathy (Gazzola, Aziz-Zadeh, & Keysers, 2006; Stern, 2004). Mirror neurons sit beside motor neurons and will fire in a person who is doing nothing other than watching another person behave or feel (Ferrari & Rizzolatti, 2014; Glenberg, 2010; Praszkier, 2016). When therapists are present and attuned, they are receiving the client's experience on a felt and neurobiological level. This is an aspect of "brain-to-brain coupling," wherein one person's perceptual system becomes linked to another's motor system and is part of how therapists experience the client *as if* they were in the other's experience (Baldini, Parker, Nelson, & Siegel, 2014; Hasson et al., 2012). Therapists are using their sensory awareness to take in the client's experience, and their mirror neurons perceive these sensations by way of the body, limbic system, and insula (which is densely populated with mirror neurons; Blakeslee & Blakeslee, 2007).

These bodily and limbic shifts in the therapist are perceived through interoception—but in these moments of interoception, part of what the therapist is sensing inwardly is the experience of the *other*, as registered in the other's brain and body. Hence, for attunement and empathy to occur, the therapist needs to be present with his or her own internal state and open to the felt experience of the other.

### Entrainment in Body and Brain

Physical entrainment is a physics phenomenon of resonance. Independent rhythms (or oscillating bodies) join in synchronized movement as one speeds up while the other slows down. When clocks are positioned next to each other, for example, their second hands will eventually move in unison independent of any intervention. The concept of physical entrainment helps us understand the psychological, physiological, and neuronal synchrony that we can experience with clients in a state of presence (Geller & Porges, 2014; Koole & Tschacher, 2016).

To take in and resonate with another human being, we need to be in synch with that person. Like a dance between two partners moving in temporal coordination, with synchronicity comes a participation in each other's experience (Stern, 2004). Adaptive oscillators could play a role in this. They act like clocks in our body that can be reset over and over so their rate of firing is adjusted to match the rate of firing of the incoming stimuli. In clinical terms, when the therapist is open and moving, speaking and feeling in synch with the client, there is a shared reality that is reflected in the adapting of the therapist's neural firing so it entrains with the client's neural firing. This deepens the sense of synchronicity and deep knowing of the other. And when there is intentionality behind the joint behavior, there is a subjective feeling of synchrony in addition to neural synchrony (Llobera et al., 2016).

Many other studies find that rhythmic interpersonal coordination, including walking, singing, drumming, and others, leads to greater prosocial behavior, cooperation, and a subjective experience of connectedness (Kirschner & Tomasello, 2010; Kokal, Engel, Kirschner, & Keysers, 2011; Valdesolo & DeSteno, 2011; Wiltermuth & Heath, 2009). This bodily and relational entrainment also has neuronal correlates: Behaviors performed together, such as in music, sports, dance, or theater, create what has been called *interbrain synchrony* (Llobera et al., 2016). For example, research with improvising musicians documents this brain synchrony in musical dialogue: A mirror state is created in the brain of each player as well as an experience of connection (Lindenberger, Li, Gruber, & Müller, 2009; Sänger, Müller, & Lindenberger, 2012).

So we can see that purposely entraining our body movements with someone else's can increase our sense of unity. Like the inanimate hands of the clock, bodies tend to naturally fall into these rhythms in relationship as well (Marsh, Richardson, & Schmidt, 2009). One example of spontaneous synchronization is the unintentional entraining of rocking chair rhythms when individuals rock with a companion (Richardson, Marsh, Isenhower, Goodman, & Schmidt, 2007). The pattern of birds in flight is another example of how there is a larger whole that emerges as different rhythms naturally entrain together.

In the therapy context, intending for presence can invite this synchrony between brain and body rhythms, along with the subjective feeling of connection and interpersonal integration. When we entrain our breath and body with our clients, there is a neurophysiological resonance created through the vocal, breath, and body movement rhythms, allowing for attunement, connection, and feelings of harmony and well-being (Cozolino, 2006; Geller & Porges, 2014; Porges, 2011; Siegel, 2010). Relational integration in the therapeutic context allows for a deepening in presence in the client, which invites change and deeper therapeutic work as both therapist and client become present in themselves and with each other.

## THE WHOLE STORY: THERAPEUTIC
## PRESENCE AND INTEGRATION

Pulling this all together, we can begin to understand how therapeutic presence is the foundation of a positive therapeutic relationship and effective therapy. When we become present within ourselves, we become more personally integrated across our brain and body. We can then receive and attune with our clients, which makes them feel felt, heard, understood, and accepted—in mind, brain, and body. This evokes a neurophysiological experience of connection and safety. In a state of safety, our clients are more able to notice and stay present with their feelings and experiences, the therapeutic relationship strengthens, deeper work becomes possible, and both internal and intrapersonal integration are further promoted. We can use our presence intentionally to invite greater safety through entraining in the relationship.

How do we do all of this good work? The focus of the next clinical section is on gaining the microskills to promote optimal therapy with therapeutic presence. Let us transition there with a practice, to support the state of presence arising in our own bodies so we can let go of this chapter and receive the next (just as we do with our clients).

## TRANSITION PRACTICE: THE RHYTHM OF BREATHING

- Pause and bring your awareness to the sensation of breathing in your belly or chest.
- Notice the rhythm of your inhale and exhale in relation to the rise and fall of your belly or chest.
- For 2–3 minutes allow yourself to just be with the gentle rhythm of breathing.
- When this feels complete, take a few deep breaths before proceeding to the next chapter or the rest of your day.

# II

## PRESENCE SKILLS
## IN SESSION

# 4

# PREPARING FOR PRESENCE PRIOR TO THE SESSION

When we are able to make ourselves as still within as an untouched mountain lake, we have an exquisite reflection of all that is in and around us.

—Laura van Dernoot Lipsky (2009, p. 191)

Let us venture now into the therapy encounter, with a focus on clinical skills to help strengthen your presence with your clients. I am presenting a model (see Figure 4.1) as a preliminary glimpse of this flow and breakdown of the therapeutic presence process as presented over the next three chapters. This begins with this chapter, preparing and approaching the session with presence, with a unique focus on the hours and moments leading up to a session itself. The following two chapters will break down the process of presence in session, as informed by the therapeutic presence model. Throughout the session you are receiving the client and attuning inwardly to what emerges (Chapter 5). Then you use the information that you attune to in yourself and in the client to respond, while maintaining right brain to right brain communication in your nonverbal expression to maintain contact and safety (Chapter 6). This includes closing the session and transitioning in intentional ways to let go and regain a sense of presence (also in Chapter 6).

http://dx.doi.org/10.1037/0000025-005
*A Practical Guide to Cultivating Therapeutic Presence,* by S. M. Geller

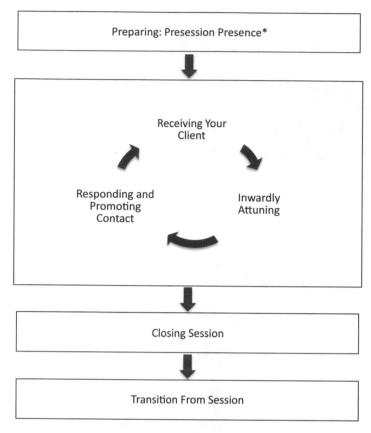

*Figure 4.1.* The skills and process of therapeutic presence. Asterisk indicates that preparing occurs in moments leading up to the session.

The clinical section will close by naming and working through some of the challenges to therapeutic presence (Chapter 7).

## THE POWER OF PREPARING PRIOR TO THE SESSION

Your therapy day begins before you even walk in the door to your office; starting with your self-care. Practices for presence in life will be offered in Chapter 8. It is suffice to say here, caring for your clients requires that you care for yourself, maintaining a focus on balance and nourishment of yourself and your relationships.

Preparing before you start your therapy day also sets the conditions for presence in the session. To do this, allow yourself time to open up the space, gather your thoughts, and attend to what you personally need to feel nourished. This also means taking time to transition between sessions, to consciously form an intention for presence, to resist busyness, and to actively clear a space inside. For example, a few minutes prior to the session, I will ensure all phones, texts, notes, and other distractions are aside and that I have also taken care of my own hunger, thirst, or bodily needs. I can then center and receive my client without distraction or irritation, which can otherwise lead to judgments, preconceptions, and agendas.

Preparing for a session can take very little time yet has great effect. Remember the research suggesting that 5 minutes of precentering or presence practice can shape the direction of your session, promoting greater alliance and positive outcomes (Dunn, Callahan, Swift, & Ivanovic, 2013). Running antiparallel to that relationship is the detrimental effect of not allowing you the time to prepare. Here is my experience of the negative impact of rushing into session.

## Clinical Vignette: The Impact of Not Preparing

One of my major challenges is allowing myself enough time in advance to arrive early. I have improved over the years, but I can remember a particular occasion when I walked in late and upset a client. Not only did I disrespect his time, but being late also impacted my focus and presence at the beginning of the session in my rush to get started. Let me tell you the story of my client "Bob" and what I won't soon forget about the importance of preparing for presence.

I hurried into the office, 10 minutes late for my first client of the day. Bob was in the waiting room taking his jacket off the coat rack. When I apologized for making him wait, he looked uncertain as to whether he was going to stay or go. In a low voice he said, "Fine, I'll come in." We sat down across from each other: I was filled with apology for my lateness, and he was silently fuming. As the session began, I could feel that he was shut down and sharing only at a surface level. Finally, I checked in and said, "I know you are upset and get the sense you felt disrespected by my being late. I went on about feeling badly and that took away from your feelings." Bob's eyes met mine and then he quickly looked away again. I continued, "I wonder if what you needed was to be angry and share your hurt. I want to know now what you feel, and I realize I did not do such a good job before in listening to your experience." After a long pause he started to tear. "Yes, I was angry, I had such a hard night last night and really needed to talk. And there I was in the hall wondering if you had forgotten about me, if you really cared."

I noticed the tension in my chest as I resonated with Bob's hurt and had a passing realization that my overapologizing might partly be an effort to protect myself from feeling the discomfort of his hurt. I authentically shared my remorse about how I had hurt and disappointed him, but this time in response to his sharing about the experience and not in a way he would feel was just a social grace. He softened and shared his appreciation that I owned my role, as he had experiences with past therapists and relationships where his upset was thrown back on him as his "pathology" and "issues" (to use his own words).

*Reflection*

This example shows how lack of preparation or presence can cause emotional harm, creating an unsafe feeling and emotional withdrawal in the client. It is important to note that if there is an upset, there is room to repair. In fact, recognizing relationship difficulties in the here and now and having honest communication, including clients sharing their emotions and therapists owning their part, can strengthen the therapeutic alliance (Safran, Crocker, McMain, & Murray, 1990). When Bob and I talked about what happened, we were able to fix the rupture. Regaining my sense of presence, noticing his withdrawal, inviting him to speak, and being authentic in acknowledging my mistake were all important parts of that process. Once Bob could name what he was feeling and sense me taking ownership of my part and really being present with him in all of that, he could start to regulate emotionally again. The same was true for me.

People who use words to describe their internal states (including their emotions and perceptions) are more flexible and capable of regulating their emotions in an adaptive way (Ochsner, Bunge, Gross, & Gabrieli, 2002). Researchers have noted in brain scans that labeling intense emotions that are triggered by evocative pictures keeps limbic firing more in balance (decreasing amygdala activity) than observing an intensely emotional experience without naming it (Hariri, Bookheimer, & Mazziotta, 2000; Lieberman et al., 2007). We then also become more able to reflect honestly and hear from others without being overly sensitive or defensive—aspects of reappraising the situation that also draw on the prefrontal cortex to help to resolve emotional distress (Burklund, Creswell, Irwin, & Lieberman, 2014). A great catch phrase for this is "name it to tame it," as coined by Daniel Siegel (Siegel & Bryson, 2012). To reap the benefits of naming feelings, however, clients need to (a) feel safe doing so and (b) feel respected and validated in the process. Both of these requirements depend on the quality of your therapeutic alliance and the client's felt sense that you are present with them. Here we circle back to the importance of preparing. If I had allowed myself time to prepare, I would have been immediately aware that overapologizing for an injury in session takes space from a client's expression of his or her own feelings about what had happened. (Preparation might also have allowed me to avoid this situation entirely.)

**Presence Reflection: Starting a Day of Therapy**

I invite you to pause now to reflect on your own preparations for a therapy day:

- Take a moment to stop and breathe, as you prepare to reflect on your experience.
- Internally ask yourself each question, while pausing for a few moments to listen for a response inside:
    - What is your normal practice at the beginning of the day or between sessions?
    - What is the way you intentionally prepare yourself to meet your clients?
    - Are there ways that you start your day that may interfere with your being fully present with your clients?
    - Are there changes you would like to make? For example, would it be helpful to add in a few minutes before or between each session to pause without distraction, sit outside, or move your body?
- Pay attention in the next week as you try something new. For example, take a few minutes before or between sessions to stretch and breathe. Notice whether your sense of presence in session changes. If you feel more present, consider how this impacts you, your client and the relationship between you.

**Intention for Presence**

Intention setting is powerful. It can act as a compass that takes you where you want to go. In musical terms, intention provides the undertone, something subtle beneath the melody line that contributes to the feel of the music. Buddhist master Thich Nhat Hanh (2003) teaches that intention toward kindness sends out kindness in all directions; the same is true for presence:

> You are like a candle. Imagine you are sending light out all around you. All your words, thoughts and actions are going in many directions. If you say something kind, your kind words go in many directions, and you yourself go with them. (p. 122)

So intention for presence involves directing all of yourself toward that which you are intending: to invite your energy, body posture, motivation, care, and focus to be in the moment with and for your client.

When you set an intention for presence, you kick-start changes at the brain level that prepare you to receive, sense, focus, and behave in a way that is therapeutically present (Hanson & Mendius, 2010; Siegel, 2007). Intention for presence also stimulates the parasympathetic nervous system (inviting calm), with a mild activation of the sympathetic nervous system (inviting alertness), which mirrors the experience of therapeutic presence.

The following are some practices to set the intention for presence. I encourage you to practice each of them for a focused time. For example, you can commit to one practice every day for 1 to 2 weeks and then try a different one. This will allow you to gain an experiential sense of what works for you.

### Preparing Practice: PRESENCE Acronym

Acronyms are excellent mnemonic devices to help the brain remember. They break the whole down into bite-sized chunks and leave you with a cue, the first letter of each component, to jog your memory. There is an acronym I use before every session that helps me to invoke the core aspects of therapeutic presence.

As you bring your attention to each step in the acronym, notice how it leads you through aspects of the experience such as opening and attuning to the moment, to yourself, to others, and to the relationship between what is inside (yourself) and what is outside of you (others). Although the PRESENCE acronym is a practice for yourself, it begins as a private preparation and ends with opening the door to greet your client. Like any practice, feel free to alter the wording if there is a way this practice can work more effectively for you.

- **P**ause.
- **R**elax into this moment.
- **E**nhance awareness of your breath.
- **S**ense your inner body; bring awareness to your physical and emotional body.
- **E**xpand sensory awareness outwards (seeing, listening, touching, sensing what is around you).
- **N**otice what is true in this moment, both within you and around you.
- **C**enter and ground (in yourself and your body).
- **E**xtend and make contact (with client, or other).

*Reflection.* The signature of relating with therapeutic presence is simultaneously holding a connection to yourself and others. The PRESENCE acronym is like a miniature guidebook to help you do just that in the moments leading up to a session. We first arrive in the moment, through the body and the breath (oxygenating the brain and body with deep inhales and activating the parasympathetic nervous system with long exhales). We then mindfully notice what is true in our body, both physically and emotionally (readying our interoceptive awareness for a bodily attunement to self and other throughout the session, which prepares us to empathize with clients). In noticing what is true, we can name our experience internally, especially if there is any distress we need to ease, as the labeling itself will help to regulate our emotions.

Next, expanding our attention outwards helps to connect us beyond ourselves (enhancing right-brain functioning). Feeling the relationship between your inner world and your outer world is a pivotal component of this practice, and it activates the social engagement system for relating with others. Returning to a grounded, centered place, feeling your feet on the ground, is a part of reestablishing your sense of personal integration—mind and body acting together, in the moment. From this grounded place you can then extend and make contact with your client, beginning the process of integrating in relationship.

It is helpful to do at this practice at the beginning of each session. When we practice this repeatedly, it can provide a conditioned response so that the act of going through the acronym invites the experience of presence to arise within. Although it takes more time initially to walk through the steps, over time presence can be activated when you only have a few minutes to prepare.

*Presence Practice: Breathing in Rhythm With Your Intention*

How else can you intend for presence? As suggested with the PRESENCE acronym, words that have an intended message, spoken inside or aloud, can be helpful cues to guide you. If you tend to be a more verbal person, adding words internally can help keep you focused on your breath and reduce mind wandering. This practice invites you to link a word or phrase to the rhythm with your breathing, such as the following:

Inhaling and saying "Letting go of busyness"
Exhaling in rhythm with the words "Arriving in this moment"

And then to continue with a briefer phrase that holds the essence of the message:

Inhaling and saying "Letting go"
Exhaling in rhythm with the word "Arriving"

You can create your own words that resonate better for you, to invite your own energy and activate your intention. Here are some other suggestions:

Inhaling: "Opening"
Exhaling: "to Being present"
Inhaling: "Receptive"
Exhaling: "Here"
Inhaling: "Being"
Exhaling: "In the moment"
Inhaling: "Grounding"
Exhaling: "Expanding"

You can add your own variations below:

Inhaling: _____
Exhaling: _____
Inhaling: _____
Exhaling: _____
Inhaling: _____
Exhaling: _____

*Reflection.* Recalling Thich Nhat Hanh's (2003) message from earlier in the section, it is perhaps clearer now how when your "words go in many directions . . . you yourself go with them" (p. 122). Setting intention through words, while pausing to breathe and arrive, invites your body, mind, and brain into the present. Intention engages the frontal lobe and gears up our neural system to be in mode of that which we are intending (i.e., to be present; Hanson & Mendius, 2010; Siegel, 2007).

You can try this as a daily practice in the morning to strengthen your ability to be present. This practice can also be used at the beginning of therapy day, or even just to pause in the middle of the day if you need to regain a sense of presence. Through repeated practice, you can discover how this seemingly simple practice over time has dramatic effects on the inside, in ways that will bolster your ability to be present.

### Bracketing Practice: Clearing a Space

*Clearing a space* means putting aside your own challenges, needs, concerns, preconceptions, or judgments that may be in the way of being fully present. Emptying yourself out and then visualizing the space inside will allow the experience of the client to enter in without interference from your personal issues, emotions, thoughts, or distractions. Try the following clearing-a-space practice when you are feeling clouded with your own issues. It is helpful to engage in this when you have more time to prepare. Optimally you should allow yourself at least 10 to 20 minutes for the practice.

- Sit or lie down in a comfortable position with your eyes soft or closed.
- Become aware of the rhythm of your inhale and your exhale.
- Ask yourself, "What is between me and feeling fully present and at ease in myself right now?" Wait to see what issues emerge. Spend a moment with each issue that arises, until you intuitively focus on one particular issue.
- Scan your body to bring awareness to how and where you carry that issue within your body, noticing the physical sensations associated with the issue and just naming them (e.g., tightness in jaw, butterflies in stomach, pit in chest).
- Ask yourself for a felt sense of what gets in the way of being present. Find words or an image that reflect an overall feel of the issue (e.g., frightened, confused, frustrated).
- Now visualize yourself putting that issue in a box or on a shelf, putting the whole sense of that issue aside (or use other images such as floating the issue down a river).
- Continue until all the issues have been acknowledged, labeled, felt, and put aside.
- After a few moments, check inside to see if there is a background sense of feeling more receptive and present.
- Notice what it feels like to have cleared out these concerns. Feel and absorb the sensations in your body.
- When you are ready, gently transition out of practice and bring this receptive openness with you into the next phase of your reading or day.

*Reflection.* The clearing-a-space practice is inspired by Eugene Gendlin's (1978, 1996) focusing technique. *Focusing* involves bringing an open and nonjudging attention to an experience that is felt but not yet clearly defined in words. This technique can help you to become clear on what you feel or want, or to gain new insights. Focusing begins from a felt sensation of your experience, which is the parallel to this practice. When you follow the felt sensation, it can help you identify and ultimately clear any residual issues you may be carrying with you into session.

## OPENING AND CLOSING YOUR THERAPY DAY

Beginning your therapy day by having a simple gesture, activity, or ritual can help you open up to presence. Similarly, closing your day with the intention to release any residual stress or emotions can help you maintain your energy as you transition into the next part of your day or evening.

Hebbian law (Hebb, 1949) tells us that cells activated in rapid succession wire more strongly together over time. The repetitive nature of rituals particularly helps in the priming of body and brain for presence, in a type of self-conditioning in which we develop associations between the rituals and the state we are invoking (Bar, 2007; Sejnowski & Tesauro, 1989).

Opening and closing a day could include any of the practices that have been shared. Making time for the ritual and sticking with it over time are more important than the specific form the ritual takes. You can choose something that works for you. Here are some suggestions:

- Take a moment to pause in your office.
- State your intention to be present with and for your clients.
- Engage in mindful breathing, with an awareness of your feet on the ground.
- Intentionally clear a space of any issues or challenges that are going on in your own life that may interfere with being present.
- Stand in a balancing yoga posture like "tree pose" for a sense of rootedness and focus.
- Light a candle (and extinguish it at the end of the day).
- Visualize the release of any residual stress or emotion melting down your body and into the ground through your feet.
- Engage in a grounding practice (see Chapter 11 for suggestions).
- Play a simple rhythm on an instrument (I have a sacred rattle that was given to me by a friend in New Mexico that I play at the beginning and end of each day).

## CREATING AN ENVIRONMENT FOR PRESENCE

Perceptual cues in an environment provide a "context frame" that readies our brain for what is to come, through the power of associative learning (Bar, 2007). So if you have the opportunity to design your therapy space, it can really aid in creating an environment that enhances presence. Art that evokes the experience of presence can help (e.g., feelings of calmness, serenity, and grounding), such as images of mountains, the ocean, or a special place you have been (or want to go). Soothing background music in the waiting room will also create an environment for presence (or lack thereof). When you choose music, remember that the feelings music can evoke are personal, so try out different sounds. (I enjoy stations that offer a Zen-Jazz to give a relaxed yet slightly energized feel.)

If you work in a community or hospital setting or a shared office, you may not have the opportunity to design your space. Yet simple things can help too, such as uncluttering the room to unclutter your mind—putting away files, papers, and excess piles that you don't need. You might have a small photo on the ledge or desk that you can put away when you do not need it, or a simple rock to invite grounding. Perhaps there is space to have books around, just a few, that invite the qualities that you wish to experience (e.g., books on mindfulness, presence, or poetry or books with images that evoke the feeling you want).

How your chairs are arranged is also important. Is there a desk or table between you and your client, which may be experienced as a barrier between you both? Are the chairs at equal heights, to eliminate any physical manifestations of a power imbalance? This will support you and your clients to feel on equal levels, as two human beings in a journey together toward their well-being. Can you take measures to eliminate outside sound, such as using a sound machine with gentle waves to raise the inside sound level in the room (which blocks out external noise)? Overall this is an invitation to be mindful of the sounds, sights, and feel of your therapy room so it invites the qualities of presence you may wish for yourself and your client to feel.

## SPACE BETWEEN SESSIONS: TRANSITION MOMENTS

Taking time to transition between sessions can make the difference between a mediocre or great session. We are constantly in flux—moving from place to place or role to role. There are the major transitions we undergo, such as illness, death, separation or divorce, job loss, retirement, a child moving away from home, loss of functioning, loss of money. We need to be more conscious of taking the time we need to process these major losses, transitioning from one stage of our life to another. There are also smaller transitions that occur throughout each day, such as shifting roles from being a parent to a daughter or son, to a therapist, to a friend, to a spouse. There are transitions before and after a meal. My most recent one I realize was a blur as I ate quickly to get on to writing—and then had to spend time preparing to write again as my mind was not engaged with the material. The practice of breathing in rhythm with my intention helped to bring my awareness back to writing about presence. There are also transitions within a workday: from arriving, to seeing your first client; the moments in between clients; shifting from lunch or breaks back into session; and eventually, ending your day.

We don't often think of daily transitions as experiences in and of themselves. We are either (unknowingly) delaying a full transition by reviewing the situation we have just left behind, or we are way ahead of ourselves, focused on what's coming up next. When we slow down transitions, and really inhabit these moments, we realize there are three components:

- noticing and letting go of what came before;
- the space between events; and
- arriving to a new moment, role, or opportunity—with intention.

To ease transitions, we need to be present to the space between what was (my last client) and what is to come (lunch). This will allow for a letting go of the emotional residue from the last moment (these could be happy or sad or neutral emotions), and an entering into the next moment (whether it be your next client, a conversation with your friend or spouse, or a meal) with a fresh sense of openness and receptivity. The best way to support your transition between sessions is through intentional transitions in daily life. The inclusion of transition moments at the end of each chapter, such as the following practice, is designed to further support your experience of pausing in between events.

TRANSITION PRACTICE: ABSORBING RELEVANCE

Allow yourself a few moments to pause and absorb what has been meaningful for you from our discussion. The following steps may help you in that process as you transition:

- Pause and take three deep and slow breaths, allowing yourself to feel the air flow in the center of your body between your inhale and exhale.
- Ask yourself: "What is important for me to take away from this chapter? Is there something I want to intentionally do to activate a sense of presence a little more consciously in my life and in my clinical practice?"

- Pause and listen deeply to what arises. Make a mental or written note.
- Take another full conscious round of breathing, to let go of what arose and create space for what is to come.
- While maintaining contact with your breath, mindfully continue to the next chapter (or to the next part of your day).

# 5

# RECEPTIVELY ATTUNING WITH CLIENTS AND OURSELVES

The art of living . . . is neither careless drifting on the one hand nor fearful clinging to the past and the known on the other. It consists in being completely sensitive to each moment, in regarding it as utterly new and unique, in having the mind open and wholly receptive.
—Alan W. Watts (2011, p. 95)

We have arrived at the session, present in the moment, and then what? What does therapeutic presence look like in the clinical encounter? These next two chapters focus on developing skill in the process of therapeutic presence in session. In this chapter we learn the process of (a) being receptive to our clients, attuning with their experience from moment to moment and (b) attuning inwardly to ourselves to help make sense of the information we receive. We build on this foundation in the next chapter with a focus on (c) extending our presence to clients through our responses and promoting contact through nonverbal communication.

## BEGINNING THE SESSION: A SHARED PAUSE FOR PRESENCE

When I begin the session, I often invite a shared moment for my client and I to consciously pause, breathe, and fully arrive (body and mind) in the room together. This helps clients to settle and go beyond the initial chatter.

http://dx.doi.org/10.1037/0000025-006
*A Practical Guide to Cultivating Therapeutic Presence*, by S. M. Geller

At the end of this practice I invite them to listen inside for the essence of what they want to explore. For example, I might say:

> Notice in your body what you are feeling right now. Ask yourself: What is important for me to discuss or explore today? (*I would then pause and if nothing arose I would continue.*) Slowly scan your body for feelings of tension or other signs of emotion. Put a gentle hand on the place you experience the feeling, as you ask: What am I feeling in this moment? Allow yourself to listen inside with acceptance and compassion.

When clients share their intent, I listen inside to how this blends with their overall therapy goals. I use myself as a clear vessel for receiving and an antenna to attune to their inner world.

## WITHIN THE SESSION: READING AND ATTUNING WITH CLIENTS

The process of attuning with my clients involves tracking their experience moment to moment, including their in-the-moment feelings and how they are receiving my interaction with them. Verbal and nonverbal expressions are all gateways to clients' experience, both surface and hidden. Let us take a microlevel look at the different aspects I am listening for.

### Emotions

Emotion is woven into all the aspects of clients' expression, yet it warrants its own section, as emotions are a guide to understanding the essence of our clients' experience. The emotional underpinning is what we seek to find within verbal and nonverbal expressions. I am thus listening for and sensing clients' core pain by attuning to both primary and secondary emotions (Greenberg, 2010). *Primary emotions* are fundamental or initial "gut responses" to a situation, such as feeling sadness to a loss. *Secondary emotions* appear in reaction to primary emotions, as in when we feel irritation or anger to cover the sadness that is difficult to bear. To identify my clients' core pain, I need to access their primary emotions. Recognizing the different and subtle ways emotions are expressed will help us to identify what is most primary, in the moment. It can also help us sense how connected our clients are to their own emotional experiencing.

Emotions are expressed as bodily shifts, so reading our clients' bodily signals is key to knowing their current feeling state. According to Damasio (1999, 2005), the brain receives continuous signals from the body, registering what is actually going on inside. It then processes these signals in neural maps, compiled in somatosensory areas of the brain. When these maps are read, they register as feelings, indicating that emotional changes are recorded as snapshots of our physical state. So reading clients' bodily cues helps us recognize their emotions and core pain.

For example, my 18-year-old client expressed anger toward her mother for stepping on stage with her during her first solo performance. She had been preparing for months to find the strength and courage to go on stage alone, as this performance was in front of an audience of her peers who had previously taunted her for being a "mommy's girl." As she spoke I noticed that her eyes were downcast, her face was red, her voice had a strain to it as if she were fighting back tears, and her shoulders were slumped forward and down. She was expressing her anger (secondary emotion) toward her mother, but I was sensing in her body cues that she was experiencing primary emotions of shame and hurt as she perceived everyone in the audience making fun of her.

We next look at specific client expressions to attend to, including verbal narratives and bodily markers of emotions, as informed by my clinical experience, research, and findings from the polyvagal theory. Although there is some evidence of specific somatic markers of emotions, the theory remains controversial (Rainville, Bechara, Naqvi, & Damasio, 2006). It is important to see these as guides while being sensitive to individual and cultural differences.

### Verbal Narrative

Attending to narrative is one of the most natural ways we listen. Markers can guide therapists as to what they are looking for in the narrative and how to move forward in light of what they find. For example, if clients are expressing the "same old story," we might feel bored and unclear on how to break the repetitive cycle. However, the repetition could be an indicator that there is unexpressed pain underneath that needs to be accessed and may serve as a portal to deeper work. Attending to markers for narrative and client process found in the Narrative-Emotion Process Coding System can be a helpful tool (Boritz, Bryntwick, Angus, Greenberg, & Constantino, 2014).

Listening to clients recount their experience is important, yet the narrative itself is not the whole story: We must listen for both what is expressed and unexpressed (Angus & Greenberg, 2011). It is the relationship between verbal narrative and body language that we want to keep gently and empathically unfolding. Attending to discord between clients' words and body language can signal something important is going on, such as feeling overwhelmed or shutting down. It is these embodied feelings that we want to attune to (Van der Kolk, 2014).

Researchers have categorized nonverbal communication according to specific functional differences (e.g., Efron, 1941; Ekman & Friesen, 1969). One example is "illustrators," which are movements that supplement speech and refine or enhance verbal communication (Ekman & Friesen, 1969). Clients' use of gestures to augment their verbal narrative can powerfully shape the intended message, and so we must watch for these. When clients struggle for words, they might use movements like cutting the air with their hand in frustration or clasping their palms to their chest when they feel grief. We can help them deliver their message by being attuned enough to notice these movements and reflective in suggesting the meaning they are trying to convey.

Ekman (1977) noted the cultural specificity of gestures used to convey specific verbal meaning. Although there are many universal categories of these "emblems" (Efron, 1941; e.g., gestures serving as greetings and communications about one's physical state), Ekman found no universally occurring emblems. For example, Ekman described culturally specific gestures signifying suicide: While Americans are likely to form a gun shape with their hand and hold it to their temple, Chinese individuals tend to depict stabbing by sword, and the South Fore of New Guinea illustrate strangling by wrapping their hands around their neck. Although clients might not gesture in ways as blatant as this, it is a helpful illustration of how gestures that contribute to storytelling are often culture bound. It is valuable to familiarize yourself with your clients' personal style and their cultural background, and attempt to clarify the meaning of recurrent gesturing if you are unsure.

## Vocal Expression

Another doorway into our clients' emotions is to attend to their vocal quality (speech rate, volume, pitch, and tone). Studies have shown that it is much harder to control the voice than other aspects of nonverbal behavior, such as facial expressions—which can be hard to control in themselves (Zuckerman, Larrance, Spiegel, & Klorman, 1981). One of the ways that research connects emotions and vocal quality is through nervous system activity (Scherer, Johnstone, & Klasmeyer, 2003). As we know, autonomic activation impacts breathing and cardiovascular activity. Sympathetic nervous system activation during emotional arousal also creates differing patterns of tension in the vocal organs that change how air moves through the respiratory tract. These changes come together in the specific quality of the vocal expression.

For example, increasing vocal pitch, changing vocal pitch, and pausing frequently are possible indicators that clients are feeling anxious about what is happening or being shared (Laukka et al., 2008). When clients are angry, they will often speak quickly at an increased pitch and amplitude (loudness; Scherer et al., 2003).

My clinical experience, combined with an understanding of polyvagal theory, has taught me several vocal cues that could convey clients' state of safety or unsafety. When their vocal tone is softer with a natural space between words, it can indicate that clients feel safe to reflect and explore their present-moment experience. The nervous system is calm, tension in the vocal tract eases, and breathing is regular. When their vocal tone is loud and booming, it may indicate that they feel unheard or disconnected from their own experience. A vocal tone that is monotonous and rambling may also be an indicator of distancing. When their voice is trailing off, it may mean that clients are tentative about sharing their experience. There may be a sense of unsafety, uncertainty about their own experience, or discomfort with you in the moment. If they are touching something highly emotional and feeling guarded, this is likely to be reflected in their voice. In contrast, a prosody (rhythm) in the voice suggests that clients are at ease (Geller & Porges, 2014). Hearing the quality of voice in relation to facial cues such as twitches in the eyes or the face can also indicate the emotional poignancy of what he or she is sharing.

Laura Rice, a student of Carl Rogers, developed the Client Vocal Quality Scale to assess the nuances that reflect the depth of client experiencing (Rice & Kerr, 1986). This scale can be a guide for learning more about the meaning of variances in vocal expression and connecting this to how deeply the client is experiencing what they are sharing.

*Breathing Patterns*

Respiratory psychophysiology research explores the connection between emotional processes and breathing. As we intuitively know, deep and slow breathing can indicate that clients feel calm and met by you (Geller & Porges, 2014; Porges, 2011). Shallow, irregular breathing and short exhalations suggest they may feel triggered or threatened.

Research on emotions and breathing originally focused on timing and volume of respiration, but there has been a recent interest in breathing variability as well. During high arousal or intense negative emotions, variability in breathing patterns tends to increase (Vlemincx, Van Diest, & Van den Bergh, 2015). Sudden breath retention suggests a holding back, a sense of being overwhelmed with what is being felt, or that your client has been caught off guard.

A more readily observable signal is the sigh, which can indicate a wide variety of emotions and mental states ranging from relief to boredom, fatigue, or dismay (Vlemincx et al., 2013). It's easier to detect than some breathing cues, but not necessarily easier to decipher. Vlemincx and colleagues (2013) suggested that the sigh acts as a physiological "reset" that lets individuals regain respiratory control after something has dysregulated them—but this could be a positive trigger or a negative one. They added that sighs might have an analogous role psychologically, helping people return to a baseline after emotional arousal.

If sighs can induce a return to calm when needed, and also signal a sense of relief, how do we know which our client is feeling? Attending to the context can help. If a client sighs or takes a deep breath following something you have empathically reflected, perhaps you have managed to articulate their felt experience in exactly the way they needed. If their breathing becomes more irregular after something you have offered, this might signal that you have led them somewhere that is emotionally laden (i.e., early trauma) or perhaps they feel misunderstood or unsafe in those feelings or with you. It is useful to become conscious of each client's unique breathing patterns, so that you can more accurately track their internal state moment to moment. If it is difficult to discern what they are feeling given the context or individual variance in expression, try expanding your focus to include other aspects of their bodily expression as the body is a gateway to emotional experience.

*Body Posture*

A lot of information can be received through attention to bodily expressions of emotional experience, such as posture and tension or softness in musculature. Certain postures, such as those conveying pride and shame, are thought to be innate. Even congenitally blind athletes puff up their chest following victory and slump their shoulders after defeat (Tracy & Matsumoto, 2008). However, societal influences can alter even these innate responses (Tracy & Matsumoto, 2008), so it is good to understand your client's particular expressions.

Despite this individual variance, there are some suggested examples of what you may notice when you attune. A closed or tight posture, for example with the arms crossed across the chest, may indicate that your client is held back, defensive, or disconnected. Vitality in the body shown through an upright posture, open and broad chest or torso, with the arms relaxed at the sides, suggests openness in the client to both his or her own experience and to you. Reading bodily cues might also indicate when an expressed primary emotion holds greater emotional charge and meaning than the words alone are conveying.

*Eyes and Facial Expression*

The upper part of the face can reflect how relaxed and safe a client feels (Geller & Porges, 2014; Porges, 2011). The eyes in particular are portals to emotion: In the eyes of my clients I look for signs of moisture, a downward cast that could indicate sadness or shame, or a widening of the eyes signaling fear, among others. In contrast, a soft gaze indicates that the client feels at ease and more able to connect and receive from you.

Emotions are expressed in facial expressions in an overt way, as suggested by Ekman and colleagues (Ekman, 2003; Ekman & Friesen, 1969), as well as in microexpressions, which may flash for just a brief moment. These microexpressions can reflect concealed emotions. Subtle emotions are also revealed through miniexpressions, which remain a bit longer and are localized to one part of the face.

Facial expressions of emotions can be seen visibly as described below:

- Happiness—This involves the upper and lower parts of the face. The corners of the mouth are raised and the muscles around the eyes contracted. The jaw is relaxed and open.
- Sadness—The corners of the mouth are lowered and the eyebrows raised. The upper eyelids drop, and there is a loss of focus in the eyes.
- Contempt—This is the only emotion that involves asymmetry in the face—it occurs on one side of face, where the corner of the lip is tightened and raised.
- Surprise—Arching of eyebrows, eyes wide open, and jaw slightly dropped.
- Fear—Eyebrows are raised and pulled together, eyes open with lower eyelids tensed, lips stretched, and mouth slightly ajar.
- Disgust—This feeling of aversion is reflected in raising of the upper lip, wrinkling of the bridge of nose, and raised upper lip and cheeks.
- Anger—Different intensities of anger have similar facial patterns. There are lowered eyebrows, upper lids pulled back, lips pressed firmly together, and bulging or glaring eyes.

So attuning to facial and bodily expressions moment to moment is imperative to understanding what is overtly as well as subtly expressed by our clients. Movies such as Disney's *Inside Out* offer an interesting glimpse of the inner emotional life that is expressed through facial and bodily cues. There are also programs designed to help military, government, businesses, and psychologists to read facial expressions of emotions.[1]

---

[1]Visit http://www.paulekman.com/ or http://www.humintell.com to learn more.

## Cultural and Individual Differences When Reading Emotional Cues

My aim is not to present this material as a deciphered code. Instead, it is to alert you to some major vehicles of client nonverbal expression and make suggestions about what these could mean, especially given the evidence from neuroscience discussed in Chapter 3 on bidirectional attunement and how we feel each other all the time, even when we are not consciously aware.

There are very real and pronounced differences in nonverbal language and how to understand it, particularly cross-culturally. I touched on this briefly in the sections on verbal narrative, where we looked at how gesturing can supplement storytelling. In his neurocultural theory of emotion, Ekman (1972) attributes differences in facial expression of emotion to "display rules" around what should be shared or hidden, rather than to anything innate. These display rules are dictated by social norms that are embedded in culture. For example, in the earlier study of pride and shame expression in athletes, sighted individuals somewhat inhibited the shame display, indicating the influence of cultural norms (Tracy & Matsumoto, 2008). Matsumoto (1989) added that there are culturally specific "decoding rules" too, dictating whether and when it is appropriate to acknowledge you have perceived specific emotions in another person. As therapists, this means we have another reason to anticipate varying degrees of comfort in our clients with being openly confronted by their own emotions—yet another reason to let therapeutic presence and reading the moment be our guides.

Individual differences can also emerge from clients' family backgrounds or societal messaging around what is acceptable and what is not. For example, if a family message is that pride should be hidden and one should be humble about their accomplishments, expressions of feeling good may be complicated by a downward glance, reflecting associated shame or merely humbleness. People with disabilities that are due to neurological or musculoskeletal differences may have different forms of expression as well. Facial features may be impinged on by muscle neurological damage, so typical facial expressions of emotions could appear differently.

Part of being fully present to your clients is taking the time to consider how their cultural and personal backgrounds might influence their modes of expression. If you and your client come from different backgrounds, be aware that you lack the ingroup advantage in deciphering the client's emotional expression and proceed with extra care (Elfenbein & Ambady, 2003). Informing yourself by consulting colleagues, friends of diverse cultural affiliation, and research sources will help you more fully attune to your client's present-moment experience. But the best source of understanding is observation of your client's patterns over time; this is a valuable way to passively acquire a felt sense of how the client's nonverbal expression connects to his or her internal state. There is also great value in having an open dialogue. This can help prevent confusion, hurt, missed opportunities to connect more deeply, and therapeutic ruptures.

## Interpreting Cues Using Polyvagal Theory

Porges's (2011) polyvagal theory sheds light on why nonverbal communication like vocal prosody, body posture, and facial expressions are such powerful conveyers of an individual's physiological and psychological states. Polyvagal theory is rooted in our mammalian wiring and is therefore relevant to all human beings; even though there can be cultural and individual differences, there are some common elements too. We are all equipped with the integrated system that connects cues in our environment to our internal sense of safety or unsafety. These manifest in how we use our faces, voices, breath, and body. The physiological changes that give us an internal sense of security or dis-ease are mediated by features in social interactions that are often outside the realm of our awareness. An interaction with another (i.e., client or therapist) can trigger a broad range of observable bodily changes; although we may be unaware of them in ourselves, we can and do interpret them in each other.

Why is this important for therapeutic presence? Think of a situation, for example, in which you have had a momentary lapse in attention when listening to a client. If you have a client who is sensitive to these moments of absence, a tightness in the edges of your client's eyes or a distant gaze may suggest he or she noticed your absence and is having a reaction—the client might feel unsafe or disconnected. Your distancing triggered physiological changes in the client revealed to you through his or her face. The functioning of the social engagement system reflects the effects of our presence on clients, and if you become familiar with universal and individual signs of expression, you can use this to inform your responses. Stay tuned for more on this in Chapter 6.

## Vignette: Misreading Client Cues

Despite our best efforts, we can at times misread our clients' experience because of our own lack of presence or individualized or cultural differences in emotional expression. The following vignette illustrates such a case.

Linzi struggled with interpersonal anxiety, expressed as intense feelings of rejection and a core belief that she was "not good enough." In a particular session, I noted that she was sitting with her body slightly turned away from me and was looking down. We had engaged in some deep therapeutic work the week before, and I had the sense that she was feeling scared to open up because going to such a deep emotional place felt vulnerable and scary to her. I sensed her unsafety as expressed in her body posture and responded in a way to evoke more safety. I leaned slightly forward in an open posture and let her know I understood how scary it must be to be vulnerable and that we could take our time in processing her anxiety and fears. She became quieter and more withdrawn. I felt confused. The session ended with a feeling of disconnection.

As she arrived at the next session, Linzi reported how angry she was. In a raised and tearful voice she said she felt misunderstood by me. She had been trying to express her grief and sadness about the loss of her mother, and I didn't notice. Instead, she felt I criticized her in saying she was vulnerable and scared from engaging in our work together. She felt hurt and wanted to end therapy. I could feel a rising sense of hurt and shame in me, in knowing I had misunderstood her and let the session progress without recognizing what was really going on for her.

*Reflection*

Sometimes emotions expressed through the body will be read one way, when there is something very different being expressed. Linzi's turning away and downward cast could have reflected a feeling of unsafety or grief (as it actually was), among other possibilities. Understanding the context of what is occurring for someone and then reflecting it out aloud with tentativeness or questioning allows the client to confirm or disconfirm and then expand in the direction of his or her feeling. Linzi was hurt by my misread, and misreading clients can feel difficult for therapists as well. Her shutting down triggered confusion in me, followed by shame when I realized I had misunderstood her. In Chapters 6 and 7, we explore how to work with these misreads and our own emotional reactions, as well as how to repair ruptures when they ensue.

**Listening and Attuning Practice: Watching a Foreign Movie**

When I was in Spain a few years back, I was fascinated by how much information I could hear and feel listening to my friends converse in Spanish, even though my knowledge of the language was limited. I learned that listening or watching people speaking a foreign language helps us fine-tune our ability to read body language, tonal qualities, and emotional expressions. Often we concentrate on the spoken word, taking these alone to be representative of others' full experience. But this approach rests on several assumptions: (a) that people are always aware of their feelings, (b) that they are able to articulate them, and (c) that they are comfortable sharing their true experience with us. These are considerable assumptions to make, especially in the therapy room. So we want to know how to read nonverbal cues as well, to complement and inform the words we hear, noticing especially any discord between verbal and nonverbal expression. Before we can use nonverbal expression as tools for emotional regulation, we must become skillful at attuning to and recognizing the cues themselves.

For this practice, watch several foreign movies with the subtitles off and try to read the emotions, bodily cues, vocal tones, rhythm of voice, and facial expressions. Then watch again with the subtitles on and see if your read of the emotions at all reflected the content expressed emotionally in the dialogue. Notice also cultural variation in nonverbal emotional expression and the layer of complexity this adds (all the more reason to practice). You can also work on this skill in daily life, whenever people are speaking a language you don't understand. Rather than tuning out, which is what we tend to do when we feel disconnected, take the opportunity to tune in, refine your skills, and reconnect by reading the bodily expression of emotions and experience.

### Recommendations for Attuning With Clients in Session

The following suggestions for practicing attunement with clients are inspired by researchers who observed empathic therapists and what they do to facilitate empathy (Greenberg & Rushanski-Rosenberg, 2002; Watson, 2007), as well as by neuroscience research on mirror neurons (Iacoboni, 2009a, 2009b; Iacoboni et al., 2005; Siegel, 2007) and interbrain synchronization (Llobera et al., 2016). For example, a study using functional MRIs has shown that empathic individuals mimic postures, mannerisms, and facial expressions of others more than nonempathic individuals (Carr, Iacoboni, Dubeau, Mazziotta, & Lenzi, 2003).

1. *Bracketing* is a way of understanding. How clients feel in a moment or situation is directly connected to the context of their life history and issues. To understand the other, we have to be able to put aside our own perspective (also called bracketing) and hold their experience in the larger context of his or her life and personal challenges. By intentionally setting aside judgment or preconceptions and taking in the feelings of the client as unique to him or her and to this moment, you will develop a clearer sense of the other's experience.
2. *Visualize* being in clients' emotions by imagining details of the situation as if you were them, in the story of their life, and how that may feel. This activates your mirror neurons, allowing you to have a felt sense of your clients' experience.

3. *Mimic*, subtly and with respect, the client's physical gestures or facial expressions. This allows for motor neurons (which are adjacent to mirror neurons) to activate, also giving us a felt sense of the experience of being the other. Mimicking bodily movements, facial expressions, and body posture can also promote a sense of interbrain synchronization, which furthers our ability to empathize. You can also ask clients what they are expressing with their gesture, even allowing them to elaborate the gesture to get more of a felt sense of their own experience.

## WITHIN THE SESSION: ATTUNING WITHIN MYSELF

What do I do with all the information I am receiving? With therapeutic presence, my whole self reverberates like a tuning fork, as I allow myself to resonate with clients' experience. It is not an easy feat to resonate fully with someone else, while being attentive to one's own experience, all without losing a sense of grounding and emotional stability. Yet this is part of the mastery of therapeutic presence. Carl Rogers (as cited in Baldwin, 2000) reflected that "in using myself, I include my intuition and the essence of myself" (p. 30).

When I attune inwardly, I may notice twinges of pain or bodily sensations and images or words that emerge in resonance with the client, or I may hear a guiding voice telling me how to respond or intervene. I am also listening to the ways in which I am absent or distracted and inviting myself and my attention back. I may need to intervene internally to put aside what is getting in the way. This thorough self scan can occur in a flash once the ability to consciously practice presence becomes stronger. Note that countertransference reactions are not the same as resonance with the client's experience and must be handled differently (see Chapter 7, this volume).

In this isolation of the therapeutic presence process, I am listening and attuning internally to emotions; body sensations; breathing patterns; and images, inner words, and insights.

### Emotions

I am attending to emotions in me that I may feel in resonance with my client. For example, I may feel sadness as a tightness or quiver in my chest or a moistening of my eyes, suggesting that I am resonating with my client's sadness. I may notice physiological sensations of fear (i.e., accelerated heart rate or tightness in the chest) if I am registering that my client is feeling afraid.

My emotions could also be an interpersonal reaction to the client and important to understand or work through. For example, if I feel angry because of my client's continued lateness, perhaps I am feeling violated in some way. This is important to address for several reasons: It impacts our bond, it might reflect a problematic pattern occurring with others in the client's life, and it could indicate the client's discomfort with the therapy process. See the section on congruence, in Chapter 6, for more information on disclosing internal responses therapeutically with clients.

I want to access my client's primary emotions, which may be hidden beneath their secondary responses. Reading my own emotions can inform me of whether my client's emotional expression is primary, secondary, or instrumental. *Instrumental* emotions are consciously or unconsciously learned emotional responses expressed with the intent of getting a reaction, such as crying to soften hurt or anger someone has toward you for something you have done. When a client responds with instrumental emotions, it can feel distancing to therapists or as if they are being manipulated (Greenberg, 2010).

A recent couples session with Sally and her partner, Jane, illustrates this. Jane had recently disclosed that she was having an affair. Sally was sharing her sadness in a loud, accelerated voice, and I found myself feeling tight and held back. I recognized from my body's response that I was reacting to an instrumental emotion (sadness expressed in a loud whining voice), and there was a more primary emotion underneath. Jane might have expressed her emotions in this way, to align me with her point of view, consistent with the presentation of an instrumental emotion. If it were genuine sadness, I would likely feel more compassion. I sensed anger and hurt to be her primary feelings and knew from past sessions these were difficult emotions for her. Reading my own bodily response let me recognize this and reflect on what she was feeling underneath. It also helped my body relax so I felt more centered.

## Body Sensations

The clinical example also illustrates how I use my body to listen, as I resonate with what is poignant for the client. This is the "essence of presence" using the implicit sensing that is available to us all the time. I also listen inside to how the information received resonates with my professional wisdom and knowledge of my client.

*Interoception*, the ability to sense internal bodily states, is your greatest tool for reading these cues in yourself. The more familiar you can become with your body's interior, how it feels to be you on the inside, and how your body states shift moment to moment, the more adept you'll become at registering your visceral responses in session. Registering the sensations is step one; they offer a read on the encounter that will ground your response.

When attending to physical sensations in my body, I may feel a passing wave of head pain and find out later that my client has been suffering with migraines. I might notice tension when I am shut down or when my client is disconnected. Sleepiness can signal emotional disconnect, either in my client or myself. I am constantly assessing what I am sensing internally and discerning inner resonance of their experience from my own reaction as I respond (or regulate).

### Breathing Patterns

Attending to my own breathing informs me of my own state as well as my connection with the client. Much of what I observe in the client's breathing (see the previous section) I also monitor in myself. When my breathing is restricted (signs of nonpresence), I consider why I feel disconnected or distant and bring my attention back. When my breath flows openly, I feel a deep connection with my client and myself, and I know that I am present and attuned.

### Images, Inner Words, and Insights

Some of us are more imagery based, others more verbal, and some more visceral. There is no right or wrong as long as you are paying attention to what is true for you. At times images act as an empathic indicator of what my client is experiencing and guide my response. For example, as my client talked about caring for her son and aged mother, I had an image of her standing alone on an island. This gave me insight into her sense of isolation. Sometimes words emerge instead. For example, inside I may hear "deeply alone" when my client is talking about not feeling understood in her relationship, or I see the twinge in her eye as tears well up. Listening to and then trusting the words that emerge intuitively are two important parts of attuning inwardly in the process of presence.

As I listen with my whole self, I may make connections, see patterns, understand something in a fresh way, or perceive opportunities for intervention. When I am in presence mode, I accept that I may need to let go of insights if the client has opened in another direction. Letting go keeps me connected to the attuning process. For example, I may get a clear sense that a difficulty in a client's relationship with a business associate is not the core problem. Instead, it is a trigger to an unresolved issue with the client's father that needs to be processed. If the client pulls back when I reflect this, I need to release the insight so that I can stay with his or her current experience.

As we have explored, there are many facets of internal expression to which we can attend. Some aspects of my inner world may call my attention more than others. Therapeutic presence requires the willingness to listen to that call: If I am deeply attuned to the client and to myself, it will reflect what is most prominent and important for understanding and supporting the client.

## Embodied Self-Awareness

To therapeutically apply what is discovered from attuning inwardly, we need to be able to discern our felt understanding of our client from our own triggers. Drawing on polyvagal theory, learning about physiological shifts mediated by our own vagal activation, and building our capacity for interoceptive awareness can help us bring our own physiological changes into awareness. Here they become tools to understand what is happening with our client and the relationship, and to adjust as needed to maintain a sense of presence.

*Embodied self-awareness* is the ability to pay attention to ourselves, including our experience, bodily sensations, movements, and inner sensory world, in the present moment (Fogel, 2009). The ability to feel or sense our physiological and emotional experiences is mostly governed by brain regions that are also implicated in the experience of empathy (Hanson & Mendius, 2009; Mutschler, Reinbold, Wankerl, Seifritz, & Ball, 2013; Wiens, 2005). Therapists' capacity to be fully aware and in contact with the other and within one's self, both in the sense of unification and separateness, depends on the experience of being in contact with one's bodily felt experience and inner being.

Stern (1985) described a basic sense of self that has the capacity to expand awareness and is at the very core of our psychophysiological being. This begins in gestation and is directly related to body schema self-awareness, which is the bodily sense of where one's own body leaves off and the other begins. Gendlin (1962) described embodied experience as existing prior to and beyond language. Language cannot fully capture this state of awareness, and when used to describe this state, it is usually evocative in nature—such as in poetry, symbols, gestures, art and personal expression. Our understanding of our inner terrain comes from experience itself.

Familiarity with our bodily felt experience is also related to self-care, health, wellness, and the therapist's neural integration. The neural pathways that allow us to feel sensations and emotions in the body are directly related to those that regulate body processes to maintain physical and emotional balance (Fogel, 2009). Health, then, depends on the ability to be aware and monitor body states, which activates neurobiological responses (autonomic, immune, and endocrine), somatic awareness (symptom monitoring, stress reduction), healthy behaviors (self-care, rest, nutrition), and the capacity to be fully alive in the emotional present (Fogel, 2009).

### Vignette: Responding From Embodied Self-Awareness

As a bridge to Chapter 6, I offer the following vignette to demonstrate how this embodied awareness can inform my responses.

I was seeing my client Linda when I became aware of feeling overwhelmed. Linda had been in a traumatic car accident and was trying to cope with many medical appointments. She was talking about a call from her boss, who wanted to know when she would return to work, and about her husband's stress over the extra financial burden and chores. As she described these conversations in detail, I became fully present to her experience. I could see her face and sense her breath retention, her vocal pitch heightening. I experienced all these without concept or symbol but more like having them enter me. I began to feel what it was like for her. I checked inside to see if it was my own feeling of being overwhelmed, but it did not feel personal. I discerned that it was my inner resonance of Linda's experience. I had a sense of panic building inside my body (tightness in my chest and my heart rate quickening). I reflected: "Just feeling so overwhelmed and panicky?" Tears began to roll down her cheeks, and she said, "I'm so scared I will never feel okay again. My dependency on other people makes me feel so vulnerable." This was an access point: She began to express her despair as a child at her father's inability to support her when she was in the hospital at age 8 years.

*Reflection*

In this critical moment in the therapy, presence, or nonpresence, could have facilitated the unfolding of the session in two different directions. If I were not receptively open and attuned with an embodied awareness, I would not have accessed this experience. If I had not understood that my panic was a present-centered experience of resonance, I may have felt overwhelmed and disconnected from sensation in my body. I would have shut down to Linda as well and been unable to help her gain access to her deeper experience. Instead, I allowed myself to trust my bodily resonance and risk sharing my intuitive sense with her.

## CHAPTER REVIEW AND PRACTICE

In this chapter I have described how I attune with my clients and then actively use myself to understand: What I receive is integrated with my professional wisdom, my training, and my prior understanding of their issues. This synthesis of information within myself provides the basis for how I respond and intervene, the topic of the next chapter. To transition there, enjoy this brief self-attunement practice.

**Transition Practice: Embodied Awareness While Listening**

This practice invites you to recall a conversation. It can also be done in an actual dialogue.

- Close your eyes and enjoy three deep breaths.
- Reflect on a conversation you had recently when someone was discussing a difficult issue.
- Bring awareness to what you feel in your physical body as you recall that dialogue.
- Become aware of what you feel emotionally as you visualize being with the other person.
- Notice any images, words, or insights that capture your experience of listening to the other.
- Let that conversation go and come back to the sensations of your breathing.
- Now transition to the next chapter or the next moment in your day.

©2016 M. Lee Freedman.

# 6

# EXTENDING, RESPONDING, AND PROMOTING CONTACT WITH CLIENTS

In the act of deeply seeing, we transcend the boundaries between the self
and the otherness of the world, momentarily merging with the thing seen.
—Alex Grey (as quoted in Phillips, 2000, p. 7)

Attending to the nuances of our clients' expressions allows us to understand and connect in ways that transcend ordinary ways of knowing. The process described in Chapter 5, of reading our clients and attuning within, shapes our responses and guides us toward what is needed in the moment. I will now share potential ways to respond to what you discover, as well as how to promote contact through your expression of presence. Communicating presence, both verbally and nonverbally, is vital to the therapy process. As we learned, clients' perception of their therapists' presence in session correlates more strongly with the therapeutic alliance and session outcome than therapists' perception of their own presence (Geller, Greenberg, & Watson, 2010).

http://dx.doi.org/10.1037/0000025-007
*A Practical Guide to Cultivating Therapeutic Presence,* by S. M. Geller
Copyright © 2017 by the American Psychological Association. All rights reserved.

## EXTENDING: USING CUES FROM CLIENTS TO RESPOND

We can optimize how we extend ourselves by using the cues we receive from our clients (i.e., verbal narrative, vocal expression, breathing patterns, posture, eyes, and facial expression), as these cues communicate their emotional state. For example, if cues alert us to our clients' feelings of being overwhelmed, we can slow down and reestablish safety. They also indicate whether our clients are expressing primary or secondary emotions, which require distinct responses on our part.

### Safety or Unsafety

Understanding the components and functioning of the mammalian nervous system gives us a set of tools to use in establishing and communicating presence to our clients. The insights of polyvagal theory help us see how in the clinical encounter we can notice our clients' state of safety or unsafety by recognizing their physiological expressions. We can use physiological modes of expressing and connecting to induce feelings of safety and ease in the client. The value of being guided by our assessment of safety, through reading bodily signals, is presented next.

*Clinical Vignette*

Freda was sharing her upset over a recent discord with her mother. We had been actively working on their relationship in prior sessions. I shared how I thought she felt unvalued in this instance, and how it linked to her experience of being not attuned to as a child. When I made this link, Freda's voice became restricted and her body tensed, her arms crossed while her eyes looked away. In a slightly raised and staccato voice she emphasized that her mom had been really cruel in her recent comments. I sensed through her body posture, raised voice, disconnected eye gaze, and tight facial expression that she was not feeling safe with me. I sensed that I missed the mark on what she needed, as I had jumped too quickly to continue our work from the last session. I had not validated her experience, furthering the injury of misattunement. I needed to help her to regain safety in our relationship through coregulation. I breathed deeply and leaned slightly toward her, ensuring my posture was upright yet open. I said in a prosodic yet soft voice, "I sense that you feel misunderstood by me in this moment too. I didn't recognize how hurt you felt by your mother's comments this week. I moved too quickly into talking about the past, and I'm sorry for that. I can feel how hard it must have been for you when she criticized you as you tried to open up to her. That must have really hurt." Freda breathed deeply and her arms relaxed as she looked up at me and said, "Yeah, that really stung, and it felt like you were also telling me it is my issue that I had those feelings." I looked at her and nodded, validating the double hurt from me and from her mom. Her facial expression softened and her breath deepened (indicating she felt safe again) as she thanked me for saying that. We had a powerful moment of feeling our connection. When she was ready, we moved with natural ease into the issues we had identified as core to her therapy.

*Reflection.* There are multiple cues our clients express in physiological states. When they are feeling triggered by our lack of presence or attunement, they can subtly (or not so subtly) shut down the therapeutic process. Had I not been attuned to Freda's expressed states (restricted and raised voice, tension in body and facial features, drifting eye gaze), I may have continued pursuing an intervention without her full engagement. Through breathing and nonverbally inviting a sense of connection between us, as well as authentically sharing my regret at missing the mark on validating her experience, our relationship became an opportunity for coregulation. Likely her neuroception of safety was activated and her social engagement system came back online, as indicated by her softened facial muscles, body posture, and deeper breathing. This returned her nervous system to an optimal state for working through the negative emotional schemas and core beliefs developed from early experiences in her family.

## Overwhelmed and Shut Down

When your client is overwhelmed, he or she may be in a dysregulated state (sympathetic nervous system activation) or may be shut down by dissociating (dorsal vagal "brake," a parasympathetic response). Even though the immobilization response of the dorsal vagal can feel like a barrier in session, remember that this was once an evolutionarily adaptive response of living creatures to extreme distress (Porges, 2011). Shutting down when overwhelmed is akin to "playing dead" when a threat or predator is lurking—something that would have spared your life in ancient past. Shutting down of the system also conserves energy and maintains blood flow to the brain if distress literally knocks you off your feet via fainting. This freezing response works in a reptilian body that can survive without oxygen for longer periods, but not for mammals like us. Shutting down signals a very high level of anxiety and feelings of being overwhelmed in a client, followed by dissociation—the ability to use more evolved self-regulatory mechanisms fails and the most primitive take over.

You may also experience shutting down in the face of this and respond in a way that furthers your clients' distancing. This may be form of misattunement, as in the case of Freda described previously, or it may be clinically informative. As we discussed, we resonate with our clients experience given the bidirectional nature of our physiology in relationship. We pick up signals in our body sometimes without conscious awareness and respond in rhythm to this embodied connection. The implicit experience may alert us to our clients' shut-down state through recognizing the shutting down with us, a concept known in the trauma world as *dissociative attunement* (Hopenwasser, 2008). Recognizing these body signals in your self is key. Then you can determine what to do to invite your client back into safety, so the relationship becomes an emotional regulator.

Being present to your clients' feeling of being overwhelmed, staying connected with them while maintaining a state of calm and equanimity within, is the stance you want. Regulating within yourself through contact with your breath or body, while reaching out to connect with your clients where they are (activating the higher order social engagement or ventral vagal system) will help them to regain composure. This is coregulation in action. By self-regulating first, you set a critical negative feedback loop in motion, and your calm presence can bring your client back to baseline. Without this step, you run the risk of coupling their emotional reactivity with your own (a phenomenon called *codysregulation*) and pushing them further from emotional homeostasis (P. Coleman, Vallacher, Nowak, & Bui-Wrzosinska, 2007; Reed, Barnard, & Butler, 2015).

There are also tools you can offer to help clients regulate, such as inviting them to take long exhalations (Geller & Porges, 2014). Naming their experience without judgment, as we learned, is also a powerful regulator (Hariri, Bookheimer, & Mazziotta, 2000; Lieberman et al., 2007). Any effort you can make to help your clients be present with their experience, name their difficult feelings, and nonverbally attune to your grounded presence is going to help them shift to a more regulated state.

**Primary Emotions: Happy, Sad, or Hurt**

When clients are able to feel and express primary adaptive emotions, such as happiness, sadness, or hurt, you typically want to help them stay with that expression. Try to encourage clients to continue to notice the sensations in their bodies so they can understand, express, and make meaning of their experience. You may feel a resonance of the feeling inside that you can empathically reflect back or just use as information to inform your understanding. Being present may also include silently sitting with them as they touch and express their affect. This requires you to notice and put aside any barriers to being present, such as your own discomfort in being with difficult emotions. Clients may express discomfort in being with primary emotions, as it is a vulnerable process to express emotions so openly. It is important to read what your client needs from you to stay present with their own experience. This could include providing a nonverbal response such as a nod, a soft gaze on your face to communicate your understanding, or a more direct facilitative intervention to deepen or process their experience.

### Secondary Emotions: Reacting With Blame, Anger, or Criticism

When clients are expressing secondary emotions, such as blame, anger, or criticism, you can help them step out of the reactive cycle and be present with the vulnerable feelings that are driving their reaction. If you feel a disharmony between the client's verbal narrative and bodily expression, this could be a cue to the presence of a hidden layer of feeling. Offering your clients awareness of the possible feeling associated with their expressed body posture might shift their verbal narrative in ways that are more aligned with their primary emotions. For example, my client Samantha had been desperately searching for a relationship for several months through online dating and had been feeling despondent about ever being in a relationship again. She finally met someone and after a few dates came in boasting, "I feel so happy in my new relationship, I met the right person at last," yet her leg was shaking and her eyes were darting around the room. I reflected that her body was expressing something different and asked her to become aware of her body sensations. She paused, and slowly started to explore the uncertainty she was feeling and her fear of getting close to him given some of his outbursts in a recent encounter. She also talked about her wish to just settle down and accept his flaws.

There are many ways to try to tune into and reflect back the primary emotion behind your clients' experience. You may sense a deep sadness and invite them to notice in their own body if that is core to their experience. You can ask them to put a hand on the physical place they are feeling the sensation, to listen with compassion, and to name their more vulnerable sadness while holding a kind and caring stance toward their suffering (see a self-compassion practice you can use with your clients and yourself in Chapter 10).

## EXTENDING: USING INTERNAL CUES TO RESPOND

In Chapter 5 we looked at microexperiences of emotions, breathing patterns, words, and images that we are attuning to within ourselves. We expand the discussion here to include broader states of being, such as when in flow, energized, tired, or bored, which encompass the microexpressions we discussed. We specifically look at how these states can guide our responses.

## Flow and Presence

Several decades ago, Mihaly Csikszentmihalyi (1996) began to study the phenomenon of individuals devoting endless hours to activities that seemed to offer limited tangible rewards and were often associated with risks. By talking to these rock climbers, dancers, and surgeons, among others, he discovered a common thread: They all claimed there was something so intrinsically rewarding about the experience itself that they felt deeply motivated to continue. They described engagement in the activity as "almost automatic, effortless, yet highly focused" (Csikszentmihalyi, 1996, p. 110). Csikszentmihalyi called this optimal experience *flow*. Its key elements overlap with elements of therapeutic presence in its purest form. These include (among others) a sense of timelessness, unification of action and awareness, disappearance of self-consciousness and distractions, and a sense of self-trust (Csikszentmihalyi, 1996).

In the therapeutic encounter, typically when I am feeling in flow and in contact with the client, I am so fully immersed that I can listen and respond with greater ease. Internally I trust the images, guidance, words, insights, and possible interventions that emerge, and I communicate them with flow in the moment. This aligns with Rogers (1980):

> I find that when I am closest to my inner, intuitive self, when I am somehow in touch with the unknown in me, when perhaps I am in a slightly altered state of consciousness, then whatever I do seems to be full of healing. Then, simply my presence is releasing and helpful to the other. (p. 129)

A therapist in my qualitative study on presence (Geller, 2001) described the inner trust and ease that emerges in this energized flow state this way: "There is sort of an openness and things are flowing through me rather than me trying to do anything . . ."

In a flow and present state, responses emerge in the moment on the basis of my sensing the client's readiness and openness to what is being offered. My use of the word *sensing* rather than *knowing* or *thinking* was purposeful—in this state of flow, overthinking actually interferes with the implicit knowing that rises inside. This reflects the paradigm shift from thinking (knowing through cognition and analysis) to knowing from the inside out or through embodiment (knowing through sensing and being in relational connection).

The subjective experience of flow in therapeutic presence aligns with proposed neural mechanisms of other flow-state experiences. It is thought that when in flow, people highly practiced at a given task experience a state of *hypofrontality* (decreased activity in the frontal lobes, where explicit processing occurs) and more automatic processing chimes in (Dietrich, 2004).

This contributes to the effortlessness of the task, in spite of the high demand for focus.

For us, this means that to experience a state of flow in the therapeutic encounter, we must build our capacity to *be* present. This might be the work of a lifetime, but it is worth it, and not only for the benefit of our clients: Flow state is enlivening and rewarding, and a powerful buffer against therapist burnout and compassion fatigue. When we experience aspects of flow state in session, this is a strong signal that we are deeply present within the therapy encounter. We can trust the guiding insights, images, and reflections that arise, even if they do not yet make complete sense in the moment.

## Vitality and Excitement

I have observed that when I feel vitality and excitement, it is an indication that something new is emerging. I am on track with how I am understanding the client, yet there is a new awareness or direction surfacing that I will trust and follow. The body sensations accompanying this feeling are heightened energy, tingling, loss of time awareness, and a deep connection with the client. Vitality and excitement are connected to the flow-state experience and indicate that we are making discoveries and moving toward our shared goal (Csikszentmihalyi, 1996). The added excitement and vitality is an indicator that there is a new "aha" moment or connections that the client and I are making. They can also signal the timeliness of particular interventions to facilitate the unfolding of this new awareness.

## Tiredness

A heavy feeling behind my eyes or a sense of heaviness in my body might not actually be genuine tiredness. Once I observe sensations associated with fatigue, I proceed through several steps to determine my response. Am I tired? Or am I actually shut down? If I am picking up genuine fatigue in myself, it is important to use this as a point of exploration later. I will inquire: Am I getting enough sleep? How is my self-care? What needs attention? Often, though, if I am deeply present and connected, I can still feel alive in session (the tiredness hits later). So tiredness in session that is not a sign of emotional disconnect within myself is likely signaling a resonance with my client's feelings, including potential emotional disconnection.

If I discern that my tiredness is an indicator of my client's emotional cutoff and not my own, I will sense and possibly check in with my client to see if I am on target. Using nonverbal means to assess this, I would be looking for a discordance between what clients are saying and their body language (see the client cues section in Chapter 5). I may also be having a felt sense of the depression and demoralization of my client, through feeling a resonance with his or her fatigue.

When reflecting back an awareness of the disconnect or resonance, the message I want to send to the client is one that reflects the truth of what I am sensing in a way that leaves the client feeling respected and supported; telling a client that you are feeling tired in session could be detrimental if not handled with exquisite care. Clients respond to how we say what we say, even more critically than what we say. Using phrasing that includes references to my body sense of my experience is an important part of this communication. Leaning into polyvagal theory here, it also helps to express with vocal prosody, body posture open and forward, gestures, and facial expressions that show we are connected, and that I am safe and interested in their experience (Geller & Porges, 2014; Quillman, 2012; Schore, 2003). For example, I may say,

> I'm noticing a feeling of tiredness, like a heavy feeling in my chest. I am wondering what this might mean in this moment in our therapy. I sense that you may be feeling distant from yourself or from me too? I really want to understand if what I just said upset you in some way and you pulled back from me.

The actual words are just an example. In the therapy room they will be personal to you, based on what you sense and what may have happened moments before. The important part when opting to explore such internal cues openly with clients is to be both genuine and sensitive in the disclosure, and to communicate with your body that you are present, open, and engaged.

## Boredom

If I am feeling bored, the first thing I need to do is reset my attention back to the present moment. I will bring awareness to my breath and to my feet on the ground, or I will focus on my client's words and bodily expressions. Once I am grounded, I start looking for any potential triggers, asking myself questions like, "Is the client feeling unsafe with me, or are they avoiding what is emotionally important within them?" I try to get a sense of the real issue that is not being addressed. As with tiredness, I might share this reflection or perhaps ask them about what the disconnection I am feeling could mean. For example, I may say:

> I find my attention drifting and recognize that I may be picking up from you that there is more to what you are sharing. I sense that the anger you are sharing is just the one layer of your experience and there are some other feelings going on that are harder to share. Some deep hurt? Are you noticing or feeling anything similar?

Exploring clients' experience may reveal that they are feeling self-protective, resistant to deeper work, or shut down with me.

Another possibility of boredom may be a shutdown in myself, which may be a resonance with a shutdown in my client. As discussed, this can be a form of dissociative attunement. It is imperative that we can discern a counter-transference response (see Chapter 7) from this resonance. We can then put into place some of the mechanisms that bring our ventral vagal nerve back on line, such as long exhalations, grounding techniques, softening our facial muscles, and reconnecting to our body in the present moment. Paying attention to our internal sense of boredom or disengagement, rather than dismissing it outright as a failure of attention, can help clarify if it is clinically useful or a call for greater self-care.

## Tension

Tension in my own self and body may indicate a resonance with the client, such as my body feeling disconnected from what the client is expressing versus feeling. I want to first pay attention to this without judgment, invite my body to relax and my awareness to come back to the moment, and then explore the underlying experience or dynamic. An example of my bodily felt tension signaling to me that my client was stuck in a secondary emotion is illustrated in the following scenario.

### Clinical Vignette

Samuel was angry at his partner. He blamed her for keeping him up at night, which resulted in his not doing well on a job interview the next day, as he was not on his game. I found myself feeling tense and wondered if this could be a reflection of Samuel's blocking his primary emotion of shame and sadness about the interview outcome, and instead expressing anger and blame. I breathed and offered him this awareness: "I hear that you are angry at your partner for keeping you up. I can feel your frustration (*validation*). My sense is that you also may be feeling more vulnerable underneath, feeling possible shame or upset for not doing well (*a rise of my voice to indicate tentative questioning*)? Or fear that you will not get another opportunity like this?" Samuel took a longer breath (*indicating he was feeling understood*) and responded with "Ya, I am really upset about how badly the interview went. I'm worried this was my only chance . . ."

*Reflection.* Noting my awareness of the tension in my own body allowed me to recognize that what Samuel outwardly expressed (anger) may not be in congruence with what he felt inwardly (sadness and shame). This is important because at times we may just ignore our tension rather than recognize the clinical information it provides. Noticing my tension also helped me to regulate, so I could authentically share my experience in a way that was facilitative.

Although I may have a sense of what is being felt underneath a client's expression, I do not want to take an authoritative stance of knowing, as it can make clients feel unsafe and shut them down (or I may be off the mark). The question mark at the end of the last two points was to communicate this inflection and my own tentativeness to the client about my response, to allow him to confirm or disconfirm and elaborate on his experience. My response supported Samuel's exploration of more primary emotions such as shame and fear. His deeper breathing indicated that he felt understood, and I was on the mark with his experience. As a result, we were able to do more active work on the shame and fear, within the safety of our therapeutic relationship.

## PROMOTING CONTACT VERBALLY WITH EMPATHY AND CONGRUENCE

Contact is key to relating with presence and an underlying way relationship is maintained and sustained. *Contact* means directly meeting the essence of your client with the essence of yourself (Geller & Greenberg, 2002, 2012). Gestalt therapists use this term to describe the experience of both a boundary and a dissolve between the self and another person (Perls, 1970; Yontef, 2005). Contact is viewed as the primary motivating force in human behavior and relationships (Erskine, 2015). It is the base from which the therapeutic process is promoted.

Contact reflects the third realm of the process of therapeutic presence (after receptivity and inward attuning). It includes being in direct connection with your client, yet remaining connected within yourself. Contact can evoke in clients (and therapists) a feeling of togetherness in relationship and a positive movement toward growth and healing. Promoting contact begins with attunement, yet it is expressed verbally through empathy and congruence as well as nonverbally through synchronization. Let us explore further these keys ways of promoting contact.

### Empathic Attunement

As highlighted in Chapter 1, you can be present without being empathic—preparing for presence through a grounding practice is an example of that—yet you cannot be empathically attuned without first being present. Research has confirmed that therapeutic presence is distinct from empathy, yet a necessary preliminary step (Geller et al., 2010; Hayes & Vinca, 2011; Pos, Geller, & Oghene, 2011). With therapeutic presence you can approach clients with a calm and receptive awareness so that you can take in the depths of their experience to hear, feel, and understand them and to express that understanding back.

Empathy has been defined by Rogers (1957) and other humanistic therapists as the ability to step into the shoes of the other person's experience as if it were your own, without ever losing the "as if" quality. It is an active way of trying to understand clients' experience and express the meaningful aspects of their experience back to them, so they feel heard and understood.

Researchers have suggested that emotions and empathy live in the body (Damasio, 1999; Gallese, 2003; Niedenthal, 2007; Van der Kolk, 2014). As shared in Chapter 3, we are born with the neural structures that allow us to feel with others in an embodied way, from just watching their experience and action: Our brains mirror the experience of others when we are in close proximity and connection (Ferrari & Rizzolatti, 2014; Glenberg, 2010; Praszkier, 2016; Siegel, 2007). There is also a positive correlation between individual empathy and the responsiveness of mirror neurons (Gazzola, Aziz-Zadeh, & Keysers, 2006). In the relational space we share, through these mechanisms and others, we can recognize when someone is or isn't "feeling with" us. So we can feel our clients experience through our bodily sensing, and they can feel when we are present and attuned with them or when we are somewhere else.

When clients sense that their therapist is present and empathic, they feel more in synch with their therapist, as skin conductance tests have shown (Marci, Ham, Moran, & Orr, 2007; Marci & Orr, 2006). The levels of arousal of client and therapist come into concordance, indicating psychological and physiological synchronicity in the therapeutic relationship. Cultivating skills in empathic attunement is therefore a fundamental way to enhance your ability to respond with therapeutic presence.

## Presence Practices for Empathic Attunement

The following three practices provide an opportunity to strengthen your empathic attunement to emotions through observing, mirroring, and embodying others' experience. They can activate mirror neurons that allow you to feel others' experience in a visceral way, further promoting empathy and contact. For example, mirroring others' facial expressions helps you recognize and understand their emotional state (Oberman, Winkielman, & Ramachandran, 2007).

  1. *Observing closely.* Watch a therapy tape with the volume off.
     First, pay attention to clients' body gestures, facial expressions,

movements, and posture to try to get a sense of their experience. What do you feel as you watch them? Then replay with volume on and try to ignore words, paying attention to vocal expression, tone, and quality. See if you can get a sense of what the client is feeling. Play it a third time, listening to what they are saying and determining if it is similar or different from what you felt the client was expressing in his or her face and body. State aloud what you think the client is feeling or communicating in his or her emotions, body, and words.

2. *Mirroring practice.* This can be done with another person. Have Person A connect to a particular feeling. Then Person A is guided to create different movements, facial expressions, and gestures reflecting that feeling. Person B is invited to mirror or imitate their gesture, speech pattern, or movement. Person B can express what they feel as they mirror Person A's experience to see if it is similar. Person A and B discuss their experience with each other, then switch roles and repeat these steps.

3. *Embodying others.* Practice entering into the experience of another by embodying the person's life and challenges. For example, spend a day in a wheelchair to embody the experience of someone with a physical disability. Imagine a close family member has died, to get an experience of what it is like to deal with loss and death. Immersing yourself in an imagined experience lets you bring that experience into your body and may heighten your understanding and enrich your experience of feeling with others.

## Congruence

Communicating skillfully with congruence is a way to express presence as well as maintain contact. Therapeutic presence is also a precondition to congruence: We need to know our experience and be willing to express it to remain in authentic connection. As Rogers (1961) said, when we are "real" with each other, this facilitates trust and communication.

*Congruence* is a complex process yet can be broken down into two separate components (Lietaer, 1993). These include (a) an inner component, the ability to be aware of one's own internal experience, and (b) an external component, transparency: the willingness and ability to effectively communicate to the other person what is going on within.

### Congruence 1: Inner Awareness

The first component requires us to connect to our inner sensory world by bringing attention to our internal sensations and discomforts, and to discern (as we did in Chapter 5) whether these are clinically informative:

1. Does your inner experience reflect how your client is making you feel through the particular way the client is relating to you (and perhaps making others feel)? For example, you may feel put down, and perhaps this reminds you of how your client has described feeling around his or her friends, which contributes to the client's sense of isolation.
2. Is your internal sense of your client a resonance of a disconnection between what your client is feeling and what he or she is expressing (i.e., the pit in your stomach may be hearing the client say he or she is great, yet you sense the client is anxious or angry)? Both of these are poignant and may be powerful if disclosed in a way that is therapeutic.
3. Is your incongruence actually a countertransference reaction? If so, you can work internally to notice this, put it aside, and shift your attention back to the moment (with a promise to come back later and work on it).

### Congruence 2: Transparency and Self-Disclosure

*Transparency* means being clear in what you are doing and feeling. You can be transparent in how you present nonverbally (see the next section) as well as verbally (e.g., with self-disclosure). Being transparent may involve disclosing what you are feeling in your body, what you are thinking, an image, a past experience that could be therapeutically helpful, or it may involve commenting on the interaction between you. It could also mean sharing a feeling that has been persisting over time, even if it is not being felt at that moment in any visceral way. Being congruent may also involve saying something that spontaneously captures your sense of the moment. The current or general feelings being expressed congruently could range from compassion to anger, from feeling threatened to feeling joyful. Each will be expressed in very specific ways depending on which is being felt, and always with an intention to draw closer to your client.

In your disclosure you might reveal how you are feeling about the client, yourself in relation to your client, or the therapeutic relationship. Such disclosures are one of several forms of *immediacy*, or ways of openly working with the therapeutic relationship in the moment (Hill, 2014; Knox & Hill, 2003).

Self-disclosure can be powerful if done well, for example, by offering correc-tive relational experiences for the client, encouraging client expression, and strengthening the therapeutic relationship (Hill et al., 2008; Kasper, Hill, & Kivlighan, 2008; Knox & Hill, 2003). It can also be detrimental if done in a reactive or nonskillful way.

Congruence is therapeutic if it is preceded and infused with therapeutic presence. It presumes a certain level of personal development and a value sys-tem that puts the client's healing at the center (Greenberg & Geller, 2001). This means responses are always guided by the intention to communicate nonjudgmentally, with respect and acceptance and validation of one's own and the other's experience. It also means sensing the right timing for the client to hear, and being willing to be with one's difficult experience. Ultimately the intention of congruence is to facilitate clients' growth and development, as well as to deepen the therapeutic relationship. Without this underlying intent, congruence could be used as a justification to say anything in order to "be one's self," which is not necessarily a therapeutic or helpful way of engag-ing. Foremost, congruence needs to be disciplined.

For example, if your client's overstepping of boundaries overwhelms you, then you may notice that you feel a bit detached in session. What does being congruent require of you in this circumstance? After noticing your dis-tance from the client and sensing that internal frustration is keeping you dis-engaged (inwardly attuning), further reflection can inform you of the cause (several lengthy messages on your voicemail that leave you feeling stressed). Internally reflecting in this way also means tolerating discomfort (the anger or frustration, so you can sort out the cause and not just react). You then need to regulate (pause, notice, and breathe) to ensure that your frustration does not get expressed in a reactive way.

Being congruent also requires you to ask yourself what you need, then to respond with sensitivity. For example, you might say,

> I notice that I am distant and I don't want to feel that way. I realize that I arrived a bit shut down. After receiving several messages from you I found myself feeling stressed and overwhelmed, with no way to respond. I want to remain close and connected. I really appreciate that you want to share your experiences and I wonder if we can find a way for you to do that when we are together. That way I can be fully available to you.

This would be said with vocal prosody, body leaning forward, in connection, and with willingness to notice or help the client if any shame emerges in him or her. Self-disclosure uses the left brain (language) to share our internal felt experience (right brain) and make it accessible to our clients (Quillman, 2012). This engages both the mind and the body and has the potential to bring you both back into a state of connection and relational integration.

There is not one way of being congruent—different situations call forth different congruent responses.

## PROMOTING CONTACT NONVERBALLY THROUGH PHYSIOLOGICAL CONNECTION

There are several nonverbal ways that I can extend myself to help my client feel that I am present and available. If you recall from Chapter 3, promoting connection nonverbally relies on right brain to right brain communication (Schore, 2009, 2012). This involves using the body intentionally to show the client you are with him or her and to bring you both into alignment and connection, leaving a deeper impression than would words alone. The following are some suggestions on how we can promote contact and express presence nonverbally. This helps us to be an emotional regulator for our clients.

### Physical Gesturing

Physical sensing and bodily communication can express to clients that I am with them in the moment. Gestures of emotions with my hands or body movements, as I empathically respond, express an understanding that exists in a visceral way. For example, I may touch my heart when sharing the sadness I hear and feel from my client, to describe my visceral understanding of their sadness and to invite a connection with their present-moment emotions. As we explored in Chapter 5, there are cultural and personal variations to gesturing that may mean different things to different clients. It is important to name the gesture early to avoid confusion. For example, I may say, "I feel compassionate to your sadness" as I rest my hand gently on my chest.

### Entrainment Breathing and Synchronization

We can intentionally mirror our clients' breath as a way to read their experience and to communicate that they are not alone (see Chapter 9 for entrainment breathing practice). Clients may pick this up purely on a visceral level, feeling the connection and contact. Entraining our breathing to our clients' breathing can promote a neuroception of safety and activate the social engagement system (Geller & Porges, 2014).

When I use my right brain to connect with their right brain, through gesture and entraining my breath with theirs, a synchrony emerges as our bodies come into rhythm with each other: Our heads move in temporal coordination, and vocal rhythms are reflective of each other (Imel et al., 2014;

Ramseyer & Tschacher, 2014). Coming into synch on a physiological level builds a sense of camaraderie. Movement synchrony at the start of psychotherapy has predicted client ratings of the alliance at the end of each session, as well as symptom reduction (Ramseyer & Tschacher, 2011). Synchrony between my body and a client's body can emerge naturally in therapeutic presence and moments of deep relating. For example, connected conversation partners may begin to breathe in synch, and those engaged in joint tasks requiring interpersonal trust show heart-rate synchrony (Koole & Tschacher, 2016; McFarland, 2001; Mitkidis, McGraw, Roepstorff, & Wallot, 2015; Warner, 1996). Research has suggested that the more one partner expects the other to show reciprocity in the joint task, the more synchronous their heart-rate rhythms became. It appears from this research that trust builds synchrony and synchrony builds trust. Synchronization of physiological rhythms could therefore be considered a "proxy for trust-building process" (Mitkidis et al., 2015, p. 105), a process that lies at the heart of the therapeutic alliance. Such entrainment can also be purposeful (i.e., entraining my breathing to clients) to help deepen the connection and contact. Whether spontaneous or intentional, synchrony provides greater access to clients' experience as we enter a shared intersubjective space together (Paladino, Mazzurega, Pavani, & Schubert, 2010; Stern, 2004).

## Eye Gaze

In Chapter 5 we looked at our read of clients' eye and facial expressions. It is important to recognize that our clients too are reading our facial expressions to sense if we are there with them or not. Typically, direct eye contact communicates presence, interest, attentiveness, and connection. It is helpful to bring awareness to your gaze—being mindful to express interest (eyes attentive, not glazed over) and care and reflection (softness in the gaze).

Research has suggested that mutual gazing results in clients feeling present and empathically attuned to (Marci, Ham, Moran, & Orr, 2007; Marci & Orr, 2006). Clients' and therapists' physiological arousal came into concordance when the therapist's eye gaze was in contact with the client's. Alternatively, clinicians who shifted their eyes and attention away from their client left clients feeling distanced, less empathically attuned to, and in discord or out of synch with their clinician. These are powerful results that reflect the impact of nonverbal cues on clients. They can detect when we maintain or subtly lose our presence and attention.

So when we attune to our clients' eyes and they feel our gaze, we both are more connected. Seeing and being seen generates security and allows clients to explore their inner emotional world. A reciprocal process emerges that invites presence in the relationship as social roles drop and client and therapist see each other as they truly are in the moment. A shared gaze lets us experience the warm accepting embrace of human connection, while meeting the pain and vulnerability of the other.

## Promoting Contact From a Place of Calm

When we as therapists cultivate presence prior to the session, we allow our nervous system to arrive in a state of calm. Then, from the beginning and throughout the session, we can express this state of calm presence through our prosodic vocal tone, facial expressions, gestures, receptive body posture, and breathing (Geller & Porges, 2014). Our responses come from this calm and centered place, offering us clarity of thought and intuition in the moment, while our presence simultaneously acts as a gentle force on our clients' nervous systems, pulling them into resonance with our own.

### Presence Practice: Long Exhalations to Activate Calm

A practice to increase calm and openness in the body so that you can stay in contact with your client is to make long exhalations. Longer inhalations with shorter exhalations, in contrast, can increase tension yet can also increase a state of alertness in the body, if greater wakefulness and energy is needed. To illuminate the difference between long inhalations and long exhalations, try the following practice. You can look in the mirror or, better yet, try this practice with a partner:

- Have your partner take 10 to 20 long inhalations and short exhalations and examine their facial expressions while they are doing so.
- Switch partners to get an experience of breathing and observing.
- Now repeat the same process while taking long exhalations and short inhalations.
- Write down or discuss what you notice in their body, facial expression, and mood while doing each.

*Reflection.* Long exhalations can be used both in preparing for presence as well as in a session when needing to regulate emotions. Long exhalations are an efficient way to turn off therapists' (and clients') sympathetic nervous system and vagal pathways of defense, inviting a sense of calm, openness, and trust (Geller & Porges, 2014; Porges, 2011).

# CLOSING THE SESSION WITH CLIENTS: ABSORBING AND LETTING GO

Closing the session with a mindful moment to intentionally let go allows both yourself and your clients to absorb the experience of the session and release what is necessary to move forward. You can also invite clients to create an intention for postsession, something they want to carry away and work with. If there are a lot of emotions opened up that are not resolved, you can guide clients through a visualization to release or put aside any unfinished emotions or challenges from the session knowing they will come back or continue to take care of them.

## A Visualization to Close the Session

You can use the following script as a guide to help your clients (and you) to close the session:

> Take a moment to pause and feel your feet on the ground. Feel the rhythm of your breath as it moves through your body. Notice what is true for you right now in your body, without judgment. What is important for you to walk away with from today's session? Listen inside to what emerges (pause). Are there any intentions you have for yourself between now and our next session? Notice what emerges (pause). Now notice if there is residual emotion or suffering that you want to put aside before you go. If there is, visualize a beautiful box or bowl and imagine placing the residual emotion there. When it feels complete, put a lid on it and put it somewhere safe, knowing you will come back to it (pause). Now return your attention to your body on the chair and the rhythm of your breathing. When you are ready, begin to wiggle your fingers and toes, and gently open your eyes more fully.

Feel free to adapt this visualization. Maintain the theme of integrating insights from the sessions and intentions for self and put aside any unfinished emotions to help clients close the session and transition to the next stage of their day.

## Transition for Therapists Postsession: Letting Go, Pausing, and Moving Forward

Letting go postsession is also helpful if there is residual emotion or tension that still exists in you. This can include a few minutes for taking process notes to record the essential aspects (insights, interventions, learning, homework) of what occurred in the session. Putting away the notes and the file can be a powerful symbolic gesture of intentionally letting go of one session so you can transition and ready yourself for the next session. Residual tension or emotion can also be released by conducting an imagery practice in a grounding posture, visualizing any leftover feelings leaving through the bottom of your feet.

## SUMMARY AND CLOSING PRACTICE

Overall, having an awareness of how we express presence and how clients receive us helps to provide the optimal conditions for growth and change. The face-to-heart connection described by the polyvagal theory (see Chapter 3) provides a portal to exercise the neural regulation of physiological states through social engagement (Geller & Porges, 2014; Porges, 2011). Over consistent, present-centered encounters in therapy, the ability to emotionally regulate strengthens, and the client's physiology begins to shift toward one of safety and engagement. However, your repeated engagement is necessary, which includes the ability to be self-regulated, open, and available in the face of your client's defense and pain. A fine-tuned awareness of the nuances of expressing presence both verbally and nonverbally requires development through consistent awareness of when we are on or off the moment.

For now, enjoy a transition practice, which mirrors what you can do at the end of a session.

### Transition Practice: Letting Go

The following transition practice can help you to let go following a therapy session. Take a moment to pause with intention before you move into the next session or close a therapy day. It is also an opportunity for you to pause and transition in this moment, as you complete this chapter.

- Begin by pausing and standing with your feet on the ground, noticing any sensation or tension in your body physically, emotionally, and cognitively.
- Consciously imagine any tension releasing through the soles of your feet.
- Take three breaths with long exhalations, inviting your awareness to the present moment by feeling your breath in your body and feet on the ground.
- With intention and awareness, move slowly to the next moment or the next part of your day.

©2016 M. Lee Freedman.

# 7

# BARRIERS AND CHALLENGES TO PRESENCE

Your task is not to seek for love, but merely to seek and find all the barriers within yourself that you have built against it.
　　　　　　　　　　　　　　　　　　—Helen Schucman (1976, p. 315)

The words in the above quote are equally true for cultivating presence. When we can be aware of barriers and how to work with them, therapeutic presence can arise as a natural state. The first step is consciously attending to what gets in the way of being fully with our clients. This chapter explores recognizing and working with internal barriers, ruptures in the relationship, and challenging clients. Let's begin by exploring your personal barriers to presence, starting with a reflection on your personal relationships.

## THERAPEUTIC PRESENCE REFLECTION: BARRIERS TO PRESENCE

- Pause and take a few deep breaths with long exhalations.
- Soften your eye gaze or close your eyes fully, to invite your attention inward.
- Pause between each question and listen to what emerges.

http://dx.doi.org/10.1037/0000025-008
*A Practical Guide to Cultivating Therapeutic Presence*, by S. M. Geller

- Ask yourself: Where do I struggle with being present in my relationships?
- Now reflect on: What can help me to be more present in my relationships?
- Let that go with a deep breath and long exhalation.

The self-awareness required to notice and work with your own barriers in relationship is a key skill in preventing and working with barriers in your clinical relationships. This can prevent them from arising and also help you notice the patterns that may emerge across other relationships.

## RECOGNIZING YOUR BARRIERS IN SESSION

Before elaborating on the challenges we may encounter, we will first look at some tools that can help us assess our state in session. This can help us to focus on which aspects of presence are strong and which need attention. It can also help us recognize when we are not present so we can bring ourselves back to the moment.

### Therapeutic Presence Inventory (TPI): A Research and Self-Auditing Tool

With my colleagues (Geller, Greenberg, & Watson, 2010), I developed a research tool to recognize therapists' presence and nonpresence, both experienced and received. We based the research tool on our qualitative study resulting in a model of therapeutic presence (Geller & Greenberg, 2002). We created and studied two versions of the Therapeutic Presence Inventory (TPI): one measured therapists' perspective of their own degree of presence (TPI-T), and the second measured clients' perception of their therapists' presence (TPI-C). This measure has been used in studies assessing therapists' presence in psychotherapy treatment and training, mindfulness, self-compassion, art therapy, and osteopathy (Bourgault & Dionne, 2016; Dunn, Callahan, Swift, & Ivanovic, 2013; Durrer & Rohrbach, 2013; Hayes & Vinca, 2011; Mander et al., 2015; Pos, Geller, & Oghene, 2011; Romanelli, Tishby, & Moran, 2015; Rozière, 2016; Schwarz, Snir, & Regev, 2016).

There is an online platform developed by Franz Fischer for therapists and their clients to use the TPI (http://www.xpsy.eu). This is currently used for quality assurance in four hospitals across Switzerland and can be extended to other health care settings.[1]

---

[1]Contact Franz Fischer (via http://www.franzfischer.name/contact) to inquire further.

## EXHIBIT 7.1
### Items on the Therapeutic Presence Inventory, Therapist Version (TPI-T)

1. I was aware of my own internal flow of experiencing
2. **I felt tired or bored**
3. **I found it difficult to listen to my client**
4. The interaction between my client and I felt flowing and rhythmic
5. **Time seemed to really drag**
6. **I found it difficult to concentrate**
7. There were moments when I was so immersed with my client's experience that I lost a sense of time and space
8. I was able to put aside my own demands and worries to be with my client
9. **I felt distant or disconnected from my client**
10. I felt a sense of deep appreciation and respect for my client as a person
11. I felt alert and attuned to the nuances and subtleties of my client's experience
12. I was fully in the moment in this session
13. **I felt impatient or critical**
14. My responses were guided by the feelings, words, images, or intuitions that emerged in me from my experience of being with my client
15. **I couldn't wait for the session to be over**
16. **There were moments when my outward response to my client was different from the way I felt inside**
17. I felt fully immersed with my client's experience and yet still centered within myself
18. **My thoughts sometimes drifted away from what was happening in the moment**
19. I felt in synch with my client in such a way that allowed me to sense what he/she was experiencing
20. I felt genuinely interested in my client's experience
21. **I felt a distance or emotional barrier between my client and myself**

*Note.* Bold items reflect nonpresence. From "Therapist and Client Perceptions of Therapeutic Presence: The Development of a Measure," by S. M. Geller, L. S. Greenberg, and J. C. Watson, 2010, *Psychotherapy Research, 20,* p. 604. Copyright 2010 by Taylor & Francis. Reprinted with permission.

For our purposes, the TPI-T can also be used as a self-auditing tool for therapists to reflect on their degree of presence with a client (Geller, 2013a; see Exhibit 7.1). Following a therapy session, rate each item from 1 (*not at all*) to 7 (*completely*). To work out a total score, reverse the items in bold (which indicate a lack of presence), then add up all the items for a total score. The higher score, the greater your subjective sense of your own presence in that session. You could also ask your clients to fill out the brief three-item TPI-C (see Exhibit 7.2) so you can gain a sense of their experience of your presence (note that Item 3 is a nonpresence item to be reverse scored). I would suggest

## EXHIBIT 7.2
### Items on the Therapeutic Presence Inventory, Client Version (TPI-C)

1. My therapist was fully there in the moment with me
2. My therapist's responses were really in tune with what I was experiencing in the moment
3. **My therapist seemed distracted**

*Note.* Bold item reflects nonpresence. From "Therapist and Client Perceptions of Therapeutic Presence: The Development of a Measure," by S. M. Geller, L. S. Greenberg, and J. C. Watson, 2010, *Psychotherapy Research, 20,* p. 607. Copyright 2010 by Taylor & Francis. Reprinted with permission.

that instead of formally calculating a score, you peruse the items and just notice areas where you may be less present, so you can use a practice to boost that quality. Translations in French (Martel, Gagnon, Bourgault, & Dionne, 2016), German (Fischer, Hunziker, Lüscher, & Eggenberger, 2013) and Hebrew (Ben Ami, 2012; Corem, 2013) are also available for use as a self-audit tool (see http://www.sharigeller.ca/publications.php for downloadable versions).[2]

## Markers of Therapeutic Presence

Another way to assess our presence or absence, and our clients' safety, is to look for specific markers, which are observable signs. They can help us to recognize the areas that need attention, both in the moment and overall in our therapeutic stance. We may think we are present, yet when guided through a self-assessment we may notice that our bodies are tight, arms crossed, or fists clenched, which sends the message to clients that we are held back.

See Appendices A and B for a list of markers for therapists' presence and clients' safety. You can use them to observe your everyday interactions to confirm or disconfirm when you are present or not, and if your client feels safe and connected with you or not. This will allow you to time your responses or intervention to bring you both back into connection. Read on for a deeper exploration of working with your own internal barriers as well as your clients.

## INTERNAL BARRIERS TO THERAPEUTIC PRESENCE

We will encounter many internal challenges to presence, only some of which we explore here: self-doubt, distraction, discomfort with uncertainty, and countertransference. They may arise from our own triggers, lack of self-care, or vicarious traumatization. Although these issues demand a longer discussion, for now I am going to focus on offering ways to work with these internal challenges.

### Internal Barrier 1: Self-Doubt and the Impostor Syndrome

Doubting ourselves is one of the biggest factors interfering with being present. Especially at early stages in our careers, we can feel overwhelmed by the level of trauma people experience and doubt our ability to help. The voice of self-doubt can tell us we are incompetent, inexperienced, or unhelpful. Regardless of the stage of career, many therapists experience feelings of fraudulence, also known as *impostor syndrome*. The catch is that it is often inadmissible to share

---

[2]To download the German TPI, see http://www.psymeta.ch/.

this doubt, as we fear we will be found out and lose our professional credibility. This deepens the doubt and "impostor cloud" that hangs overhead.

Doubt can take many forms. It can emerge in subtle moments when our clients are talking about difficult issues. For example, I recall listening to a client talk about the ritual rapes she experienced growing up and the voice in my head saying, "You're in over your head, you have no idea how to help." A similar voice taunted me when I was in the midst of my relationship breaking up, and the couple I was working with was describing difficulties in their sexual relationship. I remember my focus floating away while the voice said, "If they only knew how messed up your relationship is. They are doing far better than you . . . you are such a fake!"

Doubt can occur more broadly, such as feeling incompetent to be in a helping professional at all. What are common ways of responding to such pervasive self-doubt? It can take the form of overworking to establish or "prove" competence and credibility, and hiding behind busyness to avoid being "found out." I have heard numerous therapists (including myself) describe anxiety dreams about having to go back to school to take missed courses or having their degree taken away because they had not completed the requirements. This doubt can also be disguised as an inflated ego—feeling or presenting like the best therapist ever with a "specialty" in everything. But overconfidence is also a form of delusion, as we cannot help all people, nor are we going to have success with everyone.

Being present means being with all that arises, including moments of anxiety and doubt. We need to tolerate uncertainty as clients unpack their issues and stories, and together figure out what needs addressing. Self-doubt, if not attended to, can infiltrate our ability to be balanced or focused. It can interfere with our ability to meet our clients in the depths of their experience.

*Presence Reflection: Awareness of What Underlies Doubt*

It is helpful to know our own landmines and special form of self-doubt in the context of being a therapist. Does it emerge from a childhood issue where there was pressure to perform? Was there early trauma? Or a misattuned or critical parent (or supervisor) that left you feeling not good enough? Perhaps you have developed a habit of perpetual self-criticism or doubt.

- Take a moment to call to mind a particular doubt you wrestle with.
- Invite your awareness to the emotion that underlies your doubt, including the emotional impact inside of being criticized.
- Reflect on early experiences that may have contributed to your self-doubt.

When we can understand the source of our self-doubt, then we have something to work with, to shift the patterns that occur sometimes outside of our awareness. It is also good to understand the underlying need (e.g., for acceptance or love) that may be playing itself out.

*Antidote to Self-Doubt: Self-Compassion Practice*

A powerful antidote to the menace of self-doubt is self-compassion. This is not an easy practice, especially if we have an intense inner voice telling us we are not good enough, leaving us feeling emotionally exhausted. The work of self-compassion is feeling the pain that underlies our self-doubt and offering a kinder, softer approach to ourselves. The better we get at showing compassion to ourselves, the greater the ease in experiencing the presence that lets us extend our compassion to others.

The following exercise is adapted from Kristen Neff's (2011) work on self-compassion.

- Take a moment to pause, breathe, and go inward.
- Become aware of a doubt that you have in your therapy practice or alternatively in your life—this could be in the form of a doubting inner voice.
- See if you can float back in time to a difficult period or relationship that may have contributed to this inner doubt.
- Notice the difficult feelings and sensations that are present in your body as you do this.
- Take your hand and put it on the place in your body where you feel this doubt and/or this earlier difficulty—offering kindness to the suffering you are experiencing.
- Become aware of the shared suffering that is a part of being human.
- Find some gentle and kind words to offer to that suffering, such as "I am here for you," "I know how much pain is there," "I understand," or "I love you."
- Continue to offer your suffering compassion and love with your words and gestures.
- Allow your hand to drop away as you close this practice, while staying connected to the feeling and words of self-compassion.

*Reflection.* This practice can help you work though the deeper experiences that have contributed to your self-doubt and process some of the original emotions by accessing them with compassion. With continued self-compassion practice, this voice of acceptance can emerge in the therapy room when doubt creeps in, and we can more easily redirect attention back to the moment. It can sooth the anxiety of uncertainty, reducing the self-imposed pressure to find an answer that always seems to keep one out of reach. Offering yourself a kind and nonjudgmental phrase such as "keep breathing," "you are okay," and "come back to the moment" can help to gently guide our attention back rather than spiraling further in the feelings of inner doubt.

*Other Strategies for Managing Self-Doubt*

Some other ways to manage self-doubt and impostor syndrome qualities are

- *Accept imperfection.* Although working through the source of this self-judgment is important, there is also room for accepting your imperfections as part of being human. Often it is the reaction to doubt that furthers the feeling ("I am an experienced therapist, I shouldn't have issues"). Acceptance actually slows it down.
- *Pause and reflect on the areas in which you do have expertise.* This can shift your focus away from doubt and activate feelings of self-worth.
- *Celebrate your achievements.* Create a portfolio of work you have done or how you have successfully helped others, so you can rewire your brain to more easily retrieve memories of your accomplishments too. Include a reflection of what you are good at, as well as areas that could use more development.
- *Talk with supervisors or mentors* who can help you work through challenges and help to both normalize those feelings and reflect back to you the ways you have grown.
- *Boost education, supervision, and learning* in client issues or modalities that you think of as your "areas of weakness." This is especially helpful when the doubt is not broadly cast but shows up in particularly challenging areas.
- *Go into counseling or psychotherapy* to work through this plaguing impostor belief. Without recognizing, understanding, and working through the roots of the issue, even these suggestions can fall short in making real change.

## Internal Barrier 2: Distraction (as a Natural State)

Distraction is a challenge to therapeutic presence, whether we are internally distracted by judgments or thoughts, or externally by noise or demands on our attention. It is nearly impossible to stay in a state of presence each moment. I used to think it was a deep flaw of mine that I could not sustain a state of unwavering equanimity while my clients were laying out a cascade of pain and deep emotional challenges. If I was distracted or overwhelmed I would hear the (not so) friendly voice in my head: "How can you write about and study presence and yet not be present all the time?" This pressure and self-judgment, as we explored in the last section, was a sure-fire way to heighten my distractibility and sense of being overwhelmed.

I have since reconceptualized for myself what it means to "get off center" or become distracted. We are, in fact, wired for distraction—to always be on alert for the predator that could jump out and attack the village at any moment. Attending to multiple stimuli (both internal and external) is a natural state with an evolutionary purpose. It is also a heavily conditioned one through these little smartphones and other such devices that offer us constant messages and newsflashes. They compound the challenge because we don't need cell phones or computers to take us away from the moment—our internal theater of thoughts or worries is quite capable of doing the same thing. Given the many pulls to be anywhere but here, and our brain's wiring to constantly scan the environment, how can we not be distracted?

In the therapy room these distracting thoughts can range from "What kind of therapist are you?" to "This person is never going to get better with that attitude," or there is always, "Lunch . . . hmm . . . sushi today?" All of this internal drama may be unfolding while we are nodding and absently looking at our clients. It is an illusion to think that on some level our clients do not feel and know that we are somewhere else. The risks in not working with our distractions is that therapy proceeds at a more surface level, we miss potential opportunities to promote deeper change, and our clients feel left alone in their suffering.

*Working With Distraction: The Point of New Return*

While there are many different ways we leave the moment, there are also a few simple steps that can help us to return. One example is with the acronym PNR:

1. **P**ause.
2. **N**otice.
3. **R**eturn.

It may not be a coincidence that PNR traditionally stands for *point of no return*. I like to think that we can redefine PNR to the *point of new return*. Each moment we come back is a new opportunity for presence and connection.

This acronym can change your life and attention (with a few thousand trials, of course). By training your brain and body to notice distraction and return to the moment, this process will come to take on a level of automaticity. The more we practice, the more we can transfer the many components of the therapeutic presence experience to our implicit processing system and the more automatic the components of presence become (Dietrich, 2004). This includes noticing distractors and letting them go. Opportunities arrive constantly in daily life to pause and return to the moment. Let's break PNR down further.

*Pause* is the gateway to making a choice for a different response. Pausing can be invited through a verbal cue. Remember to make it kind, as "Stop, you dummy!" may have a counterproductive impact. Perhaps just the simple words *pause*, *stop*, or *now* can work for you as a nonjudgmental reminder. Enhance your pause by taking a deep breath, which has the additional benefit of activating the parasympathetic nervous system and providing more mental and emotional space to notice what is occurring (Hanson & Mendius, 2009).

*Notice* is to bring attention to the thoughts or emotions that are contributing to your swaying away from the moment. The aim is to notice exactly as it is, without deepening it or judging it. Delving into it beyond that—experientially or cognitively—will shift more cognitive resources to its processing and make it harder to let go of the distraction. You might recognize that the emotion, thought, or physical sensation is a resonance to what is occurring in the moment (e.g., the client's sadness or pain) and can provide useful information or feedback. Or it may simply be a distraction, serving nothing more than to shut you down to the client and his or her experience. Noticing without judgment allows the sensation to subside.

*Return* involves intentionally inviting our attention and awareness back to the moment. The doorway of the senses offers many opportunities for this. You might notice your hand resting on your leg, the touch of the keyboard, the feel of the seat beneath you, or the soles of your feet resting on the ground. Return may also be refocusing your full attention on the person you are with and the feeling of being in connection in the moment. Perhaps the rhythm of their voice or the look on their face can be an anchor for your attention. Your returned state may last for several minutes or a brief nanosecond. Here is the real key to this practice: nonjudgment. Even if your return to the moment is brief, you have trod the neural pathway to presence one more time, reinforcing a more defined path. Like the meditators we read about in Chapter 3, which slowly shifted the work of sustaining attention to regions that make focus less effortful, every time you practice PNR you are potentially shaping the neural structure that makes presence more easily accessible in time (Lutz, Jha, Dunne, & Saron, 2015).

Using PNR in session can also help overcome other clinical challenges—such as countertransference, which I demonstrate in a later case example—when we are disconnected from our clients or they are withdrawn, or we are unclear how to proceed. We can miss what is truly being felt and expressed by our client because we are uncomfortable with the process of being in the unknown with them as they discover their real feelings and experience. Let's take some time to look more closely at the challenges posed by uncertainty.

## Internal Barrier 3: Discomfort With Uncertainty

As discussed in Chapter 4, we need to put aside agenda and bracket theories, preconceptions, and therapy planning when in session. However, this requires us to really get settled in the wilderness of uncertainty and to wait patiently. Therapy direction and clients' experience can take time to unfold. We need to cultivate comfort with the unknown, or our own distress can lead us to respond in a way that is out of synch with our client.

Silence poses a similar challenge for therapists. The discomfort of this socially unacceptable way of relating runs deep. Yet being with silence and the unknown allows for experience and insight to arise. When we interfere with silence, we could impede our clients' personal reflections or learning process. For example, maybe they are looking for the right words to say something difficult—words that you can't supply or that would have less impact if you did. Maybe part of their work is learning to be with silence until they are ready to share. To be able to trust in the unknown takes practice and experience in tolerating the discomfort of silence and experiencing how it can leave space for poignant therapeutic material to emerge. As Mark Twain once said, "the right word may be effective, but no word was ever as effective as a rightly timed pause" (Powers, 1999, p. 174).

The challenge of trust in the unknown often occurs near the beginning of a session, when your client is starting to delve into his or her experience but is still unclear what he or she is feeling. Whether you are practicing from a relational- or a manual-based therapy, there needs to be time for your clients to develop comfort and safety in the relationship and bring their issues into full awareness. Your anxiety at this beginning stage can force a rushed sequence of interventions before your client has had time to build trust or the relationship has had time to develop. If you are new to being a therapist, you may overuse therapeutic techniques as a way of managing your anxiety. This could minimize your efficacy, as your interventions may not be attuned with your client.

We need to get comfortable with discomfort and learn to wait patiently for emerging material. We also need to sit with suffering without trying to instantly fix it. This takes a level of psychological resilience, emotional regulation, and mental grit, as well as trust that something healing can happen when we are compassionately feeling our clients' pain alongside with them. It can also offer an experience of how intuition and responses can arise from being in the unknown together.

The following clinical vignette reflects what happened when I imposed my own view of what needed to occur, rather than being with what was emerging.

*Clinical Vignette: Attachment to a Therapy Plan*

In preparation for a session with Mary, I reviewed the notes from the last session. I was reminded of our intention to move into emotion-focused therapy (EFT) empty chair work with her mother, to resolve her hurt and anger toward her mother for being very self-focused. Mary had a learning disability and was made fun of at school. She would often arrive home feeling depressed, anxious, and alone. Her mother would tell her "it's not so bad" and then burden Mary with her own struggles about being single and wanting to meet a man. This was important work that Mary was just now ready to start exploring.

Mary came into the session looking forlorn, her eyes downcast and her mood low. When I checked in with her she described a recent argument with her partner. She was feeling invalidated and alone. She described the events that led to her partner walking out on her. I reflected the aloneness she felt in that moment and even now, and linked this to the aloneness she felt with her mother not attending to her emotional needs. I saw this as a good entry point to engage in the unfinished business task with her mother that I had reviewed as an intention for the session in my notes. I invited Mary to visualize her mother in the empty chair and tell her how she felt being left alone and invalidated. She talked to her mother in a monotone voice, and I was struggling with how to respond, as she showed very little affect. I tried to have her engage in a different EFT therapeutic task (two-chair exercise) so she could become aware of how she blocks her own emotions. Nothing I tried helped or evoked any emotion. Instead, the session ended with Mary saying she did not think this EFT exercise would work for her and that she did not want to do it again. Following the session I felt frustrated with myself for not facilitating the therapeutic process better. Instead, the session felt stuck and regressive.

*Reflection*. This vignette speaks to a barrier to therapeutic presence: I was attached to a therapy plan and unable to just be with what Mary was experiencing. There may have been a link between the depth of her current despondency and the rejection she felt by her mother, and the timing of my response only furthered her sense of aloneness. Attachment to sharing my "smart insight" got in the way of hearing what she was expressing. It is difficult to trust that when we let go of our insights, they will return at the right time, but this trust is essential.

In retrospect, Mary needed me to be with her in her pain at this most recent event. If I had engaged in a PNR when I noticed her flat affect, I would have recognized my own inner pressure and anxiety in wanting her to resolve her issue, as well as her withdrawal and detachment from me. This practice would have allowed me to acknowledge my own barrier, put it aside, and slow down the process to be with where she was. This brief practice could have repaired the rupture in our relationship in that moment as I could have noticed my own imposition on her process and validated and attuned to where she was. If Mary had felt met by me, we might even have eventually explored an intervention (i.e., empty chair exercise) that would have allowed us to process the relationship with her mother in a way that was timed to her readiness. I won't ever know. However, I do know that my bringing an agenda and not just trusting in what was emerging made the client feel abandoned and left me feeling incompetent.

*Antidotes for Managing Anxiety in the Unknown: Trust in the Process*

Experience with trusting the process can help us manage the anxiety in being with uncertainty. Some specific tools to manage this discomfort are returning to a focus on the breath; doing full abdominal breathing; or silently reminding yourself to stay in the present, to trust in the process, and to trust in being in the moment.

*Preparing for the Session Is Imperative*

As we discovered in the model of therapeutic presence, preparing for the session by intentionally bracketing our theories, preconceptions, and therapy plans can help to prevent this kind of interference in session. This includes some intentional practices, as noted in Chapter 4, to engage in a presence practice prior to starting a session, such as the PRESENCE acronym, a mindfulness practice, or clearing a space. These can help you maintain a sense of openness and attunement to the moment, being with your clients in their difficult experience, and your own discomfort in the face of unknown.

## Internal Barrier 4: Therapeutic Presence and Countertransference

*Countertransference* is when therapists' own personal conflicts, past or current issues, are triggered in the session and shape their feelings or perspective. Initially a psychoanalytic concept, it has been recognized as occurring across all modalities (Gelso & Hayes, 2007). Countertransference reactions are an occupational hazard of relating deeply in the present moment, and you can count on this happening! How could our own unresolved experiences never be touched or triggered given the openness to emotional experience we must maintain in our role? Part of our very job description as therapists is to "feel with." And yet countertransference goes beyond "feeling with" to feeling too much of our own unresolved issues in relation to our clients, which interferes with our ability to be effective as their therapist.

Different contributions could arise to cause us to feel too much or too little (shutting down). Taking in the traumatic experiences our clients share when we are present with them can result in us carrying the trauma with us. This experience of vicarious traumatization is heightened when we are not engaging in grounding, closing down the day, or releasing the emotional impact of the work we do through intentional practice or supervision, or we are not investing in self-care or a good work–life balance. Whether it be overwhelming feelings, or reactive states, or shutting down, see the next section for some strategies to deal with any countertransference reactions.

*Antidote to Countertransference Reactions*

The prevention of and antidote to countertransference lie in self-awareness, self-insight, and commitment to one's own growth. Research has confirmed that openness to one's own feelings is associated with less countertransference behavior (Robbins & Jolkovski, 1987). The more we can familiarize ourselves with our own issues and discern these from interpersonal reading of the moment, the more we can move through the triggers that emerge and use our internal experience to facilitate the therapy process. Therapeutic presence practice helps generate awareness of our underlying unmet needs that countertransference reactions could be indicating. In Chapter 6 we looked at how to respond to internal cues in session if we discern that they are not countertransference reactions. But what if they are? Recognition is a critical first step. The next step is working with the reaction internally (and later in supervision if needed) and bringing your attention back to the moment. Therapeutic presence practice is helpful as it allows for

1. A focus on self-care, balance, and taking care of interpersonal difficulties and unresolved issues. This will ensure that reactions emerge less in session.
2. Strengthening your moment-to-moment awareness of your experience. This will help develop agility with recognizing the source of that feeling and swiftly moving your awareness back into the moment.

The following vignette illustrates how noticing my reaction helped to invite my attention back.

### Clinical Vignette: Working With Countertransference

My client Jane was describing the death of her son when he was 8 years old. She shared feeling a "deep hole" in her chest from the hurt and pain she felt. She felt overwhelmed by having to cope with everyday tasks, saying she could "barely face each day." As she spoke, I found myself emotionally distancing and instead cognitively responding to her pain by reassuring her. My attention felt like it was moving further and further out of the room. I noticed my clipboard in my hand and my pen writing furtively. I recognized that writing was a comfort to me and it was as if the clipboard was acting as a shield against my being with Jane's overwhelming pain. I brought my attention to my present-moment disconnection, and I became aware that underneath the emotional distance I felt to Jane were feelings of deep sadness and fear of loss. My distancing was serving as a blockade to that pain and fear. I also felt overwhelmed with my helplessness; I could not take away or lessen her pain in any way.

I used PNR to work with what was emerging. As I became aware of my distance and feelings of being overwhelmed, I paused (first step in PNR) and asked myself what I was feeling. That was when I noticed (second step in PNR) the underlying emotional triggers, including fear of being overwhelmed by sadness and my own sense of incompetence. I noted these feelings without judgment and imagined putting these fears on a shelf, with an intention to address them at a later time. I returned my awareness to the present (third step of PNR), by bringing my awareness to my breath and to my feet on the ground, and then back to my client. Looking up at Jane from this grounded presence, I felt close to her again. I could take in the vastness of her pain while feeling a sense of inner stability.

*Reflection.* In working with countertransference reactions, it is most helpful to pause for internal awareness before shifting attention back to your client. The ability to quickly gather attention and presence is made possible by a commitment outside of the session to tracking your inner experience, emotionally regulating and returning attention to the moment through a practice such as mindfulness. The important follow-up is to take time outside of the session to work through the fears that were triggered, so they don't reemerge in future therapy sessions.

## RUPTURES IN THERAPEUTIC RELATIONSHIPS

Ruptures in the therapeutic relationship will happen. Accepting that fact rather than feeling the therapy is doomed is key. Working skillfully through ruptures can actually strengthen the therapeutic alliance. Ruptures can take the form of confrontation, in which your client expresses criticism, anger, or hostility toward you. They can also be manifested in withdrawal, in which the client pulls back or expresses negative feelings indirectly. As a therapist it can be challenging to stay present through the discomfort and discord of a therapeutic rupture.

Therapeutic presence allows you to have greater sensitivity to here-and-now aspects of the therapeutic alliance. With presence, you can use your inner sensitivity to identify possible relationship difficulties, explore them with your client, and skillfully own your contributions to the alliance rupture to move toward repair.

Safran, Muran, Samstag, and Stevens (2002) identified three key features of the therapist response that promote a repair and positive alliance: (a) recognition of here-and-now relationship problems as they occur, (b) use of the alliance rupture to explore clients' negative experiences and feelings, and (c) ownership of personal struggles in the therapeutic relationship and how this contributes to your clients' negative experiences and feelings. The theme in working through challenges is an attunement to ruptures as they arise, with a focus on the here-and-now relationship.

### Working With Ruptures

Being skillfully attuned helps you to both notice the subtle ways that clients may be expressing this difficulty in the relationship and to address the problem while managing your own feelings about the difficulty. Steps to dealing with ruptures include the following:

1. Becoming aware of and sensing the discord or withdrawal, especially if it is not explicitly expressed and coming out in aside comments.
2. Naming and bringing attention to the difficulty with clients by describing the tension or withdrawal that you are sensing.
3. Allowing for clients' expression of feelings such as anger, hurt, or rejection. This means staying present, being nonjudgmental, and validating their feelings.
4. Attempting to repair the rupture. If you did something to cause the discord, this will mean owning and accepting responsibility for that, and for the negative impact your action has had. Clarifying the misunderstanding without being defensive is crucial. Focus on validating your client's feelings while acknowledging or reflecting triggers as well as the therapeutic value of exploring this in the here-and-now relationship. By working together collaboratively to genuinely acknowledge your feelings and those of your client, you can ultimately strengthen the therapeutic alliance.

When processing a rupture, you must bring all aspects of therapeutic presence to bear on the situation. Rupture repair requires presence with your own and your client's difficult feelings and a simultaneous seeking out of a larger spaciousness in which to work skillfully and without defense. As discussed in Chapter 6, it is important to stay in contact with your client while working through these sensitive issues and maintaining an open body posture, vocal prosody, and soft and warm gaze and facial expression (Geller & Porges, 2014; Quillman, 2012; Schore, 2003).

What happens when similarly intense challenges are not one-offs, but instead occur with a client on a regular basis? How can you remain present through the ebbs and flows of working with challenging clients? Let's transition to the next section with a personal reflection on the types of clients or issues that challenge your ability to maintain presence.

THERAPEUTIC PRESENCE REFLECTION:
PRESENCE WITH CHALLENGING CLIENTS

- Pause and take a few deep breaths with long exhalations.
- Reflect on which client issues challenge your ability to be present.
- What hijacks your focus or attention? Are certain clients more challenging to be present with?

- Pause and listen deeply for what emerges—without judgment.
- Now ask: What are the conditions that can help you be more present with your clients?
- Listen deeply to the responses and jot down some notes if it is helpful to identify your challenges and what is needed to work through these.

## WORKING WITH COMPLEXITIES IN CLIENTS' EXPERIENCE

Working with clients with diagnostic or emotional complexities can make presence harder to attain, although complexity is in the eye of the beholder. One therapist may feel challenged by certain symptoms, whereas another may have developed comfort in working with these same struggles. I will do my best to pull out some of the common challenges therapists have noted, such as hopelessness in depression, dying and death, and significant emotional dysregulation. I invite you to look at what "difficult" means to you and apply some of the principles described in the vignettes and descriptions to your unique struggles.

### Hopelessness in Depression

The extreme shutting down that can exist side by side with depression can be difficult for some therapists to navigate. It can trigger fears of being "sucked down a dark hole" if you allow yourself to be really present with your clients' pain. It can also activate a sense of powerlessness in the face of hopelessness, leaving you feeling incompetent or frustrated. Part of therapeutic presence means acknowledging when your own struggle with staying present leads to distancing in the relationship. Is the distance really about your client's depression, or is it about your fear? Therapeutic presence also allows you to sense the deeper levels of your clients' experience, without attachment to outcome or what healing means for that person. The following vignette demonstrates the struggle I had with staying present in the face of hopelessness, including the ability to recognize that struggle and return to the moment of presence in the relationship.

### Clinical Vignette

As I was preparing for my session with Isaac, I was already feeling some hesitancy. I had tried to help him for several months with his depression. As the session began, he described feeling very low, with no sense of purpose and no hope that his depression would lift. I found myself feeling frustrated and stuck. I tried again to encourage him to see a psychiatrist for a medication consult. He again refused, saying he did "not believe in meds." I encouraged him to try exercise to boost his energy, as well as practices to increase his serotonin and dopamine. He said he didn't have the motivation to do these things. I reflected on the irony that his depression left him feeling unmotivated to engage in the very things that could help. Inside I struggled, longing to find a way to activate his energy so he could work on his deeper issues. I felt tension in my body as I sensed the emotional wall between us.

At this point I realized I needed to take a PNR moment. As I paused to explore my inner tension, I recognized that my pushing him was not helping and asked myself why I persisted in doing it. I realized that my own fear of helplessness and of being pulled into the darkness were leading me to over-encourage him, just trying to muster some motivation to continue working. I was far from present and realized I needed to shift this internally. I noticed the source of this issue, with a kind gesture inside to take care of it later. Taking a few breaths to regulate and feel my feet on the ground, and then returned my awareness back to the moment with Isaac.

As I attuned with Isaac, I could tell he felt distressed and alone (rapid breathing, hands across his chest, eyes averted) as I had left him in his pain. PNR helped bring me back to the moment, but self-disclosure was needed to help repair the rupture and validate his feelings. I shared with him, "I feel some tension in my chest as we're talking and I realize I'm feeling a bit helpless seeing you in pain. I find myself pushing you, which just serves to ease my tension. I imagine that doesn't feel helpful. I imagine it has made you feel more pressured and alone." He took a breath, and his face softened, which signaled to me that he felt more understood. He looked up tearfully and said, "Yeah, I feel like I am failing at therapy too." I validated this feeling, telling him I could understand how my pushing contributed to why he felt that way. He breathed again, appearing visibly safer and more connected to me (deeper breathing, softer facial expression, arms dropped and his body leaning toward me while his gaze met mine). From this place of connection we were able to access a fear he has about feeling better. Isaac was afraid he would fail at living well—that he would not get the care and love he needed and wanted in relationships. Sometimes he felt like it was just easier to stay in the depression than face the intense fear of rejection and a loneliness he couldn't control. The authentic and present-centered sharing in our relationship opened the door to explore his fear and resistance, while I held his pain and suffering alongside him.

*Reflection.* Recognizing when we are not present and what is being triggered was key here. Emotionally regulating internally (pause, notice, breathe, and return to the moment) allowed for an awareness of what was contributing to the rupture in me and what was needed to repair and reestablish a sense of connection. My bodily felt tension was no doubt perceptible to Isaac, activating a neuroception of unsafety that barred more open sharing (Geller & Porges, 2014; Quillman, 2012). When I could recognize what was happening inside me (by regaining presence), not only did my internal strain ease, but so did Isaac's: He was now receiving my nonverbal (and verbal) expressions of presence, rather than my distance and defense. I could see this in the easing of his breath and the softening of his facial muscles. He was moving into what has been called a "window of tolerance" (Siegel, 2011)—a state where his defenses were down-regulated and he could tolerate his emotions, making it possible to engage in the work of therapy. Activating safety for both of us let Isaac explore his fear of failure both in therapy and in life. In time he was able to feel less fearful of feeling better and began engaging in activities that he personally discovered were helpful in reducing his depression.

## Dying and Death

Being with someone who is dying or facing a terminal illness is one of the most difficult human experiences, as there is nothing we can do to fix or change this reality. This can evoke a feeling of helplessness in us. As therapists, we like to see relief and to feel we can help someone navigate through intolerable feelings or situations into a new life with peace and wholeness. That is not the case when facing someone who is dying. We can't help our clients cure their terminal illness. Yet we can help them to accept their dying, come to peace with unfinished issues in their relationships, and to live fully and with peace in their final days.

Presence is imperative in working with people who are dying (Halifax, 2009). Often family members, friends, even doctors, are fearful of talking about death and avoid the topic with the dying person. This creates a feeling in clients who are dying of being deserted as they face the end of their life. Presence with your clients' feelings around this transition from life to death allows them to feel less alone.

Roshi Bernie Glassman (as cited in Halifax, 2009) teaches the three tenets of compassionate care of the dying. The first tenet, *not knowing*, reflects giving up fixed ideas of ourselves or others and opening to the spontaneity of the "beginner mind." The second tenet, *bearing witness*, asks us to be present with the suffering and joy in the world, without judgment and without attachment to outcome. The third tenet, *compassionate action*, reflects a commitment to free others and ourselves from suffering.

Glassman's tenets share similarities with the work of Frank Ostaseski, founder of the Zen hospice in San Francisco and the Metta Institute. He developed five precepts (Ostaseski, 2012) as companions on the journey of accompanying the dying. He described these as bottomless practices that can be continually explored and deepened and have to be lived into and communicated through action.

*The first precept: Welcome everything. Push away nothing.* We may not like what is arising, but it is our work to neither approve nor disapprove. We just need to listen deeply. This is a journey of continuous discovery: We have no idea how it will turn out, and it takes courage and flexibility.

*The second precept: Bring your whole self to the experience.* In the process of healing we open to both our joy and fear. This precept reflects the importance of exploring our own inner life in enabling us to be empathic and respond compassionately to the other person.

*The third precept: Don't wait.* This precept calls for patience and an honoring of present-moment experience, rather than merely waiting for death. When we just wait for the moment of death, we miss so many moments of living. This allows for the awareness of the precarious nature of this life to reveal what is most important, that calls us to enter fully.

*The fourth precept: Find a place of rest in the middle of things.* Rest is often something we associate with arriving at the end of the day or going on holiday. We look forward to it as an endpoint. We imagine that we can only find rest by changing the conditions of our life. But it is possible to discover rest right in the middle of chaos and difficult emotions.

*The fifth precept: Cultivate don't-know mind.* This precept describes cultivating an open and receptive mind that is not limited by agendas, roles, and expectations. From this open receptivity we allow the situation itself and the relationship with the other, in the moment, to inform our actions. We learn to see, feel and look with fresh eyes.

Glassman's three tenets and Ostaseski's five precepts reflect the experience of therapeutic presence. We need to be receptive and open to the unknown and to others, to be fully present and nonjudgmental with our clients and their experience of dying, without attachment to outcome. We cannot fix their dying, yet our presence is what is truly healing.

Presence with dying requires us to look deeply at our own attitude or potential fear of illness and death, as well as to recognize cultural and family attitudes that may have been internalized. Yet engaging in the work of facing our own fears helps us to truly accompany our clients, without reservation. This is the gift of presence, to bear witness to our clients' suffering without shutting down, holding back, or detaching when overwhelmed, and to walk with them in their transition from life to death.

## Emotional Dysregulation, Rage, and Suicidal Threats

Clients who experience intense emotions, rage, and suicidality pose a unique challenge to therapists. The emergence of dialectical behavior therapy (DBT), developed by Marsha Linehan (1993a, 1993b), has made working with these clients feel possible and less daunting. DBT offers a structure and skill set to validate clients, while setting boundaries (if needed) and offering tools for emotional regulation. A focus on acceptance before change is key to the therapy.

Tolerating the pain we feel in resonance with clients' suffering demands a high level of presence both with ourselves and with our clients, as well as a strong self-regulation skill set. Staying present with suffering allows our clients to feel met, seen, heard, and validated. Then, from that place, our clients can integrate the tools for emotional regulation and begin to approach their own relationships without the intense fear of abandonment that is so common.

When we as therapists are the target of a client's intense anger, arrogance, or selfishness, we can sometimes experience shame or a reactive and aversive internal response. In the face of this extremely engrained behavior, we can find ourselves feeling angry, defensive, and hopeless.

Compassion helps: Know that underneath the client's anger is deep suffering. Approach your client's suffering with sensitivity and understanding, all while holding a respect for the limits of what you are willing to tolerate. The tricky balance for us as therapists is to be aware of and nonreactive to the outward expression of arrogance, while attuning to the deeper shame or sadness that is underlying these behaviors and is highly protected by the client.

Typically, clients with these issues have had problematic early attachment relationships, which we know can lead to a chronically overactive nervous system. What feels like an innocuous comment or gesture to you could send a client into an emotional tailspin. This intense emotional arousal (and how easy it is to accidentally trip the breaker) can be scary. The process of developing the client's implicit affect regulatory capacity (right brain) through your attuned presence is a long process—much longer than offering them explicit strategies (left brain). Yet we know that this implicit, more automatic form of emotional regulation is what makes the real difference in peoples' lives (Schore, 2012; Williams, Bargh, Nocera, & Gray, 2009).

The techniques we use with clients to help them regulate are valuable (e.g., mindfulness skills, increasing interpersonal skill, self-soothing techniques, enhancing empathy, cognitive behavioral techniques). Yet what is most valuable is how you are in the room with them. The techniques do not matter if your client is not met with your warm, accepting, open, grounded presence. When working through difficulties with a dysregulated client, you need to know how and when to challenge your client, and to do so is highly dependent on your inner steadiness, compassion, and attunement to the moment. There is an even greater need to remain open, connected, grounded, yet nonreactive for your approach to be effective.

*Antidotes for Therapists: Regulate to Relate*

So you must stay present in the room, session after session, without becoming so overwhelmed that you shut down yourself. Reducing your reactivity helps you to relate and respond with greater fluidity. Earlier we looked at the PNR strategy for regaining focus and composure. Yet managing emotional reactivity is a part of the work of achieving therapeutic presence itself, and not only a strategy for returning to presence if it has been lost. This ability to regulate emotionally can keep us in connection with others, especially when we are thrown off by our own reactivity. How can you regulate regardless of your client's level of arousal?

*Therapeutic Presence Practice: SOBER.* There is a brief practice that is helpful in naming difficult emotions when you are in the throws of reactivity in relationship. It is based on the acronym SOBER, which stands for:

- **S**top—pause for a moment and step out of the cycle of emotional reactivity.
- **O**bserve—pay attention to what you are sensing, feeling, and experiencing, and what is the primary experience of emotion that underlies that reactivity.
- **B**reathe—pause for a few deep breaths to assess your situation in as calm a manner as possible.
- **E**xpand—expand your awareness and allow yourself to get a larger perspective on what is happening within you and around you.
- **R**espond—now respond, rather than react, to the situation at hand so that you are acting effectively and from a place of authenticity.

REFLECTION. Although PNR offers a pause to shift attention, SOBER can help in the midst of intense emotions. Walking through SOBER calms your nervous system, and as you expand your perspective outward, you can connect to what is really being triggered. Even when in a highly reactive state, you can check in with the underlying experience and stop the escalation. SOBER can reveal some of your habitual emotional reactions, which might repeatedly intensify the cycle of reactivity with others. SOBER was originally developed in the area of mindfulness and addiction (Marlatt & Miller, 2009), yet is highly useful in any situation you want to move from reactivity to responsiveness. It is especially useful with dysregulated clients to prevent a vicious cycle of therapist and client feeding off of each other's reactivity. As a useful aside, SOBER is also an excellent tool to offer couples when they are in the midst of a reactive fight in your office or at home.

## A Toolbox for Emotion Regulation Skills

It is valuable to have on hand an array of emotional regulation skills (for you and for your clients). Here are some suggestions for your emotional regulation toolbox:

- Breathing with long exhalations (long exhalations down-regulate the sympathetic nervous system and vagal pathways of defense, inviting a sense of calm, openness, and trust).
- Naming internally what you are feeling (modulates limbic firing, regulating emotions).
- Mindfulness practice (being with experience with acceptance promotes nonreactivity).
- Focusing on the body (i.e., feeling your feet on the ground).
- Self-compassion with difficult emotions—accepting your feelings with kindness.
- Changing your body posture to upright and relaxed (promotes a positive affect).
- Centering—visualizing your center or an image of a mountain or tree to activate a physiological sense of equanimity.

The challenges that accompany presence with difficult clients are only partially illuminated here. We all have our unique challenges, and ultimately it requires skillful practice of recognizing when we are not present, regulating, and returning to the moment. These challenges highlight the increased need for balance, self-care, and the ability to release emotional residue from a therapy day to minimize compassion fatigue.

To really be present at the level I am describing means making a commitment to practice in life and strengthening the individual qualities of therapeutic presence. The next section offers in-life practices that can help to cultivate the qualities of presence in yourself and to build the neural structure to remain present and tolerate difficulties that arise.

### TRANSITION PRACTICE: NAMING AND LETTING GO

- Pause and feel your feet on the ground.
- Notice what you feel in this moment.
- Name your experience in a few words (i.e., tight, angry, tired, calm).
- Take a deep breath and transition to the next chapter or the next moment in your day.

# III

# PRESENCE PRACTICES
# FOR DAILY LIFE

# 8

# PREPARING THE GROUND FOR PRESENCE: MINDFULNESS AND EXPERIENTIAL EXERCISES

Self-care is never a selfish act—it is simply good stewardship of the only gift I have, the gift I was put on earth to offer others. Anytime we can listen to true self and give the care it requires, we do it not only for ourselves, but also for the many others whose lives we touch.

—Parker J. Palmer (1999, p. 30)

To strengthen your presence in the clinical encounter, as we have been exploring in Part II of this book, you need an equal commitment to the life-time journey of growing as a person and in relationships. Presence in life, balance, and self-care are essential parts of this skill building. Rogers (1957) believed that there is a natural growth or actualizing tendency within all of us that emerges naturally when the conditions are right. The same is true with presence. By cultivating presence in our lives, we create the conditions for presence to be accessed in session.

This chapter offers practices to cultivate presence in your daily life. These reflect the first category in the model of therapeutic presence described in Chapter 1: Preparing the ground for presence (see also Geller & Greenberg, 2002, 2012). The next two chapters include practices designed to enhance the qualities in the second and third categories (process and the in-body experience of therapeutic presence). Together these help us to live a life, have relationships, and approach therapy in a way that is infused with presence.

http://dx.doi.org/10.1037/0000025-009
*A Practical Guide to Cultivating Therapeutic Presence*, by S. M. Geller

## PRESENCE IN LIFE

Our life is the practice ground for cultivating presence and is rich with opportunities for doing so, such as "pausing to breathe" in the line at store in the shopping mall or putting down our cell phone or work to listen deeply to a family member or friend. Life's challenges also provide fodder for practice: frustration in traffic, multiple unattended e-mails, our own self-judgments, or difficulties with a colleague or family member. I am sure that you already have many ways that you experience and invite presence in your lives, whether that is your conscious intention or not. Let us begin from where you are.

**Presence Pause: Already There**

What are the ways in which you already cultivate presence and care for yourself?

- Pause and take a few breaths, inviting your attention to this moment.
- Feel your feet on the ground, and rest your eyes as you prepare to reflect.
- Ask yourself: What is already woven into my life that supports my being present? Some examples are: taking time with loved ones, self-care, gardening, meditation, yoga, walking, being in nature, being compassionate with family members, pausing throughout the day, breathing practices, music, limitations on e-mail or Internet, to name a few.
- Acknowledge within how you already engage in positive ways to strengthen your presence.

## FORMAL PRESENCE PRACTICES: MEDITATION AND YOGA

Formal meditation is a fundamental practice that helps to embody presence. On the most basic level, it supports putting time aside on a daily basis to pause and look inward. Meditation strengthens the neural muscles that support returning to the moment (Baldini, Parker, Nelson, & Siegel, 2014; Sze, Gyurak, Yuan, & Levenson, 2010). Meditation can also help us to develop a method or way to recognize when we are distracted or involved in a self-focused emotion or something that is detracting from presence in the moment. I use the word *practice* to highlight how being present is a process, and not a perfect one. In fact, awareness of when we are not present is as beneficial, as it builds our attentional capacity and invites us to get off autopilot.

Meditation offers a formal practice to train our attention to return to the moment, again and again.

Therapists have described daily meditation practice as central to developing and sustaining therapeutic presence (Geller, 2001). This is reflected in research showing that meditation (including practices from mindfulness, concentration, Zen, and Zazen traditions and yoga) enhances therapists' attention, empathy, concentration, compassion, nonattachment, equanimity, energy, and expansion of awareness—all important components of presence (Fulton, 2005; Sweet & Johnson, 1990; Thomson, 2000; Valente & Marotta, 2005; Valentine & Sweet, 1999).

Meditation involves paying attention to your sensory experience, offering an enhanced ability to sense inside your body. Expert meditators have higher levels of visceral awareness than both dancers (who have high body awareness generally) and controls (Sze et al., 2010). Visceral awareness helps us to sense our inner world, an aspect of presence (inward attunement) and a precursor to self-awareness and empathy (reading our felt experience of our clients).

Meditation is not easy. Contrary to popular conception, it is meant to bring awareness rather than relaxation. When we let our thoughts arise and pass away, we notice the incessant chatter of our minds, and in time feelings and sensations become more noticeable. By observing and opening to our experience without judging or resisting, we gain a more intimate sense of the areas of our life where we feel afraid, fixated, or grasping.

**Mindfulness Meditation Practice**

Choose a brief time each day to practice meditation. Avoid practicing on a full stomach (e.g., not immediately after breakfast or dinner), and try to practice in the same location each day. Start with a 5-minute practice, increasing over time to 20 to 30 minutes.

- Sit in an upright yet relaxed position.
- Allow your eyes to close or to softly look at the ground, inviting your attention inward.
- Invite your attention to your breath. Find a place in the body where you experience breathing, such as the belly or the chest.
- Feel the rhythm of your breathing as it moves through your body, feeling the rise and fall of your belly or chest in rhythm with the inhale and the exhale.
- When your mind wanders, without judgment name your distracting thought in one word (thinking, planning, worrying) and without getting caught in the story of what you are thinking about. Then invite your attention back to feeling the rise and fall of your belly in rhythm breathing.

- Continue to notice when your mind goes off, and keep returning your awareness to your breath, without judgment, with acceptance.
- When your practice is complete, slowly wiggle your fingers and toes and open your eyes, staying connected to your breath as you engage with the rest of your day.

You may find that being in a group helps you sustain a regular meditation practice. Look for local mindfulness or meditation groups that you can join. You can explore longer retreats or workshops to immerse yourself in as well, such as insight meditation, mindfulness-based stress reduction, mindfulness based cognitive therapy, or therapeutic rhythm and mindfulness. See Appendix A for other resources, such as apps and guided meditations.

**Presence Through Embodied Practice: Yoga**

Mind–body practices like yoga offer a gateway to meditative focus by settling the body, which is yoga's traditional aim (Lauwers, 2015; Nangia & Malhotra, 2012). Practicing yoga poses in preparation for one of your daily presence meditations, or before you start a therapy session, can decrease your distraction throughout. You can also use simple yoga postures such as tree pose or shavasana, which is lying on the ground on your back with your arms and legs spread at 45 degrees while deeply breathing with your eyes closed, to support having a grounded presence prior to a session.

Beyond acting as a preparation, yoga is a potent presence practice in itself. It cultivates mindfulness and interoceptive awareness (Gard, Noggle, Park, Vago, & Wilson, 2014), supporting your ability to attune to emotion as felt in your body, including in resonance with your clients. It also helps you to stay present to difficult emotions as you learn to tolerate the discomfort of staying with a posture.

Yoga is a valuable adjunct to general self-care for therapists, given its operation on the physical body in ways that decrease stress and anxiety and improve mood through cultivating embodied awareness (Gard et al., 2014). You can develop your own home practice or attend instructor-led classes in studio. Classes might help you to enhance your practice through immersing in postures, being in a community, and having a teacher to guide you and support you.

## PRESENCE PRACTICE IN DAILY LIFE

Opportunities for presence are abundant. You can find them in formal practices such as meditation and yoga, natural moments such as taking in the radiant colors of a flower blooming in spring, or everyday activities like walking or washing the dishes. Yet presence can also be practiced in times of difficulty and pain. Following is my "fortuitous" moment for presence.

## Life's Challenges: My Fall Into Presence

In fall 2014, at the peak of busyness (clients, facilitating groups, writing, teaching at the university, supervising), I created a 3-day break to be in the beauty of Cape Cod. Fatigue was deep in my bones, and I was embracing time to listen to the sea and wander through the colorful fall streets. On a gorgeous walk along a rock path by the ocean, taking in the beauty of the sea, I was met with an unexpected moment that would change my life dramatically over the next year. My foot slipped, and I could hear the crack penetrating through my eardrums. I realized instantly my leg was broken, and I was overcome with unbearable pain. I could not move, as I knew it could cause further injury, and I could also feel the bone penetrating through my skin. It was nearing dark, and I was far out on the rocks. Although my friend called for help, it was hours before anyone could reach us. Finally, in the dark, paramedics pulled up to the shore in a pickup truck and hiked over to us with a large basket that they used to carry me back to the truck, then drove me to an ambulance. After a 2-hour drive to Cape Cod Hospital, I found out that I had an open fracture and multiple breaks on my left leg and that the medical staff could not treat it in their facility. Several hours later I was in a Boston hospital, managing excruciating pain from this complex leg break and ankle crack. Going into surgery the next morning, I began to face the reality that I would not be bearing weight for some time (or walking my dog!), and working would be on hold for at least 3 months.

I did not anticipate that this minivacation break would lead in an insufferable, painful leg break—and then to a much-needed (and unconsciously self-imposed) larger break from my busy life. I also did not realize how pain and injury could lead into a deeper level of presence—listening to my body and slowing down. Although I would have preferred a rest on an exotic island or white sand beach, my living room provided the retreat setting that would allow for months of slowing down, being with pain, and opening to the painful moments as my body dictated what it needed.

Multitasking was a thing of the past, and focusing on one movement at a time was all I could manage. My body demanded deep rest; merely showering or walking to the kitchen was taxing. Months of attending to the moment-to-moment needs of my body allowed me to rest in a way that I would not have been able to otherwise. I am now just a few months past that time and already fighting the strong pull to busyness that is so conditioned in me. Taking intentional pauses is a response I am now working to condition in its place. I wish to share with you several lessons I learned from this memorable time:

- Life challenges are opportunities for presence.
- Slow down before the body forces you to slow down.
- Pain is a portal to presence.

- Healing comes from deeply listening to the body, and what is needed moment to moment.
- Being vulnerable and accepting help is challenging and yet key to being supported.
- Community support and connection are important parts of healing.

Perhaps intentionally slowing down would have prevented my body from sending such an engaging message (i.e., a complex leg break) in the first place?

### Preparing Practice: Slowing Down

Integrating a daily "slowing down" practice is a creative way to incorporate pausing into your life. Take any activity (e.g., walking to the office or class, washing the dishes) and slow it down to half the pace. You will begin to notice more of the subtle aspects of that experience. Pausing and taking a breath at a regular interval every time you see a common sight (e.g., a stop sign, when reaching for a door knob to open the door of your home) will ingrain new neural pathways that will support presence awareness in your daily life. Even slowing down your vocal speech can help create greater calm. If we think back to polyvagal theory, your nervous system reacts to the way you use your voice: Slowing down your rate of speech to a calm and rhythmic rate will soothe your nervous system by activating your ventral vagal pathway.

Comfort with slowing down can help in a session when your client is anxious and speaking at an accelerated pace, causing their nervous system (and yours) to speed up. Slowing down the moment (by asking your client to pause and notice what they are feeling in their body) can help evoke calm and register and clarify the emotions they are feeling underneath the rapid sharing. Slowing down your own vocal pace to be slightly less than your client's can also help to create a calming environment, as their vocal rhythm and then nervous system entrains with yours.

### Preparing Practice: Everyday Mindfulness

Choose one activity that you engage in daily, such as any of those described previously: walking up the stairs, brushing your teeth, washing dishes, or opening your front door. When engaging in that activity, for example, when washing dishes, practice bringing your full attention to it. When you pick up the soap, notice the color of the bottle and what it feels like in your hand, becoming aware of both the weight and texture. Allow yourself to feel the temperature of the water on your skin and notice the weight of the dish in your hand. Listen to the sounds of the water and the sponge as it wipes the dish. Allow this activity to become a time to consciously pause and be present to all sensations.

When you bring intentionality to your daily activities, your everyday life becomes your training ground for presence. The dishwashing practice just described affords a glimpse into how intentionality can help. As the receptors in your fingers and hands register the heat and wetness of the water, and send afferent signals up your spinal column to the parts of the brain that map sensation, your attunement to sensation will grow (Blakeslee & Blakeslee, 2007). Slowing down to be present with what you are engaged in is rarely anything but beneficial.

### Practicing Nonjudgment: Waiting

Waiting in line (and in traffic) can evoke impatience in me, so it is my best place to practice. Historically, when a line was very slow I would feel a rising frustration in my chest, with lots of judgments about the incompetence of the serviceperson, the store, and myself for not leaving enough time and being late for where I needed to be next. I now see waiting as a good opportunity to pause and breathe, or perhaps do a stretch or grounding exercise. Learning how to wait without judgment might have surprising and cascading effects for us, given the findings reported in a book on engaged Buddhism, which poses some evocative questions:

> At its very heart, engaged Buddhism is using daily life as our practice of awakening. *U.S. News and World Report* once reported that Americans spend an average of six months of their lives waiting—waiting at the stop light, waiting in the checkout line, waiting here, waiting there. My question is, "Waiting for what?" Six months is a long time. . . . What are we doing during those moments? These are all potential moments of practice. We can't always choose our circumstances, but we can choose how to respond. (Hai & Nghiem, 2010, p. 6)

*Presence Practice: Waiting With Presence*

Find the times when judgment and frustration are coming to a boil for you, such as in a line, getting cut off on the highway, or sitting in a traffic jam. Pause in these moments and notice the sensations that arise (e.g., frustration, judgment, impatience, tightness in the body). Then return your attention to the feel of your feet on the ground (or your body in the seat if you are driving in traffic). You can also try

- feeling the rhythm of your breath in that moment;
- enhancing the breath with long soft exhalations (different from a long and drawn-out sigh);
- shifting your judgments to compassionate understanding (i.e., what may be happening to the driver that cut you off that is making him or her rush, what could be going on in the unique

lives of other people in line, what are the challenges of the checkout person's job?);

- rocking your body side to side or back and forth to find a place that feels centered or grounded (see core body centering exercise in Chapter 10);
- using the time waiting to practice the mindful breathing and long exhalations or slowing down your breathing pattern, which all activate the calming parasympathetic nervous system; or
- reflecting on what else you can do while you are waiting (a yoga or tai chi pose; exercise; engaging the person in line with you, with the intent to be present and to connect).

*Reflection.* Presence does not mean deep relaxation; it means inviting our attention to the moment and cultivating acceptance, rather than engaging in repeated frustrated thoughts about the future or the past and about what is not happening in the moment. Try using these moments instead to practice acceptance and awareness. This will help you develop strategies for regaining calm after feeling emotionally unsettled, so when you are in a therapy session and you feel unrest (i.e., triggered by clients' emotions), you will be able to return to baseline more quickly.

## CULTIVATING PRESENCE: SELF-CARE

Self-care is necessary to maintaining the balance and continued growth that underlie presence. It can also reduce the vicarious traumatization or emotional weight we may experience from engaging with our clients' pain and suffering. Intentional time put aside to have fun, play, relax, be in nature, meditate, laugh, exercise, practice yoga, eat healthfully, and engage in your personal relationships are all a part of self-care. Drs. Dan Siegel and David Rock recommend a daily balance of self-care, which include focus time, play time, connecting time, physical time, time-in (reflecting), down time, and sleep time (see the healthy mind platter at http://www.drdansiegel.com/resources/). This section highlights a few components of self-care that are essential to sustaining presence, which include having a healthy relationship with technology, sleep, and balance.

### Mindful Use of Technology

We are in an era in which we are bombarded by demands on our attention, time, and emotional energy. Computers, faxes, cell phones, landlines, e-mails, Twitter, Facebook, Instagram, and other means of technology-based communication now demand our response with an immediacy that was not expected a decade ago. It has been calculated that we spend over 5 years in our lifetime logged on to the Internet, and that is estimating 1 to 2 hours per day of use (so you can figure out how that impacts you in your life). The demands of technology and devices are here to stay. How can we use them as practice time?

*Presence Reflection: Relationship With Technology*

Take a moment to first reflect on whether your relationship with your cell phone or use of the Internet is healthy (if you don't have a cell phone, then you are already in a different place than the rest of us who are captured by these devices). Take a piece of paper and divide it into two columns.

- On the left side note the benefits you receive from your cell phone and use of the Internet (these are often integrated in a smartphone but feel free to do this exercise for each).
- On the right side note the challenges or losses you experience from time spent on your cell phone or on the Internet.
- What do you notice about the balance (or imbalance)?
- At the bottom of the page, note approximate how many hours per week you spend using the phone or surfing the net. If you want to look at real time, multiply by 52 to see how many hours you spend per year, and by 520 to see per decade, etc.
- If you wish to shift the amount of time to reduce the losses and challenges, then see the next section.

*Generating a Healthier Relationship With Your Smartphone*

One of the challenges I have had with technology is e-mail overwhelm. I appreciate the connections we can forge, and the existence of what is necessary as a form of communication, but I never feel on top of the barrage of e-mails. Even if I momentarily feel up-to-date, the flood of information maintains its speed: More responses inevitably come with a counterexpectation to respond again.

A suggestion I have been working with is to restrict e-mail to particular times of day, rather than checking it on an ongoing basis. I find that doing this frees up time for self-care and greater presence in my relationships—both of which are nourishing. Following are other suggestions for generating a healthier relationship with your device, in the hopes that these can be of some benefit for you:

- When the phone rings, pause, breathe, and consciously choose to answer it—or not.
- Pause when reaching for the phone to check e-mails, apps, or messages. Notice if this was an automatic response or intentional,

and decide whether you want to spend time in this way at this moment.

- When responding to an e-mail, ask yourself whether you have time to respond with the thoughtfulness it may require, and if not, choose another time to read and respond.
- When responding, be discerning about including only what is necessary. A good motto here is: "Brief and kind can save you time!"
- After composing an e-mail, text, or response, pause and breathe before pressing Send, to ensure you are feeling good about what you have written and are sending out to others.
- If you practice a form of e-mail containment (checking only at certain times), help manage the expectations of others by letting people know that it may take a bit of time to respond.
- Turn off your device 1 to 2 hours before bedtime (research has shown that exposure to the light can impact your ability to have a full night's rest; Harvard Medical School, 2012). More on sleep hygiene next.

**Self-Care: Good Sleep Hygiene**

My strong hunch is that many of you reading this need more sleep. I know that to be true for most therapists (including myself). We live in a time when sleep is compromised for most people. In fact, 62% of people have sleep difficulties at least a few nights a week (National Sleep Foundation, 2015). We tend to be out of rhythm with our own sleeping needs. Sleep deprivation is associated with negative thoughts, depression, anxiety, and burnout (Rosen, Gimotty, Shea, & Bellini, 2006). Good sleep hygiene is one of the most important regulators of emotion, and therefore it deeply enhances our ability to be present.

Although you can access a state of presence even when tired, having energy increases the possibility tenfold. Therapists' tiredness in session is an interesting phenomenon as it has multiple messages for the therapist (and not many positive ones for the client). We explored in Chapter 5 what therapist tiredness could indicate in the clinical encounter, other than a legitimate need for more sleep. For right now I want to focus on improving sleep so that genuine tiredness does not interfere with presence.

*Tips for Improving Sleep*

Sleep deprivation can occur from not allowing enough time to settle at night and from waking in the night. Some suggestions for good sleep hygiene are as follows:

- Make a conscious intention and decision to set aside a certain amount of hours for sleep each night. Be mindful of the time you need to go to bed and time you need to wake, and then give yourself 1 to 2 hours before that time to be off any screens (computers, smartphones, television) and allow time to settle.

- Be aware of the barriers to getting to bed on time. Strategize ways to consciously choose sleep, versus doing that one more thing or watching that additional show.
- Notice how you feel when you do get enough sleep versus when you are sleep deprived, so you have an experiential sense of well-being that occurs from getting sufficient sleep.
- Limit caffeine intake to before noon, including coffee, tea, and dark chocolate.
- Don't eat anything 2 hours before going to sleep; otherwise, digesting food during sleep time can interfere with deep rest.
- Have an environment in your bedroom that supports sleep by minimizing clutter; maintaining a dark, cool, and quiet space; and having a comfortable and supportive bed.
- Eliminate television and cell phones in your bedroom, and keep outside light from coming through the window. Light sources at night can deplete melatonin and disrupt sleep. The glow from charging phones is said to negatively affect metabolism as well (MacDonald, 2016).
- Deal with unfinished issues from the day so you are not carrying them into sleep with you and they are not keeping you awake at night.
- Practice intentional relaxation exercises before going to bed, such as a body scan (see Chapter 9). This involves bringing awareness to each body part while inviting relaxation to the area by softening your muscles and taking deep breaths to support the letting go.
- Specific yogic postures and breathing techniques can increase melatonin production—the hormone that helps you sleep (Harinath et al., 2004).
- Guided visualization can also be helpful (see Appendix A for suggested sleep apps).
- Keeping a sleep diary (how you slept; what you did before going to bed; thoughts, feelings, and/or body sensations before bed) can help you to track the conditions that support or impede your sleep so you can notice and attend to any interfering patterns.

### Balance

As health care professionals, we are focused on relieving stress for others, yet we don't always attend to ourselves in the same way. We witness high levels of emotional distress daily. The stress is intensified when working in centers that demand high-quality care at an accelerated pace. Burnout, exhaustion, and minimal quality time for one's self or family are common.

If we wish to sustain our presence and the longevity of our careers, self-care is a requirement. Balance is at the center of self-care. We may preach balance and harmony to our clients but find it hard to practice them ourselves, even when we know their value. When we do strive for balance (an oxymoron in itself), it is not easy to maintain it in the pace of today.

Self-care and balance need constant attention if we are going to serve our clients (and ourselves) in the best way possible. Research has supported this, as clients of therapists who have good emotional health and well-being have better outcomes in therapy and a more positive therapeutic alliance (Beutler et al., 2004; Coster & Schwebel, 1997; Geller & Greenberg, 2002).

To investigate where you are out of balance, take some time to listen inside to what parts of your life feel neglected. The following two practices focus on recognizing what you need.

*Presence Practice: Listen to Your Body*

- Pause and close your eyes, turning your attention inward.
- Attune to the gentle rhythm of your breath, feeling the inhale and exhale.
- Do a scan of your body, moving your attention from feet to legs to abdomen to midbody up to your shoulders and to your head. Locate any areas of tension during your scan, and when you arrive there, just breathe and visualize the area relaxing.
- Ask inside your body, what do I need to feel more balanced and to be more caring to my body? Listen for what arises.
- Explore different areas that may need care by asking yourself: How am I with my sleep? Exercise? Self-care? Relationships? Fun? Play? Downtime? Rest? Overall balance? Pause between each question while listening inside to what arises.
- Choose one small thing you can do to support your self-care. Make a silent commitment and plan to follow through on addressing this need.

*Presence Practice: Finding Balance*

- *Reflection on current balance:* On a piece of paper, draw a pie chart to visualize which aspects of your life gather the most attention and which are neglected. Portion out what takes precedence on a daily basis, including areas such as self-care, family, work, hobbies, play, exercise, relaxation, and sleep. You may want to include a section for screen time (computer or phone) to see how much time that is taking up in your life.

- *Reflection on a vision for balance:* Spend some time looking at your life balance chart. Consider whether you are happy with it, or if there are areas that need slight adjusting. Now fill out a separate pie chart depicting how your life would look if you were feeling more in balance.

- *Reflection on change to move toward vision:* Consider a couple of changes that could bring you closer to your vision for balance. Keep them small and manageable: Change is more likely when it is not a total overhaul of life but rather a small shift. Notice the barriers, with respect and without judgment. Try to focus on a small achievable shift to invite more balance. Some ideas include going to sleep 1 hour earlier, turning off your cell phone or computer at night, eating breakfast, etc. Return to this intent for balance at the beginning of each day, and nonjudgmentally reflect at the end of the day on how it went.

Slowing down, breathing, meditating, and attending to the care of ourselves and our relationships are key to allowing presence to emerge more easily in session. Now that you have a sense of where you may need more attention and balance, with some suggestions for practice, we can build on this. The next chapter offers practices specifically focused on strengthening the qualities of the therapeutic presence process and experience. Let's transition there now.

## TRANSITION PRACTICE: BREATHING INTO HERE AND NOW

- Pause and invite your attention to the pattern of your inhale and exhale.
- Feel your chest or belly expand and release in rhythm with your breath.
- Now as you breathe in, silently add the word *Here*.
- As you breathe out, silently say the word *Now*.
- Continue to silently speak these words in rhythm with your inhale and exhale.
- When complete, open your eyes and transition to the next part of your day while staying connected to the flow of your breath.

©2016 M. Lee Freedman.

# 9

# STRENGTHENING THE THERAPEUTIC PRESENCE PROCESS: RECEPTIVITY, INWARD ATTUNING, EXTENDING, AND CONTACT EXERCISES

We delight in the beauty of the butterfly, but rarely admit the changes it has gone through to achieve that beauty.
—Maya Angelou (as quoted in Beautement & Broenner, 2011, p. 49)

The practices in Chapter 8 were about generally creating a landscape in your life that is conducive to cultivating presence. The practices here are also intended for your personal life and relationships, but they focus on strengthening the particular qualities of the process of therapeutic presence: *Receiving* from the other, *attuning with ourselves* and *extending* a response while *promoting contact*. Cycling through these modes in session requires flexibility of attention and awareness, in response to what is needed at the moment. Focusing on strengthening each mode can help you to access these qualities without a structured practice when you are in session. Let us begin with a practice designed to increase plasticity in shifting attention.

http://dx.doi.org/10.1037/0000025-010
*A Practical Guide to Cultivating Therapeutic Presence*, by S. M. Geller

# THERAPEUTIC PRESENCE PROCESS PRACTICE: SHIFTING AWARENESS

This practice was designed to help with shifting awareness on different sensory levels, through listening, seeing, and sensing.

- Take a moment to stop, and gently lower your eyes.
- Take a deep breath and allow your awareness to attune to your breath, noticing the natural rhythm between inhale and exhale as it is experienced in the body.
- Notice your breathing pattern without changing it. Is it fast or slow? Deep or shallow? Pay attention without judgment.
- Notice, with acceptance, what is true in your emotional body in this moment. Internally name what you are feeling without judging or changing your feelings.
- Notice what is true in your physical body, observing any sensations that arise.
- Now turn your attention outwards. Notice any sounds around you. Notice both the subtle and the loud sounds. Be curious about the tones. Listen while not reacting, just noticing.
- Open your eyes and notice the visual landscape that surrounds you. Be curious.
- Allow your awareness to return once again to the rise and fall of your belly in synchronicity with your breathing.
- Intentionally vacillate awareness between what is inside of you, such as breathing rhythm or emotional/physical sensations, and what you notice or hear around you, such as street noise, fans, or the voices of people nearby.
- Notice the relationship between your inner world and what surrounds you.
- Gently move toward close of this practice by taking a few breaths, wiggling your fingers and toes, and more fully opening your eyes.
- Transition to the next section or next part of your day, while staying connected to your breath and in contact with yourself.

*Reflection*

The mental gymnastics of shifting awareness is highly demanding, especially in therapy sessions, where we must also maintain a calm and composed presence. Yet it is worthwhile to allow us to attend to the many sensations that we reflected on in Chapter 5 when reading our clients, attuning to

ourselves, and attending to the relationship. These include shifting awareness between words and bodily expression, emotions, breath patterns, relational difficulties, and so forth. Cognitive flexibility supports the ability
to direct and sustain attention, inhibit intrusions on consciousness, and
seamlessly shift from target to target, while keeping a representation of
the whole in working memory (Dajani & Uddin, 2015). Not an easy feat,
yet it is possible to develop cognitive flexibility with practice. Any task
that asks you to shift your focus will help—whether it's focusing on your
stride while jogging and yet being aware of the environment, maintaining
your key while singing in harmony, or conversing with a group of friends.
The more formal mindfulness and meditation practices of Chapter 8
also improve your ability to shift awareness with flexibility (A. Moore &
Malinowski, 2009).

Let us now focus on fine-tuning the particular qualities of the therapeutic presence process: receptivity, inward attuning, and extending and
contact.

## RECEPTIVITY

Being fully open and accepting of your clients and their experience is
at the core of the therapeutic presence process. To receive, you must create a
space. Receptivity also means creating a space for connection, where attunement to self and others can meet within one's self. In a receptive state, all
the dimensions of experience arise without the interference of your own
barriers, judgments, or preconceptions. You relate from a responsive rather
than reactive state.

Having an intention to be receptive primes the brain for the openness and interoception (sensing inwardly) that support receptivity (Siegel,
2007). Although the particular brain state that is associated with receptivity
is unknown, Siegel (2007) proposed that it involves an overall state of neural
integration connecting body, brainstem, limbic regions, and cortex. Hence,
practices that foster neural integration help this receptive state to emerge
more easily, so we can accurately notice and attend to the subtle expressions
of our clients' inner world.

### Receptivity Practice: Belly Beach Ball Breathing

Relaxing the mind and the body is a first step to inviting a receptive
state. The following abdominal breathing practice includes a visual component to help train the body to inhale and exhale in a way that supports
receptive openness.

- Pause and close your eyes, taking two or three full rounds of breathing.
- Place your hand on your belly to physically connect with the rhythm of breathing as it is felt in the belly.
- Now imagine a beach ball on your belly, while resting a hand on this area.
- Engage in slow and deep breathing. With each inhale, imagine the beach ball expanding, blowing up, and with each exhale, imagine the beach ball deflating, releasing air.
- Continue this practice for 5 to 10 minutes. Imagine and feel this visual and tactile image of the beach ball rising and falling in rhythm with the breath.
- As you come to close, drop your hand away from your belly and pause to notice if anything has shifted in your body, such as possibly feeling a calmer state of awareness.
- As you transition out of this practice, open your eyes slowly while staying connected to the rhythm of your breathing.

*Reflection*

This practice can be helpful when you are stressed, anxious, or having difficulty settling your mind. When you are in a state of sympathetic activation, cortisol is high, the mind is cloudy, and emotions are more likely to interfere (Henckens, van Wingen, Joëls, & Fernández, 2012). Deep and slow breathing balances the nervous system, inducing the calming parasympathetic nervous system. It also strengthens attentional capacities over time, which is another aspect of receptivity. With regular practice, the breath itself can become a vehicle to help you rapidly reenter the moment and to open more completely to your client.

Breathing with nonjudgmental awareness is the foundation of all therapeutic presence practices, yet quieting the mind can be difficult given all of our mental clutter. Including a visual component like the beach ball, or the following visual practice, can simplify the task by offering a more concrete focus. This can help you to be open as you start a therapy session and to receive your clients' experience without the filter of your own agenda.

**Receptivity Practice: Visualize a Receptive Space**

The following is an alternative visual practice for activating an open and receptive state.

- Close your eyes briefly, and begin to tune into the rhythm of your breath—particularly feeling the breath rise and fall in your belly or chest.

- Now visualize a space in the center of your body—it could be in your belly or chest. Choose an image to evoke this receptive space, such as a crevice in a rock or opening in a canyon.
- Visualize that open center place as your receptor for experience.
- Pay attention to what you see, hear, and feel around you.
- Return to the image you chose to reflect being open and receptive. As you experience that image, absorb the sensations of what being open and receptive feels like.
- Now see if you can find a word or phrase that encompasses this embodied feeling of receptivity, so that you can return to it when you are in session with your client.

## Reflection

Although reminiscent of the clearing-the-space practice offered in Chapter 4, this practice has subtle differences—it takes the space you have cleared with the word or image you have linked, and creates new neural pathways. Over time, this allows you to easily access receptivity and be ready to take in other experiences. Through the conditioning effects of repetition, the image can come to remind the body to open and let go of barriers to being fully receptive to the client. As you feel practiced with this, you can call on this image in session to reactivate a receptive state.

## Interpersonal Receptivity Practice: "Breathing With"

The following relational mindfulness practice is adapted from Surrey and Kramer (2013) and offers an opportunity to deepen your awareness in relationship. Part of being receptive is taking in the other fully, without preconceptions, while in connection with yourself. Relational practices support your ability to be present with yourself and others at the same time. This practice is conducted with a partner.

- Sit facing a meditation partner on chairs or cushions, at a comfortable distance.
- Close your eyes. Bring awareness to the internal experience of breathing—breathing in and breathing out in the presence of another person (2 minutes).
- Open your eyes. Be aware of the other person in your visual field. Continue practicing mindfulness of your own breathing as you open your awareness to the other person. Extend your awareness to notice their breathing patterns as well (2–3 minutes).
- Slowly expand the field of your awareness to both of you breathing. Notice any discomfort, pleasure, curiosity, or self-consciousness in

seeing and being seen. Notice the flow—or shifts—in awareness between internal, external, or both (2–3 minutes).

- Close your eyes and resume an internal focus on your breathing. Notice any reactions or changes in your mind or in your body (1 minute).
- Open your eyes. Without words, find a way to express gratitude to your meditation partner for this time of practicing together. Allow a heartfelt wish for his or her happiness and well-being, offering and then receiving these well wishes. Rest in the flow (2–3 minutes).

*Reflection*

This practice can evoke an array of feelings and insights. It is best done when there is time to process the experience with your partner afterward—ideally with a skilled facilitator. Within a debrief, you also have the opportunity to settle any vulnerable emotions that arise by labeling them (Hariri, Bookheimer, & Mazziotta, 2000; Lieberman et al., 2007). Debriefing can serve to create meaning of the experience, integrating left-brain understanding with right-brain sensations, so you decipher the relevance of this experience to the therapy process itself. You could also use this practice in session to enhance the connection between yourself and your client so you can more astutely read their experience.

**Which Practice Do I Do When?**

Belly beach ball breathing is particularly helpful when you are in a stressful or unsettled state. Practicing this daily will help your brain and body access this relaxed state more quickly either prior to the session or in the session itself (see the case example at the end of this chapter). Visualizing an image of receptivity can be used as an additional resource prior to the session when you have a brief time to prepare. When practiced regularly outside of the session, the image can access an open state in session as it acts as a stimulus to anchor your awareness in the present. Clearing a space is a longer practice that can help you put aside difficult emotions at the beginning of a therapy day and when you aren't on the clock—especially on days that you are feeling burdened by personal issues or distractions. The relational mindfulness practice is an excellent way to connect more deeply with your client, as it accesses a state of synchrony through the shared awareness of breathing. It is an ideal practice to offer students in training to cultivate a sense of receptivity and present-centered connection in relationship.

Even though these are in-life practices to develop your own presence process, variations of these practices could be offered to clients as well. For example, belly beach ball breathing can help clients reduce their sympathetic nervous or stress response (i.e., anxious, fearful, stressed), whether in or out of session. You can walk your clients through a briefer version of clearing a space to help them get to the core of what they want to explore in session.

## INWARDLY ATTENDING/ATTUNING

Although the initial term developed was *inwardly attending*, I have come to see this more accurately as *internal attuning*. Attunement means tuning into one's self and being in contact with the ongoing flow of moment-to-moment experience, cognitively, emotionally, and viscerally. It is dependent on being present. In this mode of the presence process, we are not just "attending to" our inner experience, we are "tuning in" to gain a felt sense of our inner terrain as it resonates with our clients in the moment. Coming into rhythm with our self, and then using our self and our sensitivity to connect and attune with others, is key to this process.

Sensitivity without awareness can be confusing and overwhelming, whereas sensitivity with an attuned self can be put to skillful use. Sensitivity can be viewed as a weakness in our society: So regularly, we hear, more often in reference to women than to men, "she is too sensitive. She takes everything to heart." I personally understand the impact of this judgment. Growing up and being the one in my family that was accused of "feeling too much" created shame and self-judgment in me. I would experience anger inside as a hot tightness in my chest when I was around angry people, or a pit of sadness when around someone suffering with their own sadness or depression. In fact, I have one of those sensitive bodies that will receive a wave of physical pain, a passing headache or pressure in my chest, to only later find out the person or client I had been with was experiencing something similar.

More than 2 decades of meditation practice has helped me to work with my sensitivity, by observing rather than by being overtaken by those feelings. The feelings are no less, yet what has increased is my skill in self-regulating and recognizing my sensitivity as a resonance with others. Meditation increases regulation partially by creating a meta-awareness that can make difficult emotional experiences feel less immediate and overpowering. Experientially, labeling the feeling without judgment or reaction, such as *sadness*, *pain*, *pressure*, *fear*, or *joy*, allows me to observe my experience rather than get overwhelmed. Recovering more quickly from an aroused emotional state is an added gain from my years of practice.

Many studies validate how strengthening brain circuitry related to emotion regulation (e.g., via meditation) not only supports a greater ability to regulate emotional arousal but also reduces time needed to recover from an aroused state (Rueda, Posner, & Rothbart, 2005). This builds resilience, with the added benefit of being able to bounce back from difficult emotions to a state of equanimity and presence. This allows you to regulate difficult emotions that arise when you empathically resonate with clients. When we can learn to trust our sensitivity and use it to read what is going on within and around us, it can be a source of information and wisdom.

## Using the Self as a Sensor: Wired to Connect and Connected to Heal

There is an emerging understanding in the neuroscience world that we are "wired to connect" (Cozolino, 2006; Fishbane, 2007; Siegel, 2007, 2010). Our brains link up when we are in contact with another person, allowing us to have an experience of what the other is feeling (recall our discussion about mirror neurons and interbrain synchrony in Chapter 3). Attuning to others facilitates a similar process in ourselves, so that our bodies resonate with what others feel.

As we discovered in Chapter 5, the ability to attune to our own internal state is the basis for attuning to and understanding others (Siegel, 2007). Skillfulness in self and other attunement forms the basis from which you can respond to your client flexibly and effectively, and deepen the connection between you. Who knew that this "shameful" sensitivity I had was actually a finely tuned receptor that could become one of my greatest tools as a therapist.

## Mindfully Listening to the Body: Embodied Self-Awareness

Mindfulness involves generating a moment-to-moment awareness of present experience with acceptance (Germer, Siegel, & Fulton, 2005). With mindfulness practice, we learn to come close to our pain and discomfort without judgment, striving, manipulation or pretense (Salzberg, 1999; Santorelli, 1999; Welwood, 1996). Mindfulness practice integrates an "observing self" with what is happening in the here-and-now "experiencing self" (Parker, Nelson, Epel, & Siegel, 2015; Siegel, 2007). This strengthens our embodied self-awareness, which helps us to attune to our bodies and to make use of the information to facilitate the therapeutic process (see Chapter 5, this volume).

When we are present, receptive, and deeply engaged in the moment with a client, we are taking in their experience not only on a felt level but also on a neurobiological level, which allows us to access a bodily sense of what the other is experiencing (Hanson & Mendius, 2009; Siegel, 2007; Wiens, 2005). We feel an emotional resonance, which reflects an intersubjective neuronal sharing. This bodily and emotional resonance is experienced as a deep connection and intuitive sensing of the other's experience. We use our bodies as a sensor to detect the emotional and physical experiences of our clients.

The following practices will help you listen to your body and heighten your experience of inward attuning. They will also support you in maintaining your sense of grounding.

*Inward Attuning Practice: Body Scan*

The body scan is traditionally conducted in a lying down position; however, if you tend to fall asleep easily, you may want to sit up. Ideally, give yourself about 20 minutes for this practice.

- Lie down on the floor or bed with your legs slightly apart, arms and hands outstretched a few inches from your sides, and a pillow or rolled towel supporting your knees.
- Close your eyes, gently bringing awareness to the rhythm of your breath as it is experienced in your belly or chest.
- Invite your awareness down to your feet. Notice, with acceptance and nonjudgment, the sensations in the bottom of your feet . . . heels . . . toes . . . tops of feet . . . ankles.
- Name what you feel as you notice the sensations in your feet, such as with words like *warm, tight, painful, tingly, soft, neutral.* Breathe deeply into each area with compassionate awareness.
- Now bring a curious attention upward to your lower legs, calves, and knees. Become aware of sensations at the outer level of the skin, and then deeper inside at your kneecap and the joints. Breathe deeply into each sensation.
- Allow your awareness to move up to your thighs . . . front and back . . . hips . . . pelvic region . . . the pelvic muscles. Move your attention back to your buttocks, naming internally the sensations in that area with compassion, without judgment.
- Breathe deeply, shifting your awareness to your abdomen and lower back, torso, midback, noticing the sensations in those areas.

- Now allow your awareness to move up to your chest . . . your upper back . . . shoulders, down to your upper arms . . . elbows . . . forearms . . . wrists . . . until slowly you arrive at your hands. Notice the back of your hands . . . palms . . . fingers. Breathe into each sensation.
- Allow your awareness to move back up to your neck . . . front of the neck . . . inside to your throat. Notice sensations in your face, beginning at your chin . . . mouth . . . jaw. Breathe deeply as you invite attention to your cheekbones . . . nose . . . eyes . . . eyelids . . . forehead . . . back of head . . . top of head.
- Now bring your awareness to the whole of your body . . . breathing deeply as you notice what the body as a whole feels like.
- When you're ready, invite your attention back to the rhythm of your breath . . . feeling the rise and fall of your belly in rhythm with the inhale and the exhale.
- As we close this practice, gently invite your awareness back to the room while staying connected to your body and breath.

*Reflection.* The effects of a body scan are measurable right away, even for novices: Indices of parasympathetic and sympathetic activity were greater in a body scan group than in those performing progressive muscle relaxation or sitting quietly (Ditto, Eclache, & Goldman, 2006). A mental scan can bring vitality to different areas and ignite an overall sense of calm. Body scans also enhance our awareness of unnoticed pain or tension so we can consider their meaning and take steps to help ourselves.

Body scans can heighten your interoception so you can read your experience of the moment with your client with greater accuracy. Body maps are so plastic that scanning the internal and external body deepens your ability to perceive these layers within yourself, and to do so more naturally and quickly. An inspiring area of research documents how the interoceptive ability to listen to your own heart—literally counting its pulsations in your body—activates regions also implicated in empathy (Blakeslee & Blakeslee, 2007; Critchley, Wiens, Rotshtein, Öhman, & Dolan, 2004). Building your own visceral awareness through body-based practices can then heighten your ability to empathically attune with your clients.

## Attuning to Our Own Rhythm: Mindful Drumming

Drumming and rhythm are potent nonverbal ways to develop deep listening, access intuition, and release stress. The health benefits of drumming and percussion are vast and include the bodily integration and engagement with the moment that occurs during creative and rhythmic play. Drumming tends to evoke a sense of engagement with the present and, combined with the physical component of movement, allows for the expression of difficult emotions coupled with a sense of enjoyment and vitality. Research by Bittman and colleagues (2004, 2005) has shown that group drumming reduces mood disturbances, stress, fatigue, and burnout and improves immune function in healthy subjects. A program combining group drumming and mindfulness (Therapeutic Rhythm and Mindfulness) to cultivate relational presence is described in Chapter 11.

The benefits of drumming can also be evoked independently, as in the following practice that focuses on creating a harmonious rhythm within your self. This practice can be done on a hand drum (i.e., djembe or ashiko) or even on a desktop or your lap. An empty large jug turned upside down also makes for a useful rhythm tool.

- Put your nondominant hand on your heart, neck, or wrist to sense your heartbeat or pulse. Try and connect to the rhythm of your pulse, as it is right now. Notice what it feels like: Is it fast, slow, deep, or narrow? Feel, and experience the rhythm of your heartbeat.
- With your dominant hand, play the rhythm of your heartbeat with a soft tap on the drum, desk, or table.
- When that feels comfortable, allow yourself to tune and feel the rhythm of your breath.
- Play your breath rhythm with your nondominant hand, by tapping at the beginning of each inhale and at the start of each exhale. Begin to distinguish the rhythm of your breath from your heartbeat or pulse, and feel how these rhythms relate with each other.
- If alone or in a group, keep playing the rhythm of your heart and breath for 10 to 15 minutes, at times inviting yourself to slow down and continue the same rhythms but at a slower pace. Notice your experience as your external rhythms slow.
- When you are ready to come to close, rest with your hands on your drum (table, lap) and sit in silence for a moment, sensing what is true in your bodily rhythms and in your experience, in this moment.

*Reflection*

This exercise can help you connect with and attune to your internal bodily terrain, first by noticing your bodily rhythms and then by externalizing those rhythms through movement and sound. The movement and expression in drumming will release tension, quiet your mind, and deepen contact with your body. Slowing down the rhythm offers more opportunity for the emergence of underlying emotions, helping to generate awareness of what is true in the emotional body as well as the physical. Slowing down external rhythm also encourages your bodily rhythms to slow down in synchronization with your playing, which creates a calmer and more stable feeling inside. It also helps you become familiar with the concept of rhythm that is so inherent in our interactions with clients.

Playing one sound for a continuous time also shifts your state of consciousness to a more expansive place, and hence a sense of joy and calm can be experienced. Mindful drumming is a wonderful integration practice as well. Coordinating the right and left hands with the heart, breath, and bodily rhythms helps to synchronize right- and left-brain hemispheric activity. This supports greater balance and mental acuity, enhancing your focus and attention.

### Which Practice Do I Do When?

Mindfulness practices of any type are best done on a daily basis to help to build the neural muscles and cognitive capacities for focusing attention in the moment. Having a set of diverse informal practices allows you to access this state in a way that is tailored to your circumstances and what you want to invite. Body scans can be done invisibly, when you are waiting to board your plane at the airport or while sitting in a meeting (unless you are leading!). This practice can be done in between sessions, at the end of the therapy day, or when settling before sleep.

Whereas body scans can induce sleepiness for some people, drumming is an energizing and invigorating practice. Drumming requires a bit more planning (i.e., some tools and a conducive environment), yet has the added feature of providing a physical and emotional outlet. The exercise aspect of rhythm making before or after a therapy day can release stress or emotional residue. You may find that certain practices feel more organic at some times than others.

There are also ways to adjust the practices so that you can access variants of them in different environments. A prime example of this is how we often drum naturally, whether on our steering wheel or lap, or tap our fingers when thinking. Even unconsciously, without a formal intention, this drumming invites a sense of self-soothing. What would it be like to catch yourself in informal practice and bring intention to this powerful gesture? Any practice that moves you toward a mindful state will enhance your ability to be present.

# EXTENDING AND CONTACT

Extending and contact reflects how we offer ourselves with our clients, as we examined in Chapter 6. This includes *extending* a response informed by our attunement with the client and within ourselves, while maintaining psychological *contact* with them. This may seem simple, but we are often clouded by our own internal ideas of what should happen or what the client should do rather than being with what is. Our own barriers can get in the way of truly connecting and responding from a place of trust. Being in deep connection with our clients asks us to be accessible to them—authentic and transparent in the connection. Practices that invite a deeper connection with others while maintaining contact with ourselves support this quality.

## Intuitive Responding

Trusting the images, insights, and responses that are emerging inside in resonance with what the client shares is at the heart of extending. One source of our in-the-moment intuitions could be our von Economo neurons, or "intuition cells," discovered for the first time in 1925 (Blakeslee & Blakeslee, 2007). These very large and well-connected neurons have retained some mystique, but they populate regions of the brain associated with empathy and social intelligence in humans and other creatures believed to be capable of more advanced forms of social behavior (Allman et al., 2011). Their size, simple structure, and the stimuli they respond to all suggest these neurons have a role in fast, "intuition-based" decision making, including the type required in situations where the outcome is uncertain.

Damasio (2005) viewed intuition as guided by somatic markers. *Somatic markers* are physiological affective states associated with a reinforcing stimuli. For example, when a decision is not a good one for us, we may get an unpleasant gut feeling that occurs before the cognitive process of "weighing our options" occurs. Similarly, a positive gut response can occur in seconds when we access a decision that is right. This stems from the idea that we feel our emotions as bodily responses, which guide our decision making.

If we think about all of the information offered to us by our bodies and senses—intuition cells, mirror neurons, adaptive oscillators, gut feelings, visual perceptions—we can begin to feel confident when truly present with clients, and we can trust the intuitions that emerge. There are a lot of systems working overtime to help us understand what could be going on and allow us access to a lot more information.

The discovery that I could trust my intuition when I was present was a life-changing insight. This stood in stark contrast to a lifetime of suffering with indecision. Whether it is what to wear that day or more comical moments of which brands of personal products to buy at the pharmacy, making decisions has always depleted me. This suffering slowly subsided when I realized this indecision did not occur in moments when I was completely present. In fact, clarity was undeniable in these moments.

Carl Rogers (1980) illuminated the capacity for healing when we trust this intuitive self:

> When I am at my best, as a group facilitator or as a therapist, I discover another characteristic. I find that when I am closest to my inner, intuitive self, when I am somehow in touch with the unknown in me, when perhaps I am in a slightly altered state of consciousness, then whatever I do seems to be full of healing. Then, simply my presence is releasing and helpful to the other. There is nothing I can do to force this experience, but when I can relax and be close to the transcendental core of me, then I may behave in strange and impulsive ways in the relationship, ways in which I cannot justify rationally, which have nothing to do with my thought processes. But these strange behaviors turn out to be right, in some odd way: it seems that my inner spirit has reached out and touched the inner spirit of the other. Our relationship transcends itself and becomes a part of something larger. Profound growth and healing and energy are present. (p. 129)

### Extending and Contact Practice: Intuition With Decisions

Intuitive responding emerges naturally in presence, yet there are ways to strengthen our intuition too. Learning to read our bodily responses helps with this. This practice was inspired by my colleague and friend Dr. Solomon Shapiro and has begun to shift my indecisive nature to one where I can listen and trust my inner world, which has strengthened my capacity for responding effectively with clients.

- Focus on a decision you have to make or on an issue that you don't know how to proceed with. Get a sense of the different directions you could take with this issue.
- Now focus on your breath, feeling the gentle rhythm of inhale and exhale in synch with the rise and fall of your belly. Keep your eyes open and notice what is present around you.
- Now close your eyes—and with certainty choose one decision. For example, if it is to rent a new home, then proceed to believe this to be true. "I am renting it, it is the right decision, and this is what I am doing."
- Notice as you choose that decision what happens in your body. Pay attention to openness or constriction in your breathing and body, and any statements or phrases you hear inside.

- Take a breath and let that go. Open your eyes and focus once again on your breath and on the room or space presently surrounding you.
- Now close your eyes—and with certainty choose a different decision. For example, "I am not renting this place, it is not the right timing for me, and I am going to let it go."
- Notice as you choose that decision what happens in your body. Pay attention to openness or constriction in your breathing or bodily sensations, any statements or phrases that come to mind, and changes in your breathing patterns.
- Notice the difference in your body when you choose one path or another. Look for signs of openness and clarity in your breathing and body when it is intuitively the right decision.

*Reflection*

Listening to your body response as a guide to decision making strengthens your ability to trust what arises in our internal world when in the room with clients. This builds on the earlier practice of listening to the body by deciphering particular responses that indicate when you are in synch with your clients and therefore can trust your responses. It is possible that learning to trust intuition through monitoring your responses to a situation can support the growth of these "intuition cells," making it easier to trust yourself when you are in session. We acquire them continuously throughout the lifespan, almost like the wisdom of lessons learned and buried in the body— starting out with 28,000 and reaching approximately 193,000 by adulthood (Blakeslee & Blakeslee, 2007).

Practice will help you to discern intuitive sensations that say something is not right from experiential anxiety. Anxiety often has a different feel, which may include heart racing, trembling in your body, and sweaty palms. If it is anxiety, then using the previous suggestion might actually further the avoidance that goes along with anxiety (i.e., I am uncomfortable in my body so I avoid this situation or decision). If you suffer from anxiety, then you must get to know your bodily state when feeling anxiety so you can differentiate this from an intuitive sense of unease that is rooted in reality. It helps to conduct this practice when you are in a relaxed state to begin with, versus starting off in an anxious state. Beginning this practice with something that helps you calm (deep breathing, meditation, yoga) can set the right conditions in your body to access your intuition. Through this you can also discern an anxious reaction to clients (countertransference) from a sense that something is amiss (i.e., they are not connected to their emotional state). You can also recognize the qualities associated with the trusting the insights or responses that emerge so that you can learn to share more freely in session.

**Extending and Contact Relational Practice: Entrainment Breathing**

A way you can cultivate the ability to become attuned and in synch with your clients is through entraining your breathing with the rhythm of their breathing. The following exercise is a dyadic one and supports the skills of nonverbally attunement that we explored in Chapter 6.

Decide in your pair who will be the receiver first (Person A) and who will be the one entraining and attuning with the receiver (Person B). Each person in the dyad takes a turn at breathing and receiving being entrained with, and intentionally entraining with their partner. Allow for 5 to 10 minutes of practice before switching roles.

- Person A breathes naturally with a vocal sound on the exhalation to mark their outbreath.
- Person B focuses on the body and vocal sounds reflecting the partners breathing rhythm and intentionally matches his or her own breathing rhythm to mirror the rhythm of their partner.
- Pause after the 5–10-minute practice and reflect what the experience was like.
- Now switch roles. Person B is the receiver, breathing in natural rhythm with a vocal sound on the exhalation to mark their outbreath. Person A is the giver, focusing on the body and vocal sounds in their partners breathing rhythm and intentionally matching their own breathing rhythm to mirror the rhythm of their partner.
- Pause after the 5- to 10-minute practice to feel what the experience was like for the receiver (Person B) and the giver (Person A).
- Share with each other your experience, while listening mindfully.

*Reflection*

Entrainment breathing is a powerful way of promoting connection because it creates a neurophysiological synchronization of rhythm in the brain and body between people (Cozolino, 2006; Geller & Porges, 2014; Porges, 2011; Siegel, 2010). Entraining your breath with your clients' can invite their nervous system to calm in resonance with yours and to experience a sense of safety in connection. It also enhances your ability to sense your clients' experience with greater accuracy, enhancing your sense of empathy.

This practice is best done when there is time and space to debrief with your partner or a facilitator.

## Which Practice Do I Do When?

You can use all of these practices in your daily life. The trusting intuition practice is valuable when you need to make decisions about important matters and don't know what to do. However, the real practice happens in the small decisions we make on a regular basis in the flurry of everyday life. Bringing this practice into the flow of your life will help you get more familiar with the bodily sensations that emerge when you trust yourself (e.g., relaxed, open, deep breathing) versus when decisions do not feel right (e.g., tightness, restricted breath, anxious). So you can learn to trust the images and insights that emerge in session and share them effectively with your clients. Entrainment breathing can be done any time you want to deepen your connection with another person. In personal and therapeutic relationships, it can be used to feel more together when there is distance or discord. It can also be done more subtly, as you invisibly entrain your breath with your client as a way of connecting with them while feeling their experience.

## PULLING IT ALL TOGETHER: THE PROCESS OF THERAPEUTIC PRESENCE

Part II of this book explored what occurs in the encounter, and these practices are focused on strengthening the qualities of therapeutic presence so that the process can unfold with greater ease. I want to relate the usefulness of these practices back to the therapeutic encounter, given that the process of therapeutic presence is at the heart of this book. The following vignette offers a glimpse of this process unfolding.

## Clinical Vignette

Georgia was describing the difficulty she was having with her stepmother. She was feeling angry and frustrated after a recent interaction. I was trying to listen to the story of what happened (*listening only to content*), yet I felt disconnected (*out of rhythm, not attuned*) and a bit frustrated with her reaction and how it diverted the focus from previous work I hoped we would continue today (*nonreceptive, preconceptions of how therapy should unfold*). I felt the frustration in me as a barrier to presence (*inward attuning to recognize disconnection from the moment*). I intentionally engaged in a few deep belly breaths to let go of expectation and judgment, and I could feel my body relax and open (*inviting parasympathetic activation and receptivity*). I then watched Georgia's breathing patterns as I listened and intentionally mirrored my breathing rhythm with her inhales and exhales (*entrainment breathing*). I could feel our connection return, and her breathing calmed and deepened in synch with mine (*coregulation*). A wave of sadness washed over me, and within moments she paused and said, "I felt so hurt and let down." I reflected her sadness and the image that was emerging in me (*inward attuning*) of her as a little girl looking up at the adults waiting to be seen (*trust in intuition/extending and contact*). A tear formed in her eyes as she replied, "Ya, it felt like my experience didn't matter to anyone, like I was 10 years old again." I recognized that she also felt let down by me in that moment of disconnection. I acknowledged her hurt (with my body open and leaned forward, prosodic voice, soft facial features) and how my expectations of what we should work on also made her feel alone. Her breathing softened and deepened (*indication of feeling "felt" and seen*). Once our bond was established again, I invited her to do some intentional work. In the past she had refused to talk about her childhood, yet she was open to it for the first time (*safety in therapeutic relationship inviting engagement in deeper work*).

*Reflection*

This example describes the value of the in-life practices offered in this chapter and how they support the process of therapeutic presence in session. The therapist was disconnected from her experience, but by inwardly attuning and noticing the disconnection, she was able to reengage an experience of receptivity (practice in therapeutic presence and belly breathing). She then used her breathing to entrain with her client's breathing, which not only invited a physiological connection, it also served to coregulate therapist and client as both calmed. Her access to her client's experience was easier as she was receptively attuned to the deeper sadness and attuned with herself to notice the feeling of sadness and related image. Once returned to presence, she trusted her self and emerging experience, offering a reflection that deepened her client's process and allowed her to feel seen, heard, and felt, ultimately feeing safe to engage in deeper therapeutic work. Also the therapist was able to read the client's readiness for an intervention through her attunement to the moment and to take a risk to invite her client to engage in the work of therapy even if her client had been resistant prior to this time. We can also see from this example that the process is not always about being completely present; it is the ability to notice when you are not in presence and bringing yourself quickly back to the moment and back in tune with your clients.

Now that we have explored practices to strengthen the process of presence, we can aim to actively enhance the in-body experience of therapeutic presence. Let's transition to this final practice chapter.

## TRANSITION PRACTICE: BREATHING IN RHYTHM

- Place your hands on your belly and soften your gaze.
- Notice how you feel in this moment.
- I invite you now to take three deep breaths, feeling the rise and fall of your belly in rhythm with your breath.
- Letting that go, transition to the next chapter or the next part of your day.

# 10

## DEEPENING THE EXPERIENCE OF THERAPEUTIC PRESENCE: GROUNDING, IMMERSION, EXPANSION, AND COMPASSION EXERCISES

Restore your attention, or bring it to a new level, by dramatically slowing down whatever you're doing.

—Sharon Salzberg (2011, p. 97)

In Chapter 9 we explored the components of the process of therapeutic presence, and practices to enhance our ability to do the specific tasks involved in therapeutic presence. In this chapter, we focus on building the in-body *experiential* qualities of therapeutic presence: (a) grounding, (b) immersion, (c) expansion, and (d) being with and for the other/compassion. Fine-tuned attention to the subtle aspects of each quality can help you recognize the subtleties, so that you can activate that particular quality in-session with greater precision and ease. I encourage you to pause while reading and focus on heightening each quality with the suggested practices.

Presence is multifaceted. Although each aspect is explored separately, it is the sum of the parts (and more) that create the whole experience of therapeutic presence. As you explore your own feelings of being fully present in your body and relationships, notice if your experience resonates with the research: That therapeutic presence is a simultaneous experience of all four

http://dx.doi.org/10.1037/0000025-011
*A Practical Guide to Cultivating Therapeutic Presence*, by S. M. Geller

areas. Also ask yourself which aspect of presence could use some attention and fine-tuning.

## GROUNDING

To feel grounded is to feel centered, steady, and in contact with a healthy and integrated self. This internal steadiness supports the ability to see and feel your clients' pain and suffering with them, without getting overwhelmed, in order to be most helpful. Grounding buffers against compassion/empathy fatigue and vicarious traumatization, which is partly characterized by a lost sense of self through exposure to the suffering of others. With presence we receive our clients' feelings in our bodies, so we need to have a way to recognize our emotional stress and release it.

### A Personal Reflection on Grounding

I spent a great deal of my life being thrown from wave to wave within the emotions of others, and so I was enthralled when I discovered that one essential quality of presence is grounding. In my early years as a therapist I spent hours each night mentally reviewing the therapy day and feeling the suffering of my clients. It was not intentional, yet images and feelings from the day would whirl through my mind and body. I was carrying my clients' emotions with me, and felt like I was living their lives during my walk home, through dinner, and all night. Then I tried my hand at shutting off by numbing myself with busyness, screens, and food, until I realized I was also numbing to myself and to the rest of my relationships. I eventually discovered that I could find a place between these extremes: I could ground myself, prior to the session and throughout my meeting with clients. With a conscious intention to close the day, I also learned to let go of any emotional residue I was carrying (recall the tips for "closing the session" in Chapter 6 and ways to "open and close your therapy day" in Chapter 4).

### Grounding in the Body

The body is a portal to accessing grounding, as presence is an embodied state. Although the mind and body are interconnected, our minds tend to be whirling dervishes when not in an embodied place of presence. Researchers say we have between 50,000 and 70,000 thoughts in a day, many of them repetitive (Davis, 2013); this is a testament to how internally busy we are. Most of our thoughts are not present focused—we dwell in the past, plan for the future, obsess about mistakes we made, fantasize, self-criticize, worry, etc. As we explored in Chapter 9, the mind can be trained, such as in mindfulness meditation, to hone in the cognitive hurricane and return to the sense of embodied presence. Yet to access a more direct state of grounding and presence, body focused practices are helpful. When in this grounded and embodied state, we can more accurately discern and trust our thoughts in session to be present centered and useful.

If we could just keep this one phrase with us—that *presence lives in the body*—we will know more intimately this portal to slowing down and grounding into the moment. The following practices can support our sense of grounding.

### Grounding Practice: Eating Grounding Foods Mindfully

Eating in a healthy and nourishing way, and having adequate water, can help us to feel grounded in our body. In fact, drops in blood sugar will not only make you feel shaky and unstable but will trigger an adrenaline and cortisol rush that increases your level of arousal. This arousal is different from the calm alertness that supports therapeutic presence—it's a stress response on your body's part (Bourne, 2005). Traditional Chinese medicine views food as having qualities and energies that support different states and systems in the body (Jacobi, 2012; M. Moore, 2012). Particular grounding foods include the following:

- Root vegetables such as beets, carrots, potatoes, parsnips, radishes, garlic, or ginger. Fresh vegetable juice can be an effective way of getting these nutrients.
- Sweet potatoes and yams. Although also root vegetables, these can satisfy craving for sweets without adding refined sugars (as refined sugars can increase hypoglycemic reactions and make some people feel spacey).
- Proteins such as eggs, beans, legumes, nuts, and organic meats.

How we eat can also support grounding:

- Food made in a healthy and loving environment, not just in one's own kitchen.
- Good dietary habits, such as having a healthy breakfast, energy snacks between clients.
- Mindful eating, such as taking time to connect in a sensory way with the food (feeling the texture, tasting the flavors), eating to two thirds of your personal capacity (being completely full can induce sleepiness), and letting the eating be the only thing you

do when you are eating (not watching television or looking at your phone or computer).

*Reflection*

Although eating healthy foods with awareness does not guarantee you will feel grounded, they support the conditions for feeling steady, especially if you feel out of balance. In one study, 30% of osteopaths reported dietary and other lifestyle choices as important preparatory factors for fostering therapeutic presence (Durrer & Rohrbach, 2013). Movement through yoga, dance, or exercise is also critical for health. We tend to focus on the emotional components of remaining steady and centered, yet food, exercise, and health habits are essential supports of our energy and ability to maintain homeostasis in the body.

## Grounding Practice: Walking Meditation

Walking is one of those everyday activities most of us do (assuming we have the physical capacity to do so). We must walk from room to room, to our car, to our job, to the kitchen to get a drink. According to the Buddhist monk Thich Nhat Hanh, "Every path, every street in the world is your walking meditation path" (as cited in Levey & Levey, 2015, p. 106). If you have a disability that prevents walking, there may still be a way you travel from place to place (i.e., by wheelchair). In turning these everyday activities into presence practices, we attend to the whole set of sensations that accompany the process, whatever form it takes. You can also bring mindfulness to any part of your body that you can comfortably move, not just during transit-related movements.

You may already find that walking is your time to collect your thoughts, or release stress or emotional residue from the day. You may appreciate an additional opportunity to invite presence in one or more of the following ways:

- Step 1—Remove distractions.
    - Power down your cell phone when you begin your walk, to prevent the pull to engage.
    - Even if your phone is on, tuck it away somewhere when walking, and notice the pull to check (without judgment), returning your awareness back to the breath again and again.
- Step 2—Add awareness.
    - Allow your attention to be with the sensations of your feet on the ground. When your mind distracts (and it will), pause, breathe, and invite your attention back to walking.

- Try aligning the rhythm of your walking pace with the rhythm of your breathing.
- Step 3—Slow down your pace.
  - Slowing down your walking pace to even half of what your usual pace is can invite a sense of grounded presence and a more spacious feeling inside your body.
  - Add a pause every so often to take a breath, and return to slower walking.

Note: If you are incorporating your walking practice into walks that you take in your everyday life (to the bus, to work, with the dog), then it would be helpful to allow yourself more time than usual to benefit from the practice.

- Step 4—Intentional walking—nowhere to go but here.
  - Traditional walking meditation involves walking slowly and with awareness, back and forth on a 10- to 20-foot path. It is a form of walking without a destination, instead with the intent of inviting awareness of presence with each step.
  - Pause and feel your feet on the ground, breathing naturally with awareness. Begin by taking a slow and conscious step, feeling the ball of your foot and your toes on the first lift and being aware of the sensation of your heel gently landing on the ground as you step down. Continue to feel the heels and balls of your feet and toes as they lift and touch the ground in slow motion. When you reach the end of your path, pause, breathe, turn around slowly with awareness, and then continue your slow conscious walking.
  - If your mind becomes distracted or you feel the pull to speed up, notice that sensation and then with kindness return your attention to the slow walking pace, being aware of the rise and fall of your feet as they touch the ground.

*Reflection*

One of our liabilities as therapists is the sedentary nature of our work. Walking as a form of cultivating presence directly counters the strain of sitting and is good for our health. Beginning the therapy day with walking meditation can invite a feeling of grounding and connection with the earth. For some, walking makes it easier to be aware of the body while promoting the inner focus and stamina needed for a busy therapy day. Walking mindfully at the end of the therapy day can release emotional residue and return you to a grounded place. Walking meditation can also be incorporated in sessions with clients to help both you and your client feel grounded and more present.

Walking can be a structured form of meditation practice, or it can informally add moments of presence in your everyday life by helping you be mindfully aware of even a few of your steps. Feel your heel as it touches down on the ground and then the lift of your toes as you take your next step.

**Grounding Practice: Core Body Centering**

Focusing on three aspects of the body—length, width, and depth—can help us to ground and center (Silsbee, 2008). This practice is initially best when standing. When you feel more skillful at centering, you can practice a sitting variant, so that you can center this way in session. This centering practice is about aligning ourselves internally, so our body feels more grounded and centered and therefore our mind can follow.

- *Pause and breathe:* Begin by feeling your feet on the ground, legs slightly bent and apart, knees unlocked, and pelvis rocked forward slightly to straighten the spine. Take three full breaths with awareness to invite your attention to your body.
- *Length:* Sense the bottoms of your feet, where the soles rest firmly on the ground. Relax your shoulders, letting them gently drop. With your eyes open, allow your gaze to soften and your peripheral vision to be available to you. Relax your jaw. Visualize a string going from the top of your head to the sky. Now move attention to your feet and feel your feet steady on the ground, held by the weight of gravity. Allow your attention to move to the center of your body, 2 inches below your navel. Be aware of the length of your body as your head is upright with your feet firmly planted.
- *Width:* Be aware of the width, or space your body takes up from side to side. Gently rock your weight from right to left. Find the neutral balanced point in the center of the width of your body. Bring consciousness to having equal weight between both feet on the ground.
- *Depth:* Now bring attention to the front and back of your body, aligning yourself in this way. Gently rock back and forth, from heels and toes, until you arrive at a balanced and centered place with both heels and toes on the ground. We tend to be more focused on what is in front of us; however, notice also the space behind your body. Sense your body's center, that point or area that aligns you from top to bottom, from side to side, and from front to back.

*Reflection*

Centering is a key aspect of grounding. Centering means feeling integrated in body and mind, with a sense of equanimity. When we embody therapeutic presence, through length, width, and depth, it activates the brain and body to access the sensations of presence. If you feel out of balance, you may feel more anxious or scattered, and not as open to your client. If you open and feel your feet on the ground, you are inviting balance, and your neural activity related to grounding begins to activate. When you lose your emotional or cognitive balance in a session, you can use this centering practice to return to a steady place.

## Grounding Practice: Tree Visualization

Visualization can result in surprising changes to the parts of the brain associated with a particular experience or function. Pascual-Leone and colleagues (1995) found that participants who mentally rehearsed a piano melody 2 hours a day for 5 days had nearly the same degree of change in their body maps as those who physically practiced. Doidge (2015) recounted how physicians successfully guided their patients toward chronic pain reduction by visualizing brain regions that register pain shrinking. These findings support the use of mental imagery to call on your presence. The following tree visualization is a practice designed for just that, as it can help evoke a state of steadiness and equanimity that is an inherent part of grounding. An alternative to reading the practice here is to listen to this practice as a guided visualization with music, which can be found on my *Cultivating Presence* CD (http://www.sharigeller.ca/cd.php). Audio versions of practices discussed later in this chapter (i.e., the mindful sensing of the moment and the expansion through visualization practices) are also available on this CD.

- Pause, soften your eyes, and connect to your breath.
- As you inhale, imagine clean fresh air filling your whole body. As you exhale, imagine stress and tension dropping away through the soles of your feet.
- Visualize roots growing from underneath your feet (or base of spinal cord if sitting). Visualize the roots burrowing into the ground, through layers of soil and bedrock, reaching deeply into the earth.
- Imagine your roots drawing cool fresh water and sustenance from the earth.
- Roots also grow laterally—visualize your roots interconnecting with the roots of people who support you, love you, and help you to feel grounded.

- Breathe in the sense of rooting in the earth and rooting in connection.
- Invite your awareness to the rest of your body, imagining your legs and torso as the trunk of the tree. Imagine your arms like the branches, your head like the flower of the tree.
- Feel the branches swaying in the wind, as difficult emotions may come and go. While they sway, notice a steadiness in your feet in connection with the earth and with those you love.
- Allow yourself to rest in that sense of grounding, feeling, and absorbing the sensations.
- As we move toward close, gently open your eyes and stay in contact with a sense of grounding and with your breath.
- Take a moment to reflect on ways that you evoke the feeling of grounding throughout your day and in your life and work.

### Reflection

This visualization can also be helpful to reduce anxiety and provide the body and brain with an experience of equanimity. Imagining yourself embodying the deep rootedness and strength of a tree can help you to meet your clients' suffering while staying centered and steady. It can also be helpful to do before entering into a difficult conversation, so you can approach the other from a grounded place.

The image of our roots interconnecting with other roots in this visualization parallels the experience of grounding in supportive relationships, where emotions and physical states of arousal are regulated (Cozolino, 2006; Geller & Porges, 2014; Porges, 2011). Whether visualizing or actually connecting with others, this is central to how we can emotionally regulate and ground.

### Other Ways to Ground

*Grounding* has been defined in the leadership literature as including "rooting ourselves in something" (Cunningham, 1992). This "something" could be physical, spiritual, professional, or locational. We have talked about *physical* manifestations of grounding, including a strong and aligned posture, strong back, and yet soft and open heart. *Spiritually* we could have a value set that guides our ethical and personal choices. *Professionally* we may be educated with strong working knowledge about psychotherapy, change, and human nature. A calm and supportive working space for both you and your clients contributes to *locational* grounding. Taking this expansive perspective of grounding can have surprising effects: When you feel grounded in one respect, you may find that it supports your ability to ground in other domains as well.

A newer concept called *earthing* involves either having direct physical contact with the earth or being connected to the ground via a conductive system (Chevalier, Sinatra, Oschman, Sokal, & Sokal, 2012; Oschman, Chevalier, & Brown, 2015). The transfer of electrons from the ground to the body is believed to be responsible for such effects as improved sleep, reduced pain and inflammation, and improved overall wellness. Grounding in our bodies, our relationships, and our ideas can help us to build and sustain this sense of being steady yet deeply connected. It is an active process that needs to be nurtured, given the many pulls out of the moment that exist.

**Which Practice Do I Do When?**

Eating mindfully and enjoying grounding foods is a healthy adjunct to your life at any time. It can be particularly supportive on a day that you are feeling unsteady and anxious, to help support your body to come into a grounded state. Mindful walking can be done even when you are on the go and when sitting in quiet pause is not an option or sitting is physically difficult for you. It is also helpful if your mind is too agitated to engage in a sitting practice. You can use centering quietly and subtly while standing in a line, before a presentation, or before a therapy session. The tree visualization can be useful if you are a visual learner or when you want to create a visceral sense of grounding in relation to others. It is very helpful to do one or more of these practices daily and in particular to take a conscious moment to ground, either before entering the therapy room or with a client at the beginning of the session.

## IMMERSION

*Immersion* is a sensory experience involving an intimacy with the moment where you can feel and sense the subtle aspects of your client's and your own experience. This absorption quality demands a high level of attention and a focus on the present. Grounding and immersion need to coexist. If you were only immersed and not grounded, you could be so absorbed with your client that you lose a sense of yourself, causing burnout and feelings of being overwhelmed. Grounding without immersion can leave you feeling separate and disconnected from your clients.

Given that immersion is such a sensory experience, consciously engaging the senses is one gateway to experiencing immersion and presence. Often we are on sensory overload, which can cause us to shut down or miss what is actually occurring. Choosing to attend to one sense at a time helps parts of your brain and sensory capacity become more finely tuned and able hear and feel the nuances of what your clients are expressing. We will start with a fundamental mindfulness meditation practice and then build on this foundation with practices focused on immersing your senses in the moment through mindful sensing, listening, seeing, and tasting.

## Immersion Practice: Mindfulness Meditation

By focusing on the breath as an anchor, mindfulness meditation helps you notice when your mind is distracted, detach from the distraction, and invite attention back to the moment. Many newcomers to these practices feel like meditation is impossible because they cannot "achieve" a state of presence. This belief becomes a mental trap. The practice is noticing when you are not aware and inviting attention back from distraction, versus achieving a permanent state of presence. This is akin to a tennis player who, after each swing, returns to the center to await the next ball. You can benefit from an ability to return to the center by reanchoring yourself in your body and breath, to work with distraction that can emerge in session or in life.

The basic mindfulness meditation practice is as follows:

- Find a comfortable and supportive space to practice that is free of distractions. Sit in an upright yet relaxed position.
- Invite your awareness to your breath by finding a place in the body, the belly, or the chest where you can feel your breath.
- Notice the rise and fall of the belly or chest in rhythm with your inhale and exhale.
- When the mind wanders off (which it will), name the distraction in one word ("thinking," "worrying," "remembering") and gently invite your attention back to the breath.
- Just like a puppy dog that runs off again and again, each time your mind wanders gently invite it back, returning to the rise and fall of your belly or chest in rhythm with the breath.
- Practice for 10 minutes during the first month, then slowly increase to 20, then 30 minutes.
- Be gentle with yourself around the level of distraction you observe. Know that you are building your neural muscles for focus and attention each time your invite your awareness back from distraction to the breath.

*Reflection*

Research on mindfulness meditation reveals neuroplastic (brain) changes in the areas associated with attention control, emotion regulation, and self-awareness, including a greater focus on the present moment. The more you experience and practice bringing your mind back to the present, the more you can notice when you are distracted so you can return your attention back to the moment. Out-of-session practice supports your sustained attention and present-moment focus with your clients in session.

This practice of present-moment attention is not limited to one body position (sitting) or to being in silent spaces. Sitting and focusing is difficult for some people, and our jobs as therapists are already quite sedentary. Alternative ways to focus attention and to open to sensory awareness through creative modalities can be helpful. Next, we explore alternative practices such as using mindful sensing, listening, seeing, and tasting.

### Immersion Practice: Mindful Sensing of the Moment

Using our senses (e.g., visual, kinesthetic, auditory) to open to the moment can heighten the absorption and focus required for being immersed in session. For this practice, have an image in front of you, either a photograph, a work of art, a window view, or an item. You can also engage in this practice on my *Cultivating Presence* CD, with guided meditation and supportive music.

- Find a comfortable place to sit, in view of your object of focus.
- Close your eyes and attune to the rhythm of your breathing, feeling the flow between your inhale and exhale.
- Staying connected to your breath, open your eyes and notice the image in front of you, including the colors, shapes, textures, and lighting.
- Open sense by sense—notice what you see, hear, taste, and feel in response to the image.
- Now allow yourself to take in a small detail of that image. Notice what stands out to you about this intricacy, with great interest and curiosity.
- Close your eyes and hold the image in your mind's eye. Pay attention to detail.
- Slowly open your eyes and look at the image as if it were the first time you saw it.
- Allow yourself to be fully aware of what you notice with fresh eyes and how it feels in your body when you relate to this image in a new way.

*Reflection*

Paying attention to the details, and sensing the dimensions of what you are present with, can help strengthen your attention in therapy. Doing so allows you to fine-tune your ability to read the varying sensations and bodily cues that your client is expressing. Reading somatic markers such as facial expressions, eye flinches, breath changes, and physical gestures can help you track your clients' (and your own) experience moment to moment. This can also help you to more acutely notice the variations in the relationship, so you can address disconnection or maintain relational connection.

**Immersion Practice: Mindful Listening to Music**

Choose a piece of music that you find particularly inspiring or moving. Allow yourself to listen to the instruments and vocal sounds (if there are any), as well as the silence between the sounds. Invite your awareness to the feel of the music. Notice where you feel the sounds and how they vibrate in different parts of your body. Intentionally focus on different parts of your body to explore how sound resonates inside of you. Practice with different forms of music or sound to explore the experience of hearing with your whole body rather than just with your ears.

*Reflection*

Mindful listening to music allows you to open to presence though the auditory senses. Listening is a fuller experience than hearing, with the latter referring to taking in the physical sounds of what is expressed, which allows for perceptual processes to activate. Listening also includes what is perceived through sound acoustics (pitch, tonality, rhythm), which can indicate emotionality and feeling, as well as the meaning of what is being expressed. Sharpening your listening sense will allow you to tune in to the multiple ways your clients express their experience with greater precision and ease.

**Immersion Practice: Mindful Tasting**

This practice is adapted from a key exercise in the Mindfulness Based Stress Reduction program (Kabat-Zinn, 1990). This classic mindfulness practice is done with a raisin, yet can also be conducted with a piece of chocolate, a grape, or some other small food item.

It is best to create a 5- to 10-minute window for this practice.

- Hold the food item (i.e., grape) in your hand, noticing the touch and texture. Let your fingers explore the grape by turning it in your fingers.
- Now bring the grape up to your nose and let yourself take in the scents.
- Now place it in your mouth, but do not chew. Move it around your inner lips and tongue so you can feel the texture. Notice any desire to chew and swallow.

- After a few moments of sensory exploration, take one bite and pause to feel the sensation of the juices in your mouth and the flavor as it enters your throat.
- Slowly chew the rest of this grape, paying attention to the different sensations.

*Reflection*

By slowly tasting an item that we often eat quickly and mindlessly, we can attend to dimensions of the experience that we usually miss. This is a way of being present with what is, and generating a beginners' mind rather than processing information in a habitual way. In the therapy setting, this attitude invites you to find new ways to understand your clients' experience, to go off autopilot where you can miss what is poignant, and to be a fully engaged participant in their therapy process. It also helps you to be open to novel ways of responding.

## Which Practice Do I Do When?

The benefits of mindfulness meditation emerge most fully when it is a daily practice. It's best to choose a consistent time to practice formally, as the continuity helps to build sustainable benefits. The practice of using your senses to consciously open to the moment can also be incorporated informally into daily life activities, such as by being more intentional in listening to a song's instruments, rhythms, and tonalities, rather than playing it as background sound, or eating mindfully at mealtimes by pausing with curiosity before you eat to look at, smell, or touch the food and allow a moment of gratitude for your meal. The Zen tradition tells us to eat when we're eating, walk when we're walking, and listen when we're listening. So not multitasking (e.g., watching television while you eat, surfing on your smartphone while talking to a friend) is one way to practice this. In fact, going beyond formal practice to bringing awareness to everyday activities is central to transferring the skills you build in practice into your relationships and to your therapy session. This can allow you to notice what is alive in the moment, bringing greater fulfillment to your in-life and therapy relationships.

## EXPANSION

Expansion is the third in-body experience of therapeutic presence. Akin to flow state (Csikszentmihalyi, 1996), in an expansive state there is a heightened awareness and sense of timelessness. Therapists have described feeling both a bodily spaciousness and an expansion of consciousness, where the details of experience are more vivid and acute (Geller, 2001).

What is the purpose of expansion? Grounding keeps you connected to yourself, immersion allows you to feel and notice the details of your client's experience so you can respond accurately, and expansion lets you feel a larger sense of awareness—that everything is OK in the midst of the suffering. This facilitates a superior state of concentration and focus, which stems from direct contact with the true nature of self and experience. Going beyond or transcending the self (i.e., expansion) is possible only if we are grounded in a healthy and mature sense of self (Geller, 2003).

This expansive state opens up greater possibilities for responding than those offered by linear ways of thinking. You can access information with acuity to the nuances of your clients' experience. An expansive state is also energizing and brings a vitality that can reduce burnout and fatigue. This section will invite you to experience a larger sense of spaciousness with practices designed to enhance right-brain, holistic, and expansive ways of seeing and being.

**Expansion Practice: A Visualization**

This practice uses visualization to heighten the experience of expansion. It can be performed lying down or sitting up. Read the practice and then find a comfortable position in a space that will be uninterrupted for 15 to 20 minutes. You can also experience this practice as a guided music meditation on the *Cultivating Presence* CD (http://www.sharigeller.ca/cd.php).

- Allow yourself to pause and move your attention inward to the breath.
- Invite your awareness to the body as a whole. If your attention wanders, return your awareness to the whole of the breath or body.
- Now with your eyes open, expand your sensory awareness to notice (see, hear, feel) what is present in the direct vicinity around you in this moment. Take in the details individually first, then shift to experiencing the whole sense of what is around you.
- You can keep expanding your awareness slowly outwards, encompassing increasingly larger spaces—from the building around you to the street, the community, the town, then the city, country, neighboring countries, the other side of the world, the whole of the earth and where it sits in the solar system.
- Allow yourself to feel an expanded state while staying in contact with this, your breath.

- Bring yourself back to the room or space you are in slowly. Before closing this practice, pause and rest in the sensation of your breath and body as a whole.

*Reflection*

This practice helps to develop the openness and sense of expansion and sensory awareness so you feel the details of your clients' suffering alongside a backdrop of well-being. This brief exercise can serve as practice ground to enhance right hemispheric activity, which is involved in sensing the body and also involved in gestalts, or wholes (Siegel, 2007). By expanding awareness outward, you have the potential of accessing a functional shift that helps to decrease verbal activity, relax the body, and open your perspective, and ultimately helps in sensing the whole of a situation, such as your client's experience or what is occurring in the therapeutic relationship. The right hemisphere is also the place where you feel the connection with your client in the realm of the nonverbals, providing the conditions for the relationship to be strengthened.

## Expansion Practice: Zoom in and out With Mindful Photography

This practice is graciously offered by M. Lee Freedman, mindfulness-based psychiatrist and photographer, whose images are woven into this book. To fully benefit from this practice, use a camera with a zoom lens or a cell phone camera with zoom capacity. Begin by familiarizing yourself with your camera's functions, particularly how to zoom in and out with the lens. You can also use your eyes and the movement of your body to zoom in and out. If you wish to take a picture, click the shutter once you feel connected to the object of your attention. Let the clicking of the shutter acknowledge your moment of presence with the subject, communicating, "I see and acknowledge you." This is about using the camera to sense the moment, a very distinct experience from our usual, where the focus is on capturing a fabulous image.

- Pause and take three full breaths, feeling your feet on the ground.
- Go for a walk, or look around your current space, to find three objects or images: one that you are attracted to, one you have an aversion to, and one you feel neutral about.
- Beginning with the first object or image of something you are attracted to, look through your camera's viewfinder and notice what you see. Be curious about this object. Allow yourself to receive the image rather than looking out at it.
- Now either zoom in or move your body physically closer to the object, focusing on one aspect. Notice what is calling your attention to the subject as you zoom in closer.

- Now zoom your lens out, or move your body further away from the image. Look and feel, with curiosity, your relationship with this image.
- Walk further away and then pause to look at the image with your eyes or the viewfinder.
- Now move closer to the image with your body and/or the view-finder of your camera. How does this image look or feel different or the same? What do you feel in your body as you use the camera or your body movements to see this object from different vantage points?
- Repeat this practice with an image of something you feel averse to and something you feel neutral about. Notice how your perspective, feeling, or relationship with the object may change as you see what is present before you from different perspectives.

*Reflection*

In this exercise, you are shifting your awareness between immersion (noticing details of experience) and expansion (having a larger view or perspective of an experience), both of which are essential to presence. In the therapeutic encounter, this shifting helps you to move your attention from the minute details that your client is sharing to their larger goals. It helps to hold a larger picture in the moment: whether it be of one exchange in the session against the entire session, one experience of your client against all experiences they have shared with you, or one disclosure from you client in the context of their whole history. It can help you to shift between being with and making meaning of the details of your clients' experience, and contextualizing them to make sense of the whole. Shifting awareness can also strengthen your executive functioning, helping you to maintain greater focus and attention in session.

Attending to images that are attractive, aversive, and neutral can build your capacity to stay with experiences that may be difficult. You can change how you approach experiences—from a stance of judgment (I like or don't like) to one that is accepting, curious, looking anew with beginner's eyes. It also shifts how you approach your clients—from preconceptions or judgment (they should feel a certain way) to acceptance and curiosity about how they feel, including being open to a therapy direction that may not yet be clear.

This practice also can remind you to allow for multiple perspectives, rather than being attached to a certain idea, impression, or way to respond. The capacity to stay with experience and view it differently than you may have expected supports the ability to be with and respond to what is emerging in the moment. It can also help you to hold experiences in a larger perspective, supporting your capacity to stay with your clients' experience without feeling overwhelmed by difficult emotions or traumatic details that may be shared.

## Which Practice Do I Do When?

The expansion visualization is a good practice for when you are feeling caught up in the details of an argument or situation and not able to see the forest for the trees. The mindful photography practice can help you to step out of pursuing something that is not working and instead shift to see other interventions or directions for therapy. It can also help to strengthen attention and the ability to have multiple perspectives. Expansion can also be facilitated through practices that focus on the body (walking, yoga, tai chi, body scan), as they invite a functional shift away from language and conceptual facts (left hemispheric functioning) toward the nonverbal imagery and somatic sensations of the right hemisphere (Siegel, 2007). These right hemispheric modes of perceiving are more holistic and will help you approach clients who may be ready to see, feel, and hold a larger perspective—which they often cannot do when they are suffering. This expanded perspective helps you, too, to generate calmness and spaciousness if you tend to get overwhelmed.

## BEING WITH AND FOR THE OTHER

The fourth quality, being with and for the other, reflects the therapeutic aspect of presence: being grounded, immersed, and spacious with the intent for your clients' healing. The relational aspect of presence begins to emerge here. This includes a sense of respect and love for the other—not a romantic love, but a love that emerges from a deep sense of connection. For this connection to occur, you must recognize where you tend to shut down, so that you can become more allowing of what arises. Danna Faulds (2002) wrote in her poem "Allow":[1]

> There is no controlling life.
> Try corralling a lightning bolt,
> containing a tornado. Dam a
> stream, and it will create a new
> channel. Resist, and the tide
> will sweep you off your feet.
> Allow, and grace will carry
> you to higher ground. The only
> safety lies in letting it all in—
> the wild with the weak; fear,
> fantasies, failures and success . . .
> In the choice to let go of your
> known way of being, the whole
> world is revealed to your new eyes.

---

[1]From *Go In and In: Poems From the Heart of Yoga* (p. 25), by D. Faulds, 2002, Kearney, NE: Morris Publishing. Copyright 2002 by Danna Faulds. Reprinted with permission.

The tendency to shield can emerge in the face of suffering, especially after repetitive exposure. The barriers to connection can be subtle, such as going into advice giving, analyzing, or detaching as ways to protect from feeling clients' pain. We can hide without knowing, even by having a clipboard or desk between clients and ourselves. To be fully present, we must engage in the inner work required to let clients in, without judgment, blame, or distance. This includes softening walls and releasing barriers to human-to-human encounters. Compassion is key here.

## Compassion

*Compassion* is "the ability to be present at all levels of suffering, to experience it, and aspire to act to transform it without being overwhelmed by emotions or circumstances" (Rushton et al., 2009, p. 408). Dass and Bush (1995) wrote that

> The powerful awakening of our own compassion can tune us not just to the nurturing and sustaining forces of the world but to the oppressive and destructive ones as well. When we open to these directly and become familiar with them, instead of avoiding them as we often do, we are more likely to hear ways to respond with love and support to relieve the suffering. (p. 4)

Compassion is said to promote positive brain functioning and be healthy for the person feeling compassion. In psychotherapy, opening to pain in a compassionate way lets you feel a deep sense of connection with your clients, without resistance to their suffering (Germer, 2012). Although presence encompasses compassion, compassion practice strengthens your presence and helps to fortify your ability to sustain compassion with clients.

Studies on compassion and the brain by Richie Davidson and colleagues (Davidson & Lutz, 2008; Lutz, Greischar, Rawlings, Ricard, & Davidson, 2004) have supported deepening of the neural substrates that strengthen compassion through related practices. Positive emotions such as loving-kindness and compassion can be learned in the same way that we learn a new task. With extensive compassion and loving-kindness meditation practice, greater empathic states can be promoted. An important first step, which can help you to bring this quality into session, is the ability to meet our own suffering with compassion.

## Being With and for the Other Practice: Self-Compassion

The following practice is intended to foster your self-compassion.

- Take a moment to pause, breath, and go inward.
- Allow yourself to become aware of a situation or relationship toward which you hold anger, resentment, or blame. It could be current or unresolved from the past.

- Become aware of what is underneath that anger—explore your more primary emotions such as vulnerability, hurt, or shame. How do these emotions feel in the body? Where do you physically feel them?
- Place a loving hand on the part of your body where you feel pain.
- Offer compassion to your pain, with words or gestures that are accepting and deeply loving. You can try, "I am here with you" or "I want to understand you."
- If there is a struggle to be with the pain, offer understanding, care, and love to that struggle.

*Reflection*

To develop and sustain true compassion for others, you need to be able to connect with your own suffering and offer it compassion and care too (Desmond, 2016; Germer, 2009; Neff, 2011). Self-compassion means caring for our suffering the way we would care for someone we truly love. Kristen Neff (2011) described three components of self-compassion: (a) offering *kindness toward ourselves* rather than self-judgment; (b) recognizing the *common humanity* in our suffering, that we are not alone; and (c) *mindfulness* practice to help be with suffering rather than avoiding or running away.

As we have discussed, our need for self-care is tremendous, yet our attention to it is often lacking. This, combined with the extensive care we give others, can lead to compassion fatigue (Figley, 2002). Self-compassion can be an antidote to the emotional work of therapy; through it we give back to ourselves and become able to approach our difficult emotions with acceptance, helping them to resolve. Research suggests that self-compassion reduces burnout and compassion fatigue[2] in health care professionals (Raab, 2014; Wiklund Gustin & Wagner, 2013).

Self-compassion also boosts positive emotions such as social connectedness, competence, curiosity, happiness, optimism, and well-being (Neff, Rude, & Kirkpatrick, 2007). It activates your caregiving system, releasing the feel-good hormones of oxytocin and opioids, and is associated with heightened parasympathetic activity (Gilbert, 2009; Stellar, Cohen, Oveis, & Keltner, 2015). It supports a vitality and flow so you can stay open to

---

[2]Compassion researchers (i.e., Germer, 2012; Klimecki & Singer, 2012) are proposing that compassion fatigue should actually be termed *empathy fatigue*, given that the positive emotions accompanying compassion can in fact increase our capacity for care.

meeting your clients and feeling their suffering with them, while remaining energized.

## Being With and for the Other Practice:
## Breathing Compassion in and out

A practice inspired by Germer (2012) is to breathe compassion for your self and others. This is adapted from traditional Tonglen practice, based in Tibetan Buddhism (Rinpoche, 1992).

- Invite yourself into a comfortable, relaxed, yet upright sitting posture.
- Take a few relaxing breaths as you settle yourself into the moment.
- As you inhale, offer compassion to your stress and difficult emotions inside.
- As you exhale, offer compassion to the challenges this other person is experiencing.
- Continuing breathing compassion in and out with a natural and relaxed breathing rhythm. Scan your body for any distress while inhaling compassion for yourself, while exhaling compassion for the other person(s) who need it.
- Allow the words to accompany your breath if it is helpful: On the inhale silently noting: "one for me," and on the exhale: "one for you."
- When that feels complete, invite your awareness back by slowly opening your eyes.

*Reflection*

This practice invites a feeling of compassion, while supporting the connection between yourself and your client. It can also be useful in therapy when you feel overwhelmed with emotion, blocked, or shut down from your client. When you notice this state and when your listening is impaired, take a deep in-breath while offering compassion to the distress, and on your out-breath offer compassion to your client (Germer, 2012). Find a natural rhythm of inhaling for yourself, and exhaling for your client, until you feel yourself connecting with your client again.

## Being With and for the Other Practice: Metta

*Metta* is Pali for "loving-kindness." It is a central practice in Buddhist traditions and is viewed as the basic underlying attitude of all mindfulness practices (Bogels & Restifo, 2014). The following metta practices is offered to keep the mind and body open, loving and accepting.

*Loving-Kindness Practice (Metta)*

- Pause and find a comfortable position for practice, either sitting upright or lying down.
- Invite your attention to your breath in your body, noticing the rise and fall of your belly and chest as you breathe.
- Gently repeat loving-kindness phrases while holding yourself in your awareness. Feel free to alter the phrases so they resonate best with what you need. Allow these phrases to rise and fall in rhythm with the breath:
  May I be happy.
  May I be well.
  May I be safe.
  May I be in peace.
- Say these phrases slowly, to allow yourself to absorb the intentions they express.
- Now invite the image of someone in your life that is suffering. Hold the image of this person while repeating phrases of loving-kindness to them.
  May you be happy.
  May you be well.
  May you be safe.
  May you be in peace.
- Now imagine a benefactor or mentor and offer metta phrases to that person.
- Repeat this practice while imagining a family member, friend, or community that is suffering.
- Now invite the image of someone you are having a difficult relationship with and offer phrases of loving-kindness to them.
- Do a final round with yourself, holding yourself in your awareness while intentionally offering the energy and words of loving-kindness.

*Metta/Loving-Kindness Walking Meditation*

- Begin by standing and offering the words and intention of loving-kindness to yourself.
- Now go for a slow, mindful walk. This can be inside or outside, yet it is best to walk where there are people around.
- Take two steps in rhythm with your inhale and three steps in rhythm with your exhale. Repeat silently to yourself the phrases of loving-kindness.

- When you come across a person, pause as you silently offer phrases of loving-kindness.
- When you complete the walk, pause, offer loving-kindness inside and outward to all beings. Notice how you feel in your body. Take that feeling of loving-kindness with you as you transition out from practice.

*Reflection*

Metta can generate feelings of positivity so that you can meet your clients with an open, nonjudgmental, and loving inner space. It is a powerful and immediate way of shifting mental and bodily states, promoting acceptance and empathy. Incorporating metta practice in your walk to work can help you start your therapy day with this open, loving acceptance.

## Being With and for the Other Practice: Holding Suffering With Love

This practice is adapted from an exercise by Hanson and Mendius (2009):

- Bring to your awareness a positive experience. Perhaps it is an experience in the past where you felt strong, whole, happy, or a larger sense of love and belonging.
- Allow yourself to connect with the positive feelings, lingering to absorb and really feel the sensations of the experience.
- Now bring to your attention a negative or painful personal experience.
- Allow yourself to be aware both of the love, strength, and wholeness and of the pain and suffering. Notice how you can hold both of these in your awareness.
- Allow your love and strength to hold your suffering. Notice what that feels like.

*Reflection*

Intentionally activating feelings of love and well-being triggers the release of the neurotransmitters oxytocin and vasopressin, deepening the social bond and attachment with your clients and strengthening the therapeutic relationship (Carter, 2014). A biological sense of connection, trust, and safety is activated. This makes deeper therapeutic work possible.

Intentionally pausing to absorb positive experiences is important to highlight here. Negative experiences are stored immediately and are rapidly available for recall. Positive ones are typically registered through standard memory systems, so they need to be held in consciousness for 10 to 20 seconds to sink in (Hanson & Mendius, 2010). When you allow yourself to pause and absorb experiences (including ones mentioned earlier, such as centeredness, acceptance, compassion, and equanimity), you are increasing the likelihood that these experiences will provide a neurological imprint, becoming more accessible in life and in session with your clients.

## Which Practice Do I Do When?

Self-compassion practice is particularly beneficial if you find yourself feeling distress and spiraling into feeling badly about yourself. If negative self-talk is a pattern for you, you might use the self-compassion practice daily. It is also a really helpful exercise to do with clients if they tend to be self-judgmental or if you sense they are stuck in a secondary emotion and you want to help them connect in an accepting way with their core pain. Breathing compassion in and out is a great way of enhancing your connection with your clients when you start to drift or shut down. Metta walking practice can be done during any walk, yet this practice is especially suited to times when you are feeling closed and want to open further to positive emotions. Holding suffering with love is also a great daily practice to rewire your brain toward positivity, given the human tendency toward negativity based on evolutionary principles. It can help you to do the simultaneous tasks of being with pain and maintaining a spacious feeling in yourself.

Sometimes during these practices, seemingly opposite feelings can arise, such as anger, grief, or sadness. These can be signs that your heart is softening, and the suffering underneath is being revealed. You can either shift to mindfulness practice (acceptance of what is there and returning to the breath), or you can direct compassion and loving-kindness toward the feelings.

Focusing on different areas allows us to build strength where it is needed. For example, if we feel spacey and uncentered, doing a grounding practice would help to bring attention back to a place of equanimity. If you are distracted, having a few mindful breaths can invite your awareness back to the moment. With practice these experiences of presence can become part of your physiological and neural network, so accessing them in session may occur with greater ease.

Now that we are becoming adept at heightening presence in our bodies and in relationships, we can take therapeutic presence a step further. As our presence deepens with our clients, a shared presence emerges that is infused with healing. Next, we will explore therapeutic relational presence. Let us transition there with a practice.

# TRANSITION PRACTICE: BREATHING IN CONNECTION WITH AN IMAGINED OTHER

This practice can be done with an imagined other who generates feelings of safety and love inside you. It can be practiced in a dyad as well, but allow more time to debrief in that case.

- Invite yourself to a brief pause.
- Imagine someone standing or sitting in front of you that you feel safe and loved by (generated in your mind's eye or a photo).
- Visualize yourself looking this person in the eyes.
- Take three deep breaths together, with long exhalations as you maintain eye contact.
- At the end of the last exhalation, notice your present experience of shared breathing.
- Name this experience with one word followed by a nod of gratitude for your partner.
- Staying connected with your experience, proceed to the next moment of your day.

# IV

# INTEGRATING THERAPEUTIC PRESENCE IN RELATIONSHIPS AND TRAINING

©2016 M. Lee Freedman.

# 11

## THERAPEUTIC RELATIONAL PRESENCE: RELATIONSHIP AS A PATHWAY TO SPIRITUALITY

There is a divine purpose behind everything—and therefore a divine presence in everything.

—Neale Donald Walsch (1996, p. 60)

When we deepen into presence in relationship with our clients, the relationship becomes a portal to something that is larger than both of us. These I–Thou encounters are profound moments in which there is a sharing of experience that is transformative for both. Buber (1958) described the spiritual electricity that surges between people when they relate with each other authentically and humanly. In the therapy encounter, there are striking moments when therapist and client are in synchronicity and a gateway opens up to wisdom and healing. We have termed these profound moments of relating *therapeutic relational presence*, or *relational presence*, for short (Geller, 2013a, 2013b; Geller & Greenberg, 2012).

http://dx.doi.org/10.1037/0000025-012
*A Practical Guide to Cultivating Therapeutic Presence*, by S. M. Geller

# THERAPEUTIC RELATIONAL PRESENCE: SELF, OTHER, AND SPIRITUALITY

The transformative state of relational presence engages a triad of relationships between your client, yourself, and a larger sense of spirituality. When in this state, there is enhanced access to the inner world of your clients, and it feels as if you are sharing the same space. This multilayered connection is a form of intersubjective consciousness, as therapist and client cocreate a shared present-moment experience (Stern, 2004). The consciousness of one overlaps with and partially includes the consciousness of the other, so that when one person has an experience, it activates almost the same experience in the other person too. Both are changed in a deeply human way in these moments of relational presence.

## How Does Relational Presence Create Change?

Research in neuroscience, such as the discovery of mirror neurons at the end of the last century, may illuminate what happens in relational presence from a scientific perspective (Ferrari & Rizzolatti, 2014; Gazzola, Aziz-Zadeh, & Keysers, 2006; Glenberg, 2010; Praszkier, 2016; Siegel, 2010, 2011). In Chapter 3 we discussed how in shared moments of presence, therapists' mirror neurons and adaptive oscillators activate in relation to their client's expressed experience, which reflects the experience of knowing the other through direct engagement. Like two people salsa dancing together or rowing in unison, there is a reading and sharing of experience. Interbrain synchrony reflects this shared neural activity (Behrends, Müller, & Dziobek, 2012; Llobera et al., 2016), which potentially deepens relational presence and promotes a state of relational integration.

Feeling felt or attuned to in these ways invites clients' social engagement system (ventral vagal) to activate, dampening defenses and inviting greater calm and connection in the relationship. It evokes a neuroception of safety along with a possible release of the hormone oxytocin (Carter, 2014; Porges, 1998), which can support clients to become softer and more open (Geller & Porges, 2014). This release of oxytocin contributes to the creation of a loving relationship between the therapist and client that is infused with healing.

From an experiential perspective, in this intersubjective state of consciousness we feel a resonance with our clients' experience as if it were our own, allowing us to see, feel, and know aspects of their inner world that we would otherwise not have access to (Stern, 2004). We can then listen to our attuned bodily resonance, which evokes responses that are intuitive and directly emergent from clients' unspoken experience. It evokes a flow and energy that is healing in and of itself.

From a spiritual perspective, presence is viewed as a divine state that emerges in relation to a higher power or larger universe. Buber (1958, 1965) described how being present with each other in the immediacy of the relationship evokes a larger sense of connection and aliveness that goes beyond the self. Boundaries are dropped, and we gain access to a larger healing that moves us naturally in the direction of growth.

Carl Rogers (1980) illuminated how our presence touches our clients, and the relationship transcends to something larger. He described his experience of being closer to his "transcendental core" and how in those moments "our relationship transcends itself and becomes a part of something larger. Profound growth and healing and energy are present" (p. 129).

## How Does Therapeutic Relational Presence Evolve?

Therapeutic presence begins in the self, as you create the conditions for presence to emerge through practice and preparation. You can offer your attunement and receptive presence, which creates safety in the therapeutic relationship. Through the depth of connection as two people become present with each other, the connection expands to a larger state of being or communion (Colosimo & Pos, 2015), evolving into a deeper relational presence.

Of course you do not typically begin a session in this deeper relational presence. Creating safety with clients begins by meeting clients where they are, starting light in your contact and then deepening with each other as the session unfolds. It is helpful to understand this process by looking at a proposed model of the various levels of presence (Geller & Greenberg, 2012).

## Levels of Presence in the Therapy Encounter

Relational presence is not binary (i.e., that we are either present or not). Rather, it is a continuous process with varying intensities that unfold in your encounter with clients. Exhibit 11.1 lists five levels of presence that occur from the first in-session moment of meeting the client. This is in part inspired by literature in the nursing field, where there is recognition of the importance of presence. These models describe different levels of presence from being there physically to going beyond the boundaries of initial contact and accessing a transpersonal presence (Gilje, 1993; McDonough-Means, Kreitzer, & Bell, 2004; Osterman & Schwartz-Barcott, 1996). Integrating this perspective with the model of therapeutic presence reflects a view of presence that deepens with contact in the therapeutic encounter (Geller & Greenberg, 2012).

The first level of in-session presence, *physical presence* or *light presence*, refers to the moment of initial contact with the client. It includes the initial welcoming of the client into the therapy space and may include general surface

EXHIBIT 11.1
Five Levels of Deepening Into Presence in Session

1. Physical presence (light presence)
   a. Contact with other—light presence (superficial or small talk)
   b. Settling into the room/chairs
   c. Awareness of own body (present moment awareness, contact with chair)
2. Psychological presence (partial presence)
   a. Hearing the story, checking in
   b. Listening, attending, attunement, caring, openness, and interest
3. Emotional presence (presence with and for the other)
   a. Understanding, compassion, acceptance, empathy, unconditional positive regard
   b. Responding or providing intervention or empathic response in resonance to what the client is sharing
4. Transpersonal presence (presence with spirit)
   a. Body as a vessel
   b. Contact with deeper connection between therapist and client
   c. Contact with deeper intuition
   d. Contact with spirituality (vitality, enhanced sensation, and perception)
5. Therapeutic relational presence (all the levels)
   a. Vacillating (dancing) between what is needed in the moment—deep contact with self, with the client, and with a deeper spirituality and intuition
   b. Being fully with and for the other yet filled with energy, vitality, and a spiritual transcendence

talk about the weather, traveling to the session, etc. Even if it is light presence, it is an important part of the process because there is human warmth that lets clients know that you are happy to see them, you are interested in their day-to-day life, and that you are two human beings in contact with each other. This stage includes physically settling into a comfortable sitting position together.

The next level is *psychological presence* or *partial presence*, which includes the initial checking in and setting an intention for the session. Therapists begin to receive clients' experience, with openness, interest, and acceptance. This is the beginning stage of therapists' presence, allowing for an attunement to what the client is bringing into this particular session.

In the third level, being *emotionally present* to the client or *present with and for the other*, therapists begin to experience an emotional resonance and empathy with the client. Responses emerge in direct resonance with what the client is sharing. Therapists are simultaneously listening and absorbing the content, and attuning to nonverbal expressions, while looking within their own sensory body for information on what the client is experiencing.

A fourth level that may emerge as the session unfolds and the relationship deepens in the moment is a *transpersonal presence*, or *presence with spirit* or something larger. In transpersonal presence, therapists recognize their body as a vessel for healing and describe feeling a larger state of energy and vitality, with enhanced sensory and perceptual awareness. Greater contact with and access to intuition emerge as both inner wisdom and professional knowledge are tapped into, resulting in responses that are resonant and healing. Transpersonal presence can emerge in special present moments or deep intersubjective sharing (Stern, 2004).

This unfolds into the fifth level, *therapeutic relational presence*, when all of the prior levels are integrated and occurring simultaneously. It means shifting between what is emerging and poignant in the moment, being in direct contact with yourself and your client, as well as in contact with a deeper sense of intuition, spirituality, and/or a transcendental force.

In this profound relational presence, a state of flow emerges. There is an automatic, effortless, and highly focused energy that drives the therapeutic process. There is also a trust in the process and in your own intuition and responses. In relational presence, healing can emerge not only from the level of multiple present-moment connections (with self, other, and transcendence or spirit) but also from the quality of therapeutic work and unfolding in the depth of the relationships between these connections.

## Clinical Vignette: Therapeutic Relational Presence and Trust in the Process

As Rogers (1980) pointed out, when we trust what emerges in a present state, even when it does not yet make perfect sense, it often turns out to be right and to propel the therapy process forward. The following clinical vignette illustrates how such insights arrive when in this state.

Megan had come to therapy to work through posttraumatic reactions that she was experiencing at home. She was having terror dreams, which interrupted her sleep. She felt hypervigilant and was easily startled by minor house and street noises. We were embarking on EMDR (eye movement desensitization and reprocessing) therapy to help work through her posttraumatic stress disorder reactions, although it was difficult to set up the protocol as she did not recall any contributing traumatic events.

I did a grounding exercise so I could feel both calm and connected with her as Megan described her terror. I felt immersed in the moment with her. I could feel a resonance of fear in my body, while simultaneously feeling grounded and spacious and not overwhelmed by the fear—as if the fear were being held in a larger space of love and connection. I was sensing and reading her bodily experience as she described her fears and noticed a twitch in her eyes. In that moment, I simultaneously became aware of an image of a house on fire. I was hesitant to share, because Megan had not discussed anything that resonated with this, but I put aside my inner judgment and told myself to trust. I shared my image with her, and she began to cry. She told me that when she was 5 years old there had been a fire in the family home that was terrifying, but everyone had gotten out safely, without harm. She had been told how lucky she was, and because no one was hurt, she never talked about the fire or even recognized the significant terror she felt at the time.

*Reflection*

This vignette illustrates an intersubjective consciousness and the possibility of accessing the experience of the client in a way that can promote healing responses. Through this depth of connection, I received an image of an experience that Megan had not yet shared. She had previously undermined the experience as unimportant and irrelevant. When I made a choice to trust my seemingly irrelevant experience and share it, it turned out to be accurate and important for her, and she was able to connect to the underlying source of her trauma.

Megan had seen several therapists prior to our work and had not mentioned the fire to them either. Our therapy could have proceeded in the way that her prior treatment had. Yet, because of my presence and our deepening into connection and relational presence together, a contact with her internal world was achieved. In that state I could trust the image and experience that was arising in me, and we could identify the source of the trauma and then work to resolve Megan's current difficulties. Over time she felt a vast reduction in the fear and was able to sleep and be in her home with ease and peacefulness.

## PRACTICES FOR CULTIVATING THERAPEUTIC RELATIONAL PRESENCE

Although all the practices offered in the book provide the conditions for presence to arise, the practices here are relationally based and are designed to cultivate the experience of the triad of relationship between self, other, and a larger sense of connection.

### Relational Music and Mindfulness to Cultivate Therapeutic Relational Presence

Therapeutic Rhythm and Mindfulness (TRM™) combines evidence-based practices of group drumming, mindfulness, visualization, and emotion-focused awareness (Geller, 2009, 2010). It is a single unified program that offers multiple benefits. It is designed to evoke positive emotions such as a joy, vitality, flow, and social connectedness while dissolving barriers to presence such as stress, tension, anxiety, and depression. TRM™ also allows for the expression of difficult emotions, including vicarious traumatization and compassion fatigue, associated with being a therapist. It offers an opportunity for therapists to build relationships and a sense of belonging in community with other therapists.

Drumming and rhythm making have been used by indigenous cultures for thousands of years to reduce disease and increase harmony with one's self, community, and nature (Clottey, 2004; Diamond, 1999). Drum circles are cross-culturally a part of some of the oldest healing rituals. Although music in general has been linearly defined in Western culture as a performance-based activity, TRM™ is not about performance; it is a form of self-expression and nonverbal communication in relationship. Its use in cultivating relational presence is ideal, as it enhances intrapersonal and interpersonal connection, as well a connection with something larger.

Group drumming can help therapists become more synchronized with their own rhythms as well as the rhythms of others. It also helps therapists to become comfortable with the rhythm between them and their client to promote greater synchrony. Research with music played in relationship shows that there is a brain phase locking process within a person and between people that increases brain coherence in self and brain synchronization in relationship (Lindenberger et al., 2009; Sänger, Müller, & Lindenberger, 2012). Drumming in particular has been shown to increase brain hemispheric synchronization and social connectedness (Winkelman, 2003), thereby increasing connectedness with self and others, while enhancing a larger state of connection.

Specific exercises in TRM™ focus on this fine balance of self and other attunement, and the ability to shift awareness between all the different present-moment experiences in a session (in self, other, and in the relationship). The sense of connection from playing with the larger group often opens up a magical space where what is cocreated feels enlivening and joyful. We can feel our selves, with others, and with a larger sense of energy and flow.

**Therapeutic Relational Presence Practices:**
**Relational Mindfulness With Rhythm**

This is a dyadic practice, but it can also be conducted in a larger group. Have within reach a small percussion instrument, such as a small djembe drum, tongue drum, shakers, or soft bells.

- Pair up and sit across from your partner.
- Each of you can close your eyes and attune to your breath.
- Then open your eyes, staying connected to your own rhythm of breathing.
- Extend awareness to the rhythm of your partner's breathing, perhaps noticing the rise and fall of his or her belly or chest.
- Now pick up your instrument.

- Begin to play a gentle rhythm in relationship with your breath.
- Allow a rhythm of conversation to emerge between the two of you—being aware of allowing space in your rhythm for listening and playing.
- Notice what emerges inside—play your present moment experience of being in relationship with your partner.
- After 5 to 10 minutes of playing, close your eyes and begin to soften the volume of your rhythm back in attunement with your breath.
- Quiet the sound even further until is barely perceptible.
- Return you awareness to your breath.
- When this practice is complete, open your eyes and with a rhythmic note or sound, thank your partner for this practice.
- Take a few moments to quietly debrief with your partner what that experience was like.

*Reflection*

Drumming practices are particularly powerful in relationship (dyad or group) as the experience of entrainment quickly occurs. As you may recall from Chapter 3, entrainment occurs when independent rhythms that are interacting both adjust continuously until they come into synch with each other. It underlies the phenomena of birds flying in unison or clocks positioned side by side eventually ticking to the same beat. Entrainment promotes a subjective sense of synchrony between people. Powerful experiences and lessons can emerge, reflecting the process of presence and contact with one's self, others, and a larger collective wisdom.

Drumming and rhythm practices can be adapted for and conducted by individuals. For example, drumming along with music provides an opportunity to use rhythm awareness to synchronize emotions to experience and cognition. It can also enhance synchronicity of left- and right-brain hemispheres, hence eliciting a clearer sense of focus, concentration, and inner harmony. It also supports familiarity with how you may lose your rhythm and presence with others (i.e., the client) and how to regain it in the session.

**Relational Presence Practice: Relational Mindfulness and Whole Body Listening**

- With a partner, sit together, face to face, a few feet apart, with the intention of listening with your whole body to your partner's whole body.
- Close your eyes to eliminate your vision, inviting an opportunity to use your other senses.

- Silently notice your experience of having your eyes closed. Notice the sensations of your breath and what you feel physically in the body.
- Person A begins to speak about the experience of having his or her eyes closed, describing the experience in the moment.
- Person B listens in a present-centered way, without interruption or feedback. The listener can focus on the voice of the speaker (rhythm, tempo, vocal quality, pauses, hesitations, etc.) and what is being expressed by the voice itself. Continue for about 5 minutes.
- Quietly discuss with each other what you noticed and were aware of. Be specific about what you were aware of in the voice, your feeling and response, and your impression of what it felt like. For instance: "I was aware of how softly you speak; I felt sleepy as I listened to your voice, like I was listening to a lullaby." Take about 5 minutes to do this.
- Switch partners and repeat the exercise.
- Now return to silence together, but this time open your eyes. Take a moment in silence to just look into the other's eyes. Allow yourself to sense what the other person is experiencing, placing close attention to nonverbal cues like body posture, facial expression, etc. Notice in your own body any sensations that are arising that are unfamiliar . . . these could be images, pains, tensions, etc.
- Share with each other your experience on a sensory level as you connected to the other. Take 5 minutes to do this. After debriefing together, return to the larger group to share.

*Reflection*

Listening as a mindful practice can help to build your neural capacity to attend to the multiple sensations that may be expressed by your client. Mindful, multisensory listening is indispensable if you want to connect in ways that lead you and your clients into a shared relational presence. It also shifts your own bodily and attentional states to a more present-centered experience, as you decenter from your cognitive understanding of experience and expand your sensory awareness.

This intensity of practice can initially be very uncomfortable, as you face the barriers to being this intimate with someone. The fears, vulnerabilities, and shame that may be felt when being heard and seen are part of the practice. Initially paying attention to what arises, while being accepting of these potentially difficult states, can eventually give way to a deeper state of connection that transcends each person. Like any of the mindful practices that initially evoke discomfort when slowing down, we need to stay with the difficult feelings with love and acceptance for them to transform. In *10% Happier*, Dan Harris (2014) humorously described his initial experiences with meditation practice: "It was the longest, most exquisite high of my life, but the hangover came first!" (p. 121).

### Therapeutic Relational Presence Practice: Relating With Nature

Experiences in nature can provide you with a powerful sense of expansion and inter-connectedness. This practice is simple: Spend time in nature, in silence with yourself or others, to evoke and feel a connection with something larger.

M. Coleman (2006) offered the following description:

> When we are distressed, going outside for some fresh air, taking a walk in the park, or wandering deep into the woods quickens our attention, bringing us instantly into the present. Being outdoors provides mental space and clarity, allowing our bodies to relax and our hearts to feel more at ease. Putting ourselves in the midst of something greater than our personal dramas, difficulties, and pain—as we do when we walk in the open plains, hike in rarefied mountain air, or ramble on an empty beach—can give us a sense of space and openness, lifting us out of our narrow selves. Similarly gazing up at the vast night sky helps us to see our problems and concerns with greater context and perspective. The natural world communicates its profound message: things are okay as they are; you are okay just as you are; simply relax and be present. (p. xvi)

*Reflection*

In our postmodern world, we have lost touch with the ability to access, be open to, sense, and feel the essence of nature. Many people are uncomfortable with spaciousness, stillness, and interconnectedness. It is difficult to keep the mind and body still amidst the stimulation of constant busyness. Putting that all aside and being immersed in the outdoors helps the body attune to the rhythms of nature, enhancing a sense of relational presence.

Nature can be a powerful teacher of expansion as well as other qualities of therapeutic presence. The trees can evoke a feeling of grounding and centering. Mountains mirror an experience of equanimity and steadiness, teaching you to find stillness amidst storms and changing weather. Gazing out at the ocean, onto a horizon, or up to the sky helps to connect to the sense of expansion. The river shows you how to flexibly flow around obstacles, such as rocks and sticks or challenges in session, so that we can adapt to what arises in the moment. Walking along a path helps to remind you to take one step at a time, enjoying the process and not just the destination or outcome. Flowers reflect inner beauty, the essence of human nature that is whole and complete, supporting your compassionate understanding of your clients. The earth reminds you of what is under your feet, a sense of grounding that keeps you steady and centered. The darkness can hold your fears and the sunlight mirror your joy. Whether taking a longer excursion in nature or daily visits to a park, attuning to nature can help calm distraction and attune you to the present moment and the larger interconnectivity of life, activating an interconnected state for the brain to encode and return to.

## THE FERTILE GROUND OF THE PRESENT MOMENT

Therapeutic relational presence reflects how we are interconnected beings, resonating moment to moment on the level of dialogue, and in our bodies, emotions, and brains. As you deepen in presence, so do your clients, and the relationship transcends itself, becoming larger. It is experienced as overlapping with the other, feeling or resonating a part of your client's experience in your own being. Concepts described in this chapter and elsewhere in the book, such as mirror neurons and adaptive oscillators and interbrain synchrony, reflect how your brain mirrors and experiences resonance with your clients' states when you are in relational presence.

So how can you optimize this intersubjective consciousness and the fertile ground of the present moment? Stern (2004) described the ancient Greeks' notion of *kairos*, which is a moment of opportunity. Events come together, and there is opportunity to act or respond that could change the course of your destiny, either for the next moment or a lifetime. In psychotherapy, your attunement to the fertile ground of the present moment, and both the visible and invisible expressions of your client's experience, allow your client to feel deeply felt, seen, and understood. Attuning to and responding from these present-moment experiences deepen into a relational presence. This larger sense of interconnection invites a state where you can trust that what arises is in the direction of growth and healing.

## TRANSITION PRACTICE: RETURNING TO THE RHYTHM OF BREATHING

- Pause and take three deep breaths.
- Invite an image of interconnectivity, with others that you love and/or with nature.
- Feel the qualities of this interconnectivity—breathe and absorb the positive feelings that arise when you feel connected.
- Now take three deep breaths, letting that image go, yet allowing the feelings to linger.
- Transition to the next chapter or the next moment of your day.

# 12

## CONTINUING THE JOURNEY: TRAINING AND EXPANDING THERAPEUTIC PRESENCE TO ALL RELATIONSHIPS

Your hand opens and closes and opens and closes.
If it were always a fist or always stretched open,
you would be paralyzed.
Your deepest presence is in every small contracting and expanding,
the two as beautifully balanced and coordinated
as birdwings.

—Rumi (trans. 1995, p. 174)[1]

As Rumi so eloquently wrote, the dance of presence is one of immersing and expanding, moving in rhythm with our clients and within ourselves. Our awareness moves fluidly with the moment, always guided by what is truly in service of our clients' healing. This commitment to being steady within yourself, yet feeling deeply with your clients, invites a safety to the relationship that is healing in and of itself. Yet it goes beyond just the healing in connection, as effective responses and interventions emerge naturally when you listen to the moment.

This journey of relating with presence is a lifetime's work. I hope that engaging with this book and its practices has given you a deeper understanding of how practicing presence supports change, and you feel equipped with the tools and skills to strengthen your presence both in therapy sessions and in your daily life and relationships.

---

[1]From *The Essential Rumi* (p. 174), trans. C. Barks, 1995, New York, NY: HarperCollins. Copyright 1995 by Coleman Barks. Reprinted with permission.

http://dx.doi.org/10.1037/0000025-013
*A Practical Guide to Cultivating Therapeutic Presence*, by S. M. Geller

## PRESENCE IS POSSIBLE WITH INTENTION AND PRACTICE

Practice makes presence. It is trainable, as witnessed in (a) several workshops and courses I have offered in which people have experienced a change in their ability to be grounded, connected, and open in the therapeutic relationship and (b) extensive research illustrating the brain changes that occur when engaging in practices that cultivate presence (Hölzel et al., 2011; Lazar et al., 2005; see also Chapter 3, this volume). Presence practices, such as mindfulness, balance the autonomic nervous system and support the ability to take in the depths of the client's pain with greater intimacy and less reactivity. Practices of self-attunement create a neural state of integration that forms the basis for receptive awareness and attunement to the other. They also enhance interoception, including your ability to inwardly sense the experiences of others. Being present with others evokes safety, which is the most important mediator for growth and change (Geller & Porges, 2014).

Therapeutic presence and the depth of relationships it produces require a level of openness and intimacy that can feel vulnerable and anxiety provoking. It can be challenging to rely less on a precise plan and more on yourself to listen and respond to the moment. Training in presence needs to include recognition and support for working through these barriers, with practices that induce self-regulation and emotional regulation such as mindfulness and self-compassion meditation. Cultivating positive qualities like love, compassion, equanimity, receptivity, and healthy intimacy is an important part of cultivating presence in relationship. Mastering your inner world in these ways and taking care of yourself are key to strengthening your therapeutic presence.

With intention and commitment, you can deepen the therapeutic relationship in ways that are profoundly healing. Your clients can flourish in the safe encounter with you, while their bodies and brains restore and grow in ways that only this type of connection can activate. Your responses or techniques will be in direct resonance with what is being expressed and needed in the moment, enticing positive therapeutic movement. As a bonus, your own health, well-being, and relationships will benefit from attention to being present, preventing burnout and supporting a therapy practice that is sustainable and vital.

This book is not a call to throw out techniques or minimize interventions. It is an invitation to include therapeutic presence as part of the foundation in strengthening your therapy practice, whatever it may be. In fact, I suggest learning new therapeutic interventions through and through, then throwing out any particular agenda when you walk into the room and relying on your *presence*. It will attune you to the moment and allow your skill in intervention to emerge in response to your clients' readiness to receive, promoting positive change and outcomes.

# SUGGESTIONS FOR COUNSELOR TRAINING

This book is an appeal to include therapeutic presence training as equal value to learning interventions in psychotherapy training, as it can and does enhance the efficacy of therapeutic technique. Psychotherapy training programs would benefit from integrating a foundational training module, to balance the doing mode of therapy with the being mode. I wish to offer a framework for this module that involves a three-pronged approach: (a) a focus on theory of therapeutic presence; (b) clinical role-plays and practice; and (c) in-life practice, including a deepening of presence through retreat and workshops. Let us expand further as to what these steps could offer.

*The theory of therapeutic presence* would include teaching the model, the research, and an explication of the neurophysiological and experiential process involved in creating safety for clients in the therapeutic relationship. This section could include watching video clips of sessions where the therapist is present and not present. The American Psychological Association video *Presence in Psychotherapy* (APA, 2015) could be used as a teaching aid to show therapeutic presence in action via session clips, including a debrief where client and therapist markers of presence are discussed (see the markers in Appendices B and C). Videos by Stephen Porges on compassion and polyvagal theory or Daniel Siegel on interpersonal neurobiology can greatly aid this learning. Clinical vignettes could provoke discussion on presence in the therapeutic encounter and the challenges that ensue.

*Clinical role-plays and practice sessions* can provide the groundwork to develop an ability to attune to self and other in the present moment and deepen the therapeutic relationship. These include the following:

1. Practices to exemplify the different components of therapists' in-body experience of presence (grounding, immersion, expansion, and being with and for the other). An opportunity to practice preparing for presence prior to the session—for example, through intention, visualization, or presession centering—can give trainees a felt sense of how preparing ahead can invite presence to emerge more readily in the moment.
2. Dyadic encounters in which therapists role-play sessions provide opportunities to build attunement skills. These could include attending to the different ways to attune with your client and with yourself in the present moment. Dyadic role-plays would also focus on responding to clients from this attuned place, and practicing listening to the different aspects of experience to guide responses such as emotions, images, breathing patterns, etc. (Information in Chapters 5–6 can provide

guidelines for this step in the training.) Contact with neuro-physiological practices like entrainment breathing and relational mindfulness can be promoted in these dyadic encounters, as well as actual role-play sessions with feedback provided by an observer and "clients."

It is important that the teacher or facilitator be skilled at debriefing these dyad practices for several reasons. First, they can evoke vulnerability and emotions that are important to process. Naming these emotions helps trainees self-regulate. Creating meaning of the experience through discussion also integrates left-brain understanding with right-brain sensations for an integrated learning experience and illustrates the clinical relevance of the experience. Mindful inquiry, which is a method of inquiry offered in mindfulness-based cognitive therapy (Segal, Williams, & Teasdale, 2002), is one method that can help guide this.

*In-life practices* include practicing presence in relationships and in everyday life. These could either happen simultaneously with the first two steps or be ongoing throughout the training program, and might include a daily in-life practice project. For the latter, students choose a quality of therapeutic presence that they could benefit from as a part of their personal development (i.e., grounding, self-care, equanimity, compassion). They then come up with a 15- to 20-minute daily practice to build this quality. For example, cultivating grounding may include a daily mindfulness practice or a grounding meditation. Another example could be cultivating receptive listening by sitting down with a grandparent each day to listen without judgment. A past student focused on presence through compassion by pausing to talk with elders, as he would find himself feeling impatient. His empathy and compassion expanded through this practice as he tearfully described the wisdom and relationships he gathered when he showed this respect. Students are also asked to keep a daily reflection journal on their experience and challenges and to write a short paper on their learning and how it relates to their development as therapists. The rich experience of interweaving a daily practice with daily life provides a glimpse of both the challenges and positive neuroplastic change that can occur through intentional practice.

Retreats and workshops that focus on opening to the moment are optional yet highly recommended to strengthen the development of therapeutic presence. Mindfulness workshops and group retreats, particularly with a relational focus, can allow for an opportunity to cultivate relational presence. For example, the Therapeutic Rhythm and Mindfulness (TRM™) program described in Chapter 11 experientially teaches trainees to come into rhythm with self and other, while experimenting with a larger relational presence in a safe group context.

Overall, foundational training needs to take a multipronged approach offered early in counselor training, as it is precedes developing a therapeutic relationship/alliance, empathy training, and training in specific psychotherapeutic techniques (e.g., cognitive behavioral therapy, emotion-focused therapy, psychodynamic approaches, dialectical behavior therapy). Creative modalities, such as art and other music-based programs, can also complement this training.

## Cultivating Presence With Expressive Arts

Engaging in the artistic process can help us to gain a sense of comfort with the unknown. Learning to trust in the process through artistic expression is reminiscent of the trust we need to develop in therapy. We can allow for the unexpressed to take form and for novel responses to emerge only when the canvas is blank, free of expectations. Art in various forms, such as painting on canvas, drawing in a sketchbook, or sculpting, offers rich opportunities to see and experience the world with a beginner's mind, an open heart, and fine-tuned attention without preconceptions. From this place of deep presence with your medium, creativity emerges. Reciprocally, when we are immersed in the artistic endeavor of creating, without attachment to a particular end product, then flow and presence can emerge.

Improvisational theater focuses on cocreating the moment and is a promising adjunct to training. The responsiveness and focus on the here-and-now that this provides can potentially build the experience and neural structures for flexibility and adaptability in relationship. A 16-week course offering improvisational skills to therapists supported this method of heightening key qualities of therapeutic presence, such as receptivity; self-awareness; contact with therapists' own emotions and body sensations; and empathy, spontaneity, ease, and congruence when extending and making contact with clients (Romanelli, Tishby, & Moran, 2015).

## Cultivating Presence With Music

The power of music to change the brain and promote health is an up-and-coming topic in the area of neuroscience and psychology. Music (both listening to and making music) is uniquely effective because it recruits almost every region of the brain (Thompson & Schlaug, 2015). Music can induce various emotional states and promote movement, social engagement, vitality, positive brain functioning, and synchronization of rhythms.

Creating music in rhythm with others heightens the experience of synchronization within our own brains and body, and with those of others (Lindenberger et al., 2009; Sänger, Müller, & Lindenberger, 2012). As described in Chapter 3, musicians who play improvisational music together start to generate shared experience as their internal body and brain rhythms mirror each other in rhythm and tempo. This is a deep way of connecting in the moment in relationship. Experiencing rhythmic synchrony with others through music helps to cultivate the ability to entrain in other types of rhythms too, which is key to relational presence.

TRM™ is an example of a single unified program offering multiple benefits. It invites greater ease in coming into rhythm with our bodies (grounding and centering, attunement with self), while synchronizing with the rhythm of others (attunement with others promoting right brain to right brain communication) and activating a larger sense of connection through group drumming in community with other therapists. Mindfulness instruction is embedded in the program to enhance focus and present-moment awareness, both in traditional forms of meditation and relational practices in group and in everyday life. Both music and art offer us fun, engaging, and effective ways to promote relational presence experientially and neurobiologically.

**Supervision With Presence**

For the psychotherapy trainee to truly experience the fruits of presence, it is important that therapeutic presence and the relational connection between supervisor and supervisee also be infused with presence. If you are a supervisor, then commitment to the value of presence in your own life and practice supports your presence with your trainees as well. This provides both a safe place for their exploration and a model for trainees to experience receiving presence. As with your clients, you must be open to what emerges in the supervisory relationship, attuning to your supervisee and the present moment with acceptance and nonjudgment.

Supervision with presence creates the conditions for your trainee to feel open and safe to express the issues that need addressing. This requires a balance between teaching them technique and offering guidance and allowing for exploration in the present-centered relationship so your trainee can find his or her own answers. Attuning to your supervisee without a preconceived plan or direction, and receiving and listening to his or her experience while creating safety through connection, invites growth and modeling of a relationship infused with presence.

Acknowledging equality and the human-to-human encounter in the supervisory relationship is central to training. It models the kind of present-centered authentic relationship that you want trainees to be able to create with their clients. Through your supervisory presence, willingness to be there as a whole person, and deep listening with and for your trainee, wisdom and direction can emerge.

# PRESENCE BEYOND THE THERAPY ENCOUNTER

Presence is healing in all relationships that involve a human-to-human encounter. As psychologists we can help to facilitate present-centered relationships in other disciplines too. For example, family and child psychologists, school psychologists, and psychologists in interdisciplinary care teams could help to build presence in family, school, and health care settings. Additionally, many psychologists wear multiple hats: You may be a therapist as well as a teacher or a parent, so building presence in your life requires you to consider these roles too. Here are some ways that presence can be beneficial in these important relationships.

## Parenting Presence: Strengthening Parent and Child Relationships

Family therapists who include a focus on relational presence can help foster healthier relationships between parents and children. Parenting presence is about how to be with children—turning your full awareness and self toward them and being able to receive and listen with kindness, compassion, and acceptance. Helping parents to engage with full awareness allows them to more clearly notice their thoughts, feelings, and body sensations, so they can see, hear, and feel their children's experiences more clearly too. The invaluable gift of presence builds children's resilience, helping them to thrive through difficult experiences and to navigate the challenging terrain of growing up (Freedman, 2013). It also strengthens the relationship between parents and children, providing kids with the safety and security to move out into the world. Secure attachment is the basis for a healthy and emotionally resilient child and a strong predictor of emotional health and well-being in adulthood.

A newer movement toward mindfulness for parents offers a way to develop patience, nonjudgment, presence, and deep understanding with children (Duncan, Coatsworth, & Greenberg, 2009; Freedman, 2013; Kabat-Zinn & Kabat-Zinn, 1998; Race, 2013; Siegel & Bryson, 2012; Stiffleman, 2015). It requires parents to intentionally bring moment-to-moment awareness to the parent–child relationship, as well as deep listening, compassion for self and other, and the ability to self-regulate in the relationship (Duncan et al., 2009). This allows space for attuned responses that are skillful and wise, rather than unconscious habitual reactions. A similar focus emerges from emotion-focused therapy for families, which in part offers this same intent with a focus on working through parents' fears and unresolved childhood emotions that get in the way of listening and being present with their children.

Parenting with presence can facilitate healing and growth for parents, as well as for children, by encouraging self-acceptance, self-compassion, emotional and attention-regulating skills, stress reduction skills, and improvements in overall health. Research has shown that mindfulness practice helps parents feel less anxious and stressed, more calm and focused, and more present and helpful (Race, 2013). Parenting offers abundant possibilities for practice, given the many transient moods, experiences, and emotions that can arise with children. It also demonstrates in a poignant way that interconnectedness and interdependence in relationships allow for both parents and children to learn and grow together (Kabat-Zinn & Kabat-Zinn, 1998).

## Teachers' Presence: Creating Optimal Conditions for Learning Through Safety

School psychologists who promote presence can help teachers value this quality in the classroom. Teachers who feel grounded with equanimity, yet connected and immersed, can maintain a steadiness in the classroom so as not be thrown off by the chaotic moments that can occur. Engaging students with kindness, respect, and openness supports the ability to see the strengths within each child. This level of care, focus, attunement, and joining—with individual students and the whole group—helps to create a safe classroom to optimize students' learning and recognize opportune teachable moments (Rodgers & Raider-Roth, 2006).

To do the best job teaching, teachers need their students' brains to be functioning optimally, and children need to feel safe in the classroom for this to occur. Their nervous systems can then calm, which allows for health and growth in a way that is similar to clients' in therapy (Porges, 2015). With presence, teachers are also attuned to their students' needs and capacity in opportune moments—which can differ drastically depending on the subject, the task, and the time of day, among other variables. This present-moment attunement also allows teachers to be aware of how teaching technique and material are impacting students, so both are geared toward optimizing safety and learning. Teachers' presence can create conditions for students to thrive.

In a classroom where the teacher is grounded, connected to the class and to the moment, students can feel heard, respected, and known. This ignites interest, excitement, and motivation, all of which contributes to an energized classroom environment (Hart, 2004). It also creates an atmosphere where spontaneity is valued and students feel free to express themselves (Solloway, 2000). Students can ask questions without embarrassment and share feelings and views that differ from those of their peers, without worry about judgment or intimidation. This environment supports the most meaningful interactions for both teachers and students, as students develop their own sense of identity as a person and in relationship with others.

Education for teachers is mostly focused on the development of skills and acquisition of information. However, education needs to focus too on developing the person and his or her own presence, including the ability to focus in environments that may, at times, be chaotic. If teachers are to cultivate and practice presence, they also need their working environment to support this. School psychologists could help teachers learn how to develop their own presence and self-care through workshops and programs designed for this purpose. This structured programming could help teachers feel less isolated in their own efforts to develop their presence in the classroom and provide a space for meaningful resource sharing and collaboration. Helping teachers to understand how they can use themselves to embrace uncertainty and flexibly respond to what emerges in the moment will also help them adjust lessons plans to best meet the needs of students (Mayes, 1998). Learning self-care and remaining grounded and centered in the classroom setting would also provide teachers sustainability in a demanding profession.

## Physicians' Presence: Improving Doctor–Patient Relationships and Outcomes

Physician presence involves being attentive, present, and attuned to patients. Presence can reduce burn-out for medical professionals and evoke healthy doctor–patient relationships. Physicians who have positive relational styles, demonstrated through empathy, caring, and attunement, have improved patient outcomes. Recall the earlier study showing that a brief moment of presence and empathy from the physician helped patients with cold symptoms to heal in 2 days versus 3 (in the latter case, doctors were distant and technical in their approach; Rakel et al., 2009). A genuine doctor–patient relationship motivates patients to be more engaged in their own health care, as they feel safer and more trusting of the guidance their physicians offer.

The cultivation of physician presence can enhance empathy and patient trust, which leads to more appropriate prescribing, reduced health care disparities, and lowered health care costs (Krasner et al., 2009). Doctors' presence can also improve diagnostic impressions, as they attend more closely to what the patient is saying and what the patient's body is expressing. Lack of presence can cause medical errors and poor outcomes (R. M. Epstein, 2003). Misdiagnosis can result from inattention to the subtle cues within patients' verbal and bodily expression of symptoms. An objective and rote response or intervention can lead to ineffective treatment options. By listening deeply to the patient and to one's own self in resonance with the patient in the moment, what is going on for the patient and what they need will emerge (R. M. Epstein, 2003).

Psychologists in interdisciplinary care teams can provide workshops for health care staff to support their cultivation of presence and well-being. The importance of the relational aspect of health care is generally undervalued at the government level with respect to a lack of training in this capacity and cut backs and high demands for doctors to see many patients in a short time. In fact, research has suggested that physicians are at greater risk of burnout than workers of the same age group in other professions (Shanafelt et al., 2012). Ironically, this pressure and stress interferes with doctors' ability to meet their patients' pain in direct human-to-human encounters, which affects quality of care (and patients' experience of feeling heard and cared about) and increases health costs.

Training doctors to be present and empathic can decrease patients' distress around their illness, improving their health and reducing demands on the health care system. It is also helpful for the physician's self-care. Training in present-centered attention is associated with reduced stress, depression, anxiety, and burnout and improvements in overall well-being and resiliency for primary care physicians (Fortney, Luchterhand, Zakletskaia, Zgierska, & Rakel, 2013). Psychologists can help physicians and medical staff to focus on presence and self-care and educate them on how this can be a valuable resource for their well-being and for the benefit of their patients.

## CONTINUING THE JOURNEY . . .

This shift in priority to being before doing, relating rather than reacting, interdependence over independence, and connecting over correcting requires a paradigm shift in our day-to-day living and relationships. We need to be actively aware of the fears, busyness, and what pulls us away from being in the moment, so that we can bring our receptive awareness to others and ourselves. Engaging with presence is the key to letting your clients feel safe in your present arms, allowing the relationship between you to expand and strengthening your ability to respond effectively.

The power of presence is in the pause and with compassionate and kind awareness. Pausing allows us to see, hear, feel, and experience with greater acuity. It also allows us to reconnect with ourselves, so we can make conscious choices on how we want to respond or proceed in the next moment. This has application beyond moments of presence with our clients. It helps us slow down enough to care for ourselves and foster fulfilling lives while, paradoxically, being more effective. My learning of this is ongoing, as I have been completing this book in Mexico to put aside clinical and other demands and be present to the writing process. Yet, in the pressure of timelines, I lost sight of the beauty around me. After I spent the morning pausing, taking in the sounds of the waves, the expansive sky, the details in the blush-colored shell on the ground, I felt more able to return to this chapter and say what I really wanted, to write with more flow and ease, and to feel healthier and more nourished.

As with your therapeutic relationships, presence allows your personal relationships to flourish too. Through deep listening and present-centered relating, your loved ones can feel heard, felt, and safe, and the relationship can open to new depths. Try and explore the impact you have on them when you pick up your cell phone while they are speaking, or glaze over with distraction from your own flurry of planning or worrying thoughts. You may begin to notice how they respond by disconnecting too, and how your relationships may be suffering. Relationships with presence are fulfilling and meaningful, yet not easy. You must attend to your unresolved hurt and pain, which can create distance when ignored, like the wedge that countertransference drives between therapist and client. Being present means recognizing and expressing your authentic experience, with kindness, and also listening to how you may have hurt those you care about, so that the barriers can dissipate and the connection can deepen.

Pause to reflect now: Who in your life have you felt distant from? Who would you like to show up for more, to listen to more deeply, and share more fully with about how you feel? The chasm may feel great, yet it can be bridged with presence. Creating safe relationships can be your greatest tool, to have a life that thrives and relationships that deepen and grow. This nourishment of your own life and relationships is a direct gift for your clients.

Presence offers a healing way of relating to our broader society and planet as well. We are in a time when resources are being depleted at a rapid pace, resulting in climate changes that are unsettling. This is in part due to the quick pace and disposable attitude that we live with, unaware of the impact our actions have on future generations, or at least unwilling to be inconvenienced by making changes. In pausing and considering our impact, we can make conscious choices, however small, that are grounded in awareness of reality and our values. The power of pausing and becoming aware is boundless, as we can discover infinite choices for living more meaningful lives and having our relationships injected with greater vitality and joy. As discussed in Chapter 11, what we infuse with presence transcends itself to something larger. Relational presence offers a portal to a larger spiritual plane. This invites greater meaning in our lives and brings interconnection with others and with our larger world—so we are living fully in connection, not in isolation.

Change begins with each of us, with the recognition that our clients, our own relationships and lives, and our wider society and planet can benefit from the safety and kindness that presence offers. This very moment is an opportunity to pause, invite presence, and recognize that such opportunities are always available, where we can make a choice that influences the next in profound ways. Thank you for traveling this way together. May your journey with presence continue and infuse all of your relationships, both professionally and personally, having ripple effects on society and our planet as a whole.

## TRANSITION PRACTICE: TAKING IT WITH YOU

- Pause now to take a few deep breaths.
- Ask yourself if there is something you wish to take with you from what you read, into your life or even just into the next moment.
- Invite a word or phrase to arise that captures your experience and intention in this moment.
- Letting that go, proceed to the resources offered next or to the rest of your day.

# APPENDIX A: ADDITIONAL RESOURCES FOR CULTIVATING PRESENCE

## ONLINE PROGRAMS FOR CULTIVATING PRESENCE

The following online workshops are different series to help you cultivate qualities of presence.

- Awakening Joy: https://www.awakeningjoy.info
- Mindsight: https://www.mindsightinstitute.com/
- NeuroScience, Mindfulness, and Psychotherapy: http://www.nicabm.com
- Foundations of Well-Being: http://fwb.rickhanson.net

## GUIDED MINDFULNESS AND SELF-COMPASSION MEDITATIONS (AUDIO)

These are guided meditations to supplement your mindfulness and self-compassion practice to cultivate presence. Some are downloadable so you can listen on your audio device.

- http://www.freemindfulness.org/download
- https://www.tarabrach.com/guided-meditations/
- http://marc.ucla.edu/body.cfm?id=22
- http://franticworld.com/free-meditations-from-mindfulness/
- http://elishagoldstein.com/ecourses/basics-of-mindfulness-meditation/resources/
- http://www.mindfulselfcompassion.org/meditations_downloads.php
- http://self-compassion.org/category/exercises/#guided-meditations
- http://www.sharigeller.ca/cd.php

## APPS FOR MEDITATION (FOR YOUR SMARTPHONE TO REALLY BE SMART!)

This is a way to use technology in a positive way. Instead of your phone being a distraction or way of disconnecting, you can use it to promote your presence practice. These apps range from brief to longer meditation practices, for adults and teens, and include an aid for sleep.

- Insight Timer: https://insighttimer.com/
- Calm: http://www.calm.com/
- Headspace: https://www.headspace.com
- Stop, Breathe, and Think: http://stopbreathethink.org
- Sitting Still (for adolescents): http://www.mindapps.se/nyhet.php?id=19
- For Sleep: http://www.healthjourneys.com/Store/Healthy-Sleep/4

## E-NEWSLETTER WITH SUPPORTIVE PRACTICES

You can sign up for the following newsletters to get daily or weekly tips for cultivating presence.

- Just One Thing: http://www.rickhanson.net/writings/just-one-thing/
- Weekly Now Effect: http://elishagoldstein.com/the-mindful-living-community/
- Happify: http://my.happify.com
- Mindful Practice Daily Reminder (MPDR): http://www.mpdr.ca
- Tips for Cultivating Presence: http://www.sharigeller.ca

## INTERESTING AND INFORMATIVE VIDEOS

These brief and longer videos provide both a fun and an informative way of gaining information on the value of presence.

- Multi-Tasking as a Barrier to Presence: http://www.youtube.com/watch?v=KzbxpzKwDXA&sns=em
- Empathy Fuels Connection: https://www.thersa.org/discover/videos/rsa-shorts/2013/12/Brene-Brown-on-Empathy/
- Your Body Language Shapes Who You Are: https://www.ted.com/talks/amy_cuddy_your_body_language_shapes_who_you_are?language=en
- Compassion and Polyvagal Theory: https://www.youtube.com/watch?v=MYXa_BX2cE8

# APPENDIX B: MARKERS OF THERAPISTS' PRESENCE

There are particular bodily expressions, or somatic markers, that help to recognize therapists' communicated presence as well as clients' experience of safety. Markers are experiential indicators that can help you assess your own presence, how safe your clients feel, and how they receive you (see Appendix C for client markers).

Markers for therapists' presence allow you to recognize and fine-tune the physiological ways you can express presence or to notice if you are absent so you can adjust. A model of expressed therapeutic presence partially informs these (Colosimo & Pos, 2015). It can be helpful to understand presence itself by understanding its component parts and whether they are being displayed. You can also view a demonstration and discussion of markers of therapeutic presence in the American Psychological Association video *Presence in Psychotherapy* (APA, 2015). Markers of therapists' presence include the following:

**Body**
- Leaning slightly forward, toward client
- Relaxed and in open posture, faced toward the client
- Posture—open, grounded—relaxed yet alert
- Ability to shift when out of presence—realigning with a grounded, relaxed, and alert posture
- Level of arousal in synch with clients

**Face**
- Soft yet interested, open and curious facial expression
- Caring through soft eyes and facial expression
- Ear turning toward the client when trying to understand
- Soft yet open eye gaze
- Head nodding or facial expressions that are in synch with client narrative

**Vocal quality**
- Prosody of voice—in a rhythmic pattern (not monotone)
- Vocal tone shows interest and with space to listen
- Adjusting moment to moment the vocal quality or responses in synch with clients (i.e., quieting or quickening in synch with clients' voice or expression)

**Attentional qualities**
- Visual focus on client
- Responses clearly aligned with clients' experience
- Ability to maintain details of clients' experience and history

**Verbal responses**

- Responses attuned to the present moment (could include now statements—"Notice your experience right now . . ." or present reflections "What I hear you saying is . . ." or "What I just noticed was . . .")
- Responses on leading edge (not far behind or ahead of what client is expressing)
- Minimal encouraging responses attuned to the moment ("right," "um-hum")

## THERAPIST MARKERS OF ABSENCE

**Body**

- Signs of distractibility (looking at clock, looking away for extended time)
- Physical signs of distance (body tightness or pulled back)
- Frequent shifting of body, fidgety, checking the time
- Tension in body, crossing of arms and legs, tightness

**Face**

- Flat or nonresponsive expression
- Tension in face indicating fear or annoyance or rejection
- Signs of boredom or fatigue (drowsy, yawning, eyes glazed or heavy)
- Eyes wide open (shock) or tight, shifty
- Frequent head nodding or shaking not in resonance with clients' expressions
- Breaking eye contact
- Turning to check the clock frequently

**Vocal quality**

- Vocal tone, pitch, and rhythm (high, loud, fast, or monotone)
- Vocal quality not in synch with clients' tempo or narrative (choppy, delayed)
- Tone of annoyance, agitation, or disinterest

**Verbal responses**

- Minimal encourager or head nod automatic and not in synch with clients' expression or narrative
- Responses that are not in synch with clients' narrative (delayed, off topic, repetitive, not reflective of clients' experience)
- Responses interruptive or talking over clients speech
- Failure to respond to clients' expressions when appropriate, nonresponse to questions

# APPENDIX C: MARKERS OF CLIENTS' SAFETY

Client markers tell you about how safe your clients feel. They occur pan theoretically, across therapies. Whether it is a cognitive–behavioral therapy intervention, an emotion-focused therapeutic task, or an empathic exploration, markers help you determine (a) your clients' readiness to engage in a particular therapeutic intervention and (b) how particular responses or interventions are received. The following is a list of client markers of safety that reflect clinical experience, training, and research:

### Body
- Clients more present in their body, posture open, relaxed
- Settling, relaxed, open, signs that the person is becoming more in contact with self in the moment

### Breath
- Breath deepens and slows; a deep breath or sigh following a response or an intervention indicates a shift or feeling understood

### Face
- Eye gaze and face soften, or eye gaze internal and/or connected with the therapist

### Vocal quality
- Voice softens and deepens; a slow pace between words indicates the client is in a reflective mode, connected to his or her emotional state

### Verbal responses
- Focused on further exploration of experience; in synch with response from therapist

## CLIENT MARKERS OF NONSAFETY

### Body
- Arms or legs tightly crossed and body is tense; there may be rigidity or shifting around, signs of being distracted

### Breath
- Breath is shallow and irregular; breathing is at the upper part of the diaphragm

**Face**

- Tightness in face
- Jaw clenched
- Eye gaze narrow or shifting around, not connected with the therapist
- Expression flat with minimal expression
- Fatigue indicated by yawning, eyes glazed over, eyelids heavy
- Signs of boredom or fatigue (drowsy, yawning, eyes glazed or heavy)
- Minimal eye contact or eyes wide open

**Vocal quality**

- Voice tone, pitch, and rhythm is high, loud, fast, or monotone
- Agitation in tone of voice or distant and trailing off

**Verbal responses**

- At a surface level
- Not talking
- Talking over the therapist
- Nonresponsive

# APPENDIX D: A MODEL FOR OPTIMIZING PRESENCE IN YOUR THERAPY SESSION

This model offers a consolidated version of what was explored in the clinical chapters (4–6). I offer this as a supportive tool to draw on, as a brief step-wise guide for infusing your therapy sessions with presence.

- **Presession**—Five-minute grounding practice; PRESENCE acronym
- **Beginning of session**
  - Approaching clients with openness and receptivity, bracketing preconceptions, therapy plans, agendas for session
  - Tuning into clients, inviting a mindful moment to arrive into the moment together
- **In session**
  - Receptively listening to your clients, attuning and taking in their experience with acceptance, curiosity, and interest
  - Reading clients' experience moment to moment, verbally and nonverbally what they are expressing, their vocal quality, gestures, breathing patterns, noticing what is poignant for them or when they are shutting down
  - Attuning to yourself, listening inwardly to how the clients' issues are resonating inside, what is emerging in relation to what they are sharing
    - Checking in when not present and inviting yourself to reset your attention and return to the moment
  - Responding or offering an intervention based on what you are receiving from your clients and attuning inwardly to within yourself
  - Reading and attuning with your clients as to how responses/ interventions are landing on them, being received (also reading their readiness to receive a response or intervention)
  - Keeping an eye or therapeutic pulse on the emotional quality of their experience and on the relationship itself; noticing if they feel open and safe with you, or shut down
  - Entraining your breath to their breath if you want to read their experience and connect more deeply; alternatively inviting a slightly slower breathing pattern in yourself that they can nonverbally attune to if you are helping to calm or regulate

- **Closing session**—mindful moment together with clients to absorb what clients have learned, inviting an intention for postsession (homework); also to release or put aside any unfinished emotions or challenges from session knowing they will come back or continue to take care of them
- **Transition** to next session or part of your day
    - Few moments to consciously/intentionally close session internally (finish notes, release residual emotions or tensions you may be carrying from session, wishing clients well as you release image/feelings/experience of them)
    - Reenter/ground; PRESENCE acronym
    - Step into the next moment (new client, lunch break, end of day, etc.)

# REFERENCES

Allison, K. L., & Rossouw, P. J. (2013). The therapeutic alliance: Exploring the concept of "safety" from a neuropsychotherapeutic perspective. *International Journal of Neuropsychotherapy, 1*, 21–29. http://dx.doi.org/10.12744/ijnpt.2013.0021-0029

Allman, J. M., Tetreault, N. A., Hakeem, A. Y., Manaye, K. F., Semendeferi, K., Erwin, J. M., . . . Hof, P. R. (2011). The von Economo neurons in the fronto-insular and anterior cingulate cortex. *Annals of the New York Academy of Sciences, 1225*, 59–71. http://dx.doi.org/10.1111/j.1749-6632.2011.06011.x

American Psychological Association (Producer). (2015). *Presence in psychotherapy* [DVD]. Available from http://www.apa.org/pubs/videos/4310927.aspx

Angus, L. E., & Greenberg, L. S. (2011). *Working with narrative in emotion focused therapy: Changing stories, healing lives.* Washington, DC: American Psychological Association. http://dx.doi.org/10.1037/12325-000

Bacal, H. A., & Newman, K. M. (1990). *Theories of object relations: Bridges to self psychology.* New York, NY: Columbia University Press.

Baldini, L. L., Parker, S. C., Nelson, B. W., & Siegel, D. J. (2014). The clinician as neuroarchitect: The importance of mindfulness and presence in clinical practice. *Clinical Social Work Journal, 42*, 218–227. http://dx.doi.org/10.1007/s10615-014-0476-3

Baldwin, M. (2000). Interview with Carl Rogers on the use of the self in therapy. In M. Baldwin (Ed.), *The use of self in therapy* (2nd ed., pp. 29–38). New York, NY: Haworth Press.

Bar, M. (2007). The proactive brain: Using analogies and associations to generate predictions. *Trends in Cognitive Sciences, 11*, 280–289. http://dx.doi.org/10.1016/j.tics.2007.05.005

Barrett-Lennard, G. T. (1981). The empathy cycle: Refinement of a nuclear concept. *Journal of Counseling Psychology, 28*, 91–100. http://dx.doi.org/10.1037/0022-0167.28.2.91

Beautement, P., & Broenner, C. (2011). *Complexity demystified: A guide for practitioners.* Exeter, England: Triarchy Press.

Begley, S. (2008). *Train your mind, change your brain: How a new science reveals our extraordinary potential to transform ourselves.* New York, NY: Ballantine Books.

Behrends, A., Müller, S., & Dziobek, I. (2012). Moving in and out of synchrony: A concept for a new intervention fostering empathy through interactional movement and dance. *The Arts in Psychotherapy, 39*, 107–116. http://dx.doi.org/10.1016/j.aip.2012.02.003

Ben Ami, N. (2012). *The relationship between therapeutic presence, as measured by an independent observer, and the therapeutic alliance and treatment outcome* (Unpublished master's thesis). Hebrew University of Jerusalem, Israel.

Beutler, L. E., Malik, M., Alimohamed, S., Harwood, T. M., Talebi, H., Nobel, S., & Wong, E. (2004). Therapist variables. In M. J. Lambert (Ed.), *Bergin and Garfield's handbook of psychotherapy and behavior change* (5th ed., pp. 227–306). New York, NY: Wiley.

Bittman, B., Berk, L., Shannon, M., Sharaf, M., Westengard, J., Guegler, K. J., & Ruff, D. W. (2005). Recreational music-making modulates the human stress response: A preliminary individualized gene expression strategy. *Medical Science Monitor, 11*(2), BR31–BR40.

Bittman, B. B., Snyder, C., Bruhn, K. T., Liebfreid, F., Stevens, C. K., Westengard, J., & Umbach, P. O. (2004). Recreational music-making: An integrative group intervention for reducing burnout and improving mood states in first year associate degree nursing students: Insights and economic impact. *International Journal of Nursing Education Scholarship, 1*(1), e12.

Blakeslee, S., & Blakeslee, M. (2007). *The body has a mind of its own.* New York, NY: Random House.

Bogels, S., & Restifo, K. (2014). *Mindful parenting: A guide for mental health practitioners.* New York, NY: W. W. Norton. http://dx.doi.org/10.1007/978-1-4614-7406-7

Booth, D., & Hachiya, M. (2004). *The arts go to school.* Markham, Ontario, Canada: Pembroke.

Bordin, E. S. (1979). The generalizability of the psychoanalytic concept of the working alliance. *Psychotherapy: Theory, Research & Practice, 16*, 252–260. http://dx.doi.org/10.1037/h0085885

Boritz, T. Z., Bryntwick, E., Angus, L., Greenberg, L. S., & Constantino, M. J. (2014). Narrative and emotion process in psychotherapy: An empirical test of the Narrative-Emotion Process Coding System (NEPCS). *Psychotherapy Research, 24*, 594–607. http://dx.doi.org/10.1080/10503307.2013.851426

Bourgault, M., & Dionne, F. (2016, April). *Therapeutic presence and mindfulness: Mediating role of self-compassion and psychological distress amongst psychologists.* Paper presented at the annual meeting of the SQRP, Trois-Rivières, Québec, Canada.

Bourne, E. (2005). *The anxiety and phobia workbook* (4th ed.). Oakland, CA: New Harbinger.

Buber, M. (1958). *I and Thou* (2nd ed.). New York, NY: Charles Scribner's Sons.

Buber, M. (1965). *Between man and man.* New York, NY: Macmillan.

Bugental, J. F. T. (1978). *Psychotherapy and process.* Menlo Park, CA: Addison-Wesley.

Bugental, J. F. T. (1983). The one absolute necessity in psychotherapy. *The Script, 13*, 1–2.

Bugental, J. F. T. (1987). *The art of the psychotherapist.* New York, NY: W. W. Norton.

Burklund, L. J., Creswell, J. D., Irwin, M. R., & Lieberman, M. D. (2014). The common and distinct neural bases of affect labeling and reappraisal in healthy adults. *Frontiers in Psychology, 5*, 221. http://doi.org/10.3389/fpsyg.2014.00221

Butler, E. A., & Randall, A. K. (2013). Emotional coregulation in close relationships. *Emotion Review, 5*, 202–210. http://dx.doi.org/10.1177/1754073912451630

Cahn, B. R., & Polich, J. (2006). Meditation states and traits: EEG, ERP, and neuroimaging studies. *Psychological Bulletin, 132*, 180–211. http://dx.doi.org/10.1037/0033-2909.132.2.180

Carr, L., Iacoboni, M., Dubeau, M. C., Mazziotta, J. C., & Lenzi, G. L. (2003). Neural mechanisms of empathy in humans: A relay from neural systems for imitation to limbic areas. *Proceedings of the National Academy of Sciences, USA, 100*, 5497–5502. http://dx.doi.org/10.1073/pnas.0935845100

Carter, C. S. (2014). Oxytocin pathways and the evolution of human behavior. *Annual Review of Psychology, 65*, 17–39. http://dx.doi.org/10.1146/annurev-psych-010213-115110

Chevalier, G., Sinatra, S. T., Oschman, J. L., Sokal, K., & Sokal, P. (2012). Earthing: Health implications of reconnecting the human body to the Earth's surface electrons. *Journal of Environmental and Public Health, 2012*, 291541.

Clottey, K. (2004). *Mindful drumming: Ancient wisdom for unleashing the human spirit and building community.* Oakland, CA: Sankofa.

Coleman, M. (2006). *Awake in the wild: Mindfulness in nature as a path of self-discovery.* Maui, HI: Inner Ocean.

Coleman, P., Vallacher, R., Nowak, A., & Bui-Wrzosinska, L. (2007). Intractable conflict as an attractor: A dynamical systems approach to conflict escalation and intractability. *American Behavioral Scientist, 50*, 1454–1475. http://dx.doi.org/10.1177/0002764207302463

Collard, P. (2007). Skillful means at the intersection of neuropsychology and the contemplative disciplines: Patrizia Collard interviews Rick Hanson and Richard Mendius. *Counselling Psychology Quarterly, 20*, 169–175. http://dx.doi.org/10.1080/09515070701405930

Colosimo, K. A., & Pos, A. W. (2015). A rational model of expressed therapeutic presence. *Journal of Psychotherapy Integration, 25*, 100–114. http://dx.doi.org/10.1037/a0038879

Cooper, M. (2005). Therapists' experiences of relational depth: A qualitative interview study. *Counselling & Psychotherapy Research, 5*(2), 87–95.

Corem, S. (2013). *The influence of therapeutic presence and patient attachment style on patients' reaction to creative process* (Unpublished master's thesis). University of Haifa, Israel.

Coster, J. S., & Schwebel, M. (1997). Well-functioning in professional psychologists. *Professional Psychology: Research and Practice, 28*, 5–13. http://dx.doi.org/10.1037/0735-7028.28.1.5

Covey, S. R. (2004). *7 habits of highly effective people.* New York, NY: Free Press.

Cozolino, L. J. (2006). *The neuroscience of relationships: Attachment and the developing social brain.* New York, NY: W. W. Norton.

Critchley, H. D., Wiens, S., Rotshtein, P., Öhman, A., & Dolan, R. J. (2004). Neural systems supporting interoceptive awareness. *Nature Neuroscience, 7*, 189–195. http://dx.doi.org/10.1038/nn1176

Csikszentmihalyi, M. (1996). *Creativity: Flow and the psychology of discovery and invention*. New York, NY: HarperCollins.

Cunningham, I. (1992). The impact of leaders: Who they are and what they do. *Leadership & Organization Development Journal, 13*(2), 7–10. http://dx.doi.org/10.1108/01437739210009554

Dajani, D. R., & Uddin, L. Q. (2015). Demystifying cognitive flexibility: Implications for clinical and developmental neuroscience. *Trends in Neurosciences, 38*, 571–578. http://dx.doi.org/10.1016/j.tins.2015.07.003

Damasio, A. (1999). *The feeling of what happens: Body and emotion in the making of consciousness*. New York, NY: Harcourt Brace.

Damasio, A. (2005). *Descartes' error: Emotion, reason, and the human brain*. New York, NY: Penguin Books.

Dass, R., & Bush, M. (1995). *Compassion in action: Setting out on a path of service* (2nd ed.). New York, NY: Knopf.

Davidson, R. J., & Lutz, A. (2008). Buddha's brain: Neuroplasticity and meditation. *IEEE Signal Processing Magazine, 25*, 176–174. http://dx.doi.org/10.1109/MSP.2008.4431873

Davis, B. (2013, July 23). *There are 50,000 thoughts standing between you and your partner every day!* Retrieved from http://www.huffingtonpost.com/bruce-davis-phd/healthy-relationships_b_3307916.html

Desmond, T. (2016). *Self-compassion in psychotherapy: Mindfulness-based practices for healing and transformation*. New York, NY: W. W. Norton.

Diamond, J. (1999). *The way of the pulse: Drumming with spirit*. Bloomingdale, IL: Enhancement Books.

Dietrich, A. (2004). Neurocognitive mechanisms underlying the experience of flow. *Consciousness and Cognition, 13*, 746–761. http://dx.doi.org/10.1016/j.concog.2004.07.002

Ditto, B., Eclache, M., & Goldman, N. (2006). Short-term autonomic and cardiovascular effects of mindfulness body scan meditation. *Annals of Behavioral Medicine, 32*, 227–234. http://dx.doi.org/10.1207/s15324796abm3203_9

Doidge, N. (2007). *The brain that changes itself: Stories of personal triumph from the frontiers of brain science*. New York, NY: Viking Books.

Doidge, N. (2015). *The brain's way of healing*. New York, NY: Penguin.

Duncan, L. G., Coatsworth, J. D., & Greenberg, M. T. (2009). A model of mindful parenting: Implications for parent–child relationships and prevention research. *Clinical Child and Family Psychology Review, 12*, 255–270. http://dx.doi.org/10.1007/s10567-009-0046-3

Dunn, R., Callahan, J. L., Swift, J. K., & Ivanovic, M. (2013). Effects of pre-session centering for therapists on session presence and effectiveness. *Psychotherapy Research, 23*, 78–85. http://dx.doi.org/10.1080/10503307.2012.731713

Durrer, M., & Rohrbach, U. (2013). *Therapeutic presence: Therapeutic presence in osteopathy: A qualitative research to prepare the base for an evaluation model of therapeutic presence in osteopathic treatments* (Unpublished doctoral dissertation). Swiss International College of Osteopathy, Switzerland.

Efron, D. (1941). *Gesture and environment.* New York, NY: King's Crown Press.

Ekman, P. (1972). Universals and cultural differences in facial expressions of emotion. In J. Cole (Ed.), *Nebraska Symposium on Motivation, 1971* (Vol. 19, pp. 207–282). Lincoln: University of Nebraska Press.

Ekman, P. (1977). Biological and cultural contributions to body and facial movement. In J. Blacking (Ed.), *Anthropology of the body* (pp. 39–84). New York, NY: Academic Press.

Ekman, P. (2003). *Emotions revealed: Recognizing faces and feelings to improve communication and emotional life.* New York, NY: Owl Books.

Ekman, P., & Friesen, W. V. (1969). The repertoire of nonverbal behavior: Categories, origins, usage, and coding. *Semiotica, 1,* 49–98. http://dx.doi.org/10.1515/semi.1969.1.1.49

Elfenbein, H. A., & Ambady, N. (2003). Universals and cultural differences in recognizing emotions. *Current Directions in Psychological Science, 12*(5), 159–164. http://dx.doi.org/10.1111/1467-8721.01252

Epel, E., Daubenmier, J., Moskowitz, J. T., Folkman, S., & Blackburn, E. (2009). Can meditation slow rate of cellular aging? Cognitive stress, mindfulness, and telomeres. *Annals of the New York Academy of Sciences, 1172,* 34–53. http://dx.doi.org/10.1111/j.1749-6632.2009.04414.x

Epstein, M. (2007). *Psychotherapy without the self: A Buddhist perspective.* London, England: Yale University Press.

Epstein, R. M. (2003). Mindful practice in action (1): Technical competence evidence based medicine and relationship-centered care. *Families, Systems & Health, 21,* 1–9. http://dx.doi.org/10.1037/h0089494

Erskine, R. G. (2015). *Relational patterns, therapeutic presence: Concepts and practice of integrative psychotherapy.* London, England: Karnac Books.

Escuriex, B. F., & Labbé, E. E. (2011). Health care providers' mindfulness and treatment outcomes: A critical review of the research literature. *Mindfulness, 2,* 242–253. http://dx.doi.org/10.1007/s12671-011-0068-z

Eysenck, M. W., Derakshan, N., Santos, R., & Calvo, M. G. (2007). Anxiety and cognitive performance: Attentional control theory. *Emotion, 7,* 336–353. http://dx.doi.org/10.1037/1528-3542.7.2.336

Fairbairn, W. R. D. (1952). *Psychoanalytic studies of the personality.* London, England: Routledge & Kegan Paul.

Farb, N. A. S., Segal, Z. V., & Anderson, A. K. (2013). Mindfulness meditation training alters cortical representations of interoceptive attention. *Social Cognitive and Affective Neuroscience, 8,* 15–26. http://dx.doi.org/10.1093/scan/nss066

Faulds, D. (2002). *Go in and in: Poems from the heart of yoga.* Greenville, NC: Peaceable Kingdom Books.

Ferrari, P. F., & Rizzolatti, G. (2014). Mirror neuron research: The past and the future. *Philosophical Transactions of the Royal Society B: Biological Sciences, 369*(1644), 20130169. http://dx.doi.org/10.1098/rstb.2013.0169

Figley, C. R. (2002). Compassion fatigue: Psychotherapists' chronic lack of self care. *Journal of Clinical Psychology, 58,* 1433–1441. http://dx.doi.org/10.1002/jclp.10090

Fischer, F., Hunziker, M., Lüscher, T., & Eggenberger, N. (2013). *A German translation of the Therapeutic Presence Inventory.* Unpublished manuscript, Sankt Georgen Graduate School of Philosophy and Theology, Frankfurt, Germany.

Fishbane, M. D. (2007). Wired to connect: Neuroscience, relationships, and therapy. *Family Process, 46,* 395–412. http://dx.doi.org/10.1111/j.1545-5300.2007.00219.x

Flynn, F. G. (1999). Anatomy of the insula functional and clinical correlates. *Aphasiology, 13,* 55–78. http://dx.doi.org/10.1080/026870399402325

Fogel, A. (2009). *The psychophysiology of self-awareness: Rediscovering the lost art of body sense.* New York, NY: W. W. Norton.

Forsyth, J. P., & Eifert, G. H. (2007). *The mindfulness and acceptance workbook for anxiety: A guide to breaking free from anxiety, phobias, and worry using acceptance and commitment therapy.* Oakland, CA: New Harbinger.

Fortney, L., Luchterhand, C., Zakletskaia, L., Zgierska, A., & Rakel, D. (2013). Abbreviated mindfulness intervention for job satisfaction, quality of life, and compassion in primary care clinicians: A pilot study. *Annals of Family Medicine, 11,* 412–420. http://dx.doi.org/10.1370/afm.1511

Fox, J. (1995). *Finding what you didn't lose.* New York, NY: TarcherPerigee.

Fox, K. C. R., Dixon, M. L., Nijeboer, S., Girn, M., Floman, J. L., Lifshitz, M., . . . Christoff, K. (2016). Functional neuroanatomy of meditation: A review and meta-analysis of 78 functional neuroimaging investigations. *Neuroscience and Biobehavioral Reviews, 65,* 208–228. http://dx.doi.org/10.1016/j.neubiorev.2016.03.021

Fox, K. C. R., Nijeboer, S., Dixon, M. L., Floman, J. L., Ellamil, M., Rumak, S. P., . . . Christoff, K. (2014). Is meditation associated with altered brain structure? A systematic review and meta-analysis of morphometric neuroimaging in meditation practitioners. *Neuroscience and Biobehavioral Reviews, 43,* 48–73. http://dx.doi.org/10.1016/j.neubiorev.2014.03.016

Freedman, M. L. (2013). *Mindful parents: Resilient children. Principles and practices for clinicians/educators working with parents and children.* Unpublished manuscript.

Freidberg, R. D., Tabbarah, S., & Poggesi, R. M. (2013). Therapeutic presence, immediacy, and transparency in CBT with youth: Carpe the moment! *The Cognitive Behaviour Therapist, 6*(12), 1–10.

Freud, S. (1930). *Civilization and its discontents: Standard edition* (J. Strachey, Trans.). New York, NY: W. W. Norton.

Friedman, M. (1985). *The healing dialogue in psychotherapy.* New York, NY: Aronson.

Friedman, M. (1996). Becoming aware: A dialogical approach to consciousness. *The Humanistic Psychologist, 24,* 203–220. http://dx.doi.org/10.1080/08873267.1996.9986851

Fulton, P. R. (2005). Mindfulness as clinical training. In C. K. Germer, R. D. Siegel, & P. R. Fulton (Eds.), *Mindfulness and psychotherapy* (pp. 55–72). New York, NY: Guilford Press.

Gallese, V. (2003). The roots of empathy: The shared manifold hypothesis and the neural basis of intersubjectivity. *Psychopathology, 36*, 171–180. http://dx.doi.org/10.1159/000072786

Gard, T., Noggle, J. J., Park, C. L., Vago, D. R., & Wilson, A. (2014). Potential self-regulatory mechanisms of yoga for psychological health. *Frontiers in Human Neuroscience, 8*(770), 770.

Gazzola, V., Aziz-Zadeh, L., & Keysers, C. (2006). Empathy and the somatotopic auditory mirror system in humans. *Current Biology, 16*, 1824–1829. http://dx.doi.org/10.1016/j.cub.2006.07.072

Geller, S. M. (2001). *Therapeutic presence: The development of a model and a measure* (Unpublished doctoral dissertation). York University, Toronto, Ontario, Canada.

Geller, S. M. (2003). Becoming whole: A collaboration between experiential psychotherapies and mindfulness meditation. *Person-Centered and Experiential Psychotherapies, 2*, 258–273. http://dx.doi.org/10.1080/14779757.2003.9688319

Geller, S. M. (2009). Cultivation of therapeutic presence: Therapeutic drumming and mindfulness practices. *Dutch Tijdschrift Clientgerichte Psychotherapie (Journal for Client Centered Psychotherapy), 47*, 273–287.

Geller, S. M. (2010). *Clearing the path of therapeutic presence to emerge: Therapeutic rhythm and mindfulness practices*. Unpublished manuscript.

Geller, S. M. (2013a). Therapeutic presence: An essential way of being. In M. Cooper, P. F. Schmid, M. O'Hara, & A. C. Bohart (Eds.), *The handbook of person-centered psychotherapy and counseling* (2nd ed., pp. 209–222). Basingstoke, England: Palgrave Macmillan.

Geller, S. M. (2013b). Therapeutic presence as a foundation for relational depth. In R. Knox, D. Murphy, S. Wiggins, & M. Cooper (Eds.), *Relational depth: Contemporary perspectives* (pp. 175–184). Basingstoke, England: Palgrave Macmillan.

Geller, S. M., & Greenberg, L. S. (2002). Therapeutic presence: Therapists' experience of presence in the psychotherapeutic encounter. *Person-Centered and Experiential Psychotherapies, 1*, 71–86. http://dx.doi.org/10.1080/14779757.2002.9688279

Geller, S. M., & Greenberg, L. S. (2012). *Therapeutic presence: A mindful approach to effective therapy*. Washington, DC: American Psychological Association. http://dx.doi.org/10.1037/13485-000

Geller, S. M., Greenberg, L. S., & Watson, J. C. (2010). Therapist and client perceptions of therapeutic presence: The development of a measure. *Psychotherapy Research, 20*, 599–610. http://dx.doi.org/10.1080/10503307.2010.495957

Geller, S. M., & Porges, S. W. (2014). Therapeutic presence: Neurophysiological mechanisms mediating feeling safe in therapeutic relationships. *Journal of Psychotherapy Integration, 24,* 178–192. http://dx.doi.org/10.1037/a0037511

Geller, S., Pos, A., & Colosimo, K. (2012). Therapeutic presence: A fundamental common factor in the provision of effective psychotherapy. *Psychotherapy Bulletin, 47*(3), 6–13.

Gelso, C. J. (2011). *The real relationship in psychotherapy: The hidden foundation of change.* Washington, DC: American Psychological Association. http://dx.doi.org/10.1037/12349-000

Gelso, C. J., & Hayes, J. A. (2007). *Countertransference and the therapist's inner experience: Perils and possibilities.* Mahwah, NJ: Erlbaum.

Gendlin, E. T. (1962). *Experiencing and the creation of meaning: A philosophical and psychological approach to the subjective.* New York, NY: Free Press of Glencoe.

Gendlin, E. T. (1978). *Focusing.* New York, NY: Everest House.

Gendlin, E. T. (1996). *Focusing oriented psychotherapy: A manual of the experiential method.* New York, NY: Guilford Press.

Germer, C. K. (2009). *The mindful path to self-compassion: Freeing yourself from destructive thoughts and emotions.* New York, NY: Guilford Press.

Germer, C. K. (2012). Cultivating compassion in psychotherapy. In C. K. Germer & R. D. Siegel (Eds.), *Wisdom and compassion in psychotherapy: Deepening mindfulness in clinical practice* (pp. 93–110). New York, NY: Guilford Press.

Germer, C. K., Siegel, R. D., & Fulton, P. R. (Eds.). (2005). *Mindfulness and psychotherapy.* New York, NY: Guilford Press.

Gilbert, P. (2009). *The compassionate mind.* London, England: Constable.

Gilje, F. L. (1993). A phenomenological study of patients' experience of the nurse's presence (Doctoral dissertation, University of Colorado Health Sciences Center). *Dissertation Abstracts International, 54*(08), 4078B. (UMI No. 9401784)

Glenberg, A. M. (2010). Embodiment as a unifying perspective for psychology. *Wiley Interdisciplinary Reviews: Cognitive Science, 1,* 586–596.

Goldfried, M. R., & Davila, J. (2005). The role of relationship and technique in therapeutic change. *Psychotherapy: Theory, Research & Practice, 42,* 421–430. http://dx.doi.org/10.1037/0033-3204.42.4.421

Greenberg, L. S. (2007). Emotion in the therapeutic relationship in emotion focused therapies. In P. Gilbert & R. L. Leahy (Eds.), *The therapeutic relationship in the cognitive behavioral therapies* (pp. 43–62). New York, NY: Routledge.

Greenberg, L. S. (2010). *Emotion-focused therapy.* Washington, DC: American Psychological Association. http://dx.doi.org/10.1037/e602962010-001

Greenberg, L. S., & Geller, S. M. (2001). Congruence and therapeutic presence. In G. Wyatt (Ed.), *Congruence* (pp. 148–166). London, England: PCCS Books.

Greenberg, L. S., Rice, L., & Elliott, R. (1993). *Facilitating emotional change: The moment-by-moment process.* New York, NY: Guilford Press.

Greenberg, L. S., & Rushanski-Rosenberg, R. (2002). Therapist's experience of empathy. In J. C. Watson, R. N. Goldman, & M. S. Warner (Eds.), *Client-centered and experiential psychotherapy in the 21st century: Advances in theory, research and practice* (pp. 168–181). Ross-on-Wye, England: PCCS Books.

Hai, B. P., & Nghiem, S. T. (2010). This is it. In T. N. Hanh & the Monks and Nuns of Plum Village (Eds.), *One Buddha is not enough* (pp. 5–25). Berkeley, CA: Parallax Press.

Halifax, J. (2009). *Being with dying: Cultivating compassion and fearlessness in the presence of death.* Boston, MA: Shambhala.

Hanh, T. N. (2003). *No death, no fear: Comforting wisdom for life.* New York, NY: Riverhead Trade.

Hanson, R., & Mendius, R. (2009). *Buddha's brain: The practical neuroscience of happiness, love, & wisdom.* Oakland, CA: New Harbinger.

Hanson, R., & Mendius, R. (2010). *Meditations to change your brain: Rewire your neural pathways to transform your life* [CD]. Boulder, CO: Sounds True.

Harinath, K., Malhotra, A. S., Pal, K., Prasad, R., Kumar, R., Kain, T. C., . . . Sawhney, R. C. (2004). Effects of Hatha yoga and Omkar meditation on cardiorespiratory performance, psychologic profile, and melatonin secretion. *Journal of Alternative and Complementary Medicine, 10,* 261–268. http://dx.doi.org/ 10.1089/107555304323062257

Hariri, A. R., Bookheimer, S. Y., & Mazziotta, J. C. (2000). Modulating emotional responses: Effects of a neocortical network on the limbic system. *NeuroReport, 11,* 43–48. http://dx.doi.org/10.1097/00001756-200001170-00009

Harris, D. (2014). *10% happier: How I tamed the voice in my head, reduced stress without losing my edge, and found a self-help that actually works—A true story.* New York, NY: HarperCollins.

Hart, T. (2004). Opening the contemplative mind in the classroom. *Journal of Transformative Education, 2,* 28–46. http://dx.doi.org/10.1177/1541344603259311

Harvard Medical School. (2012, May). *Blue light has a dark side.* Retrieved from http://www.health.harvard.edu/staying-healthy/blue-light-has-a-dark-side

Hasson, U., Ghazanfar, A. A., Galantucci, B., Garrod, S., & Keysers, C. (2012). Brain-to-brain coupling: A mechanism for creating and sharing a social world. *Trends in Cognitive Sciences, 16,* 114–121. http://dx.doi.org/10.1016/j.tics.2011.12.007

Hayes, J., & Vinca, J. (2011, June). *Therapist presence and its relationship to empathy, session, depth, and symptom reduction.* Paper presented at the Society for Psychotherapy Research meeting, Bern, Switzerland.

Hayes, J. A., Gelso, C. J., & Hummel, A. M. (2011). Managing countertransference. *Psychotherapy, 48,* 88–97. http://dx.doi.org/10.1037/a0022182

Hebb, D. (1949). *The organization of behavior.* New York, NY: Wiley.

Henckens, M. J., van Wingen, G. A., Joëls, M., & Fernández, G. (2012). Time-dependent effects of cortisol on selective attention and emotional interference: A functional MRI study. *Frontiers in Integrative Neuroscience, 6*(66), 66.

Hill, C. E. (2014). *Helping skills: Facilitating exploration, insight, and action* (4th ed.). Washington, DC: American Psychological Association. http://dx.doi.org/10.1037/10624-000

Hill, C. E., Sim, W., Spangler, P., Stahl, J., Sullivan, C., & Teyber, E. (2008). Therapist immediacy in brief psychotherapy: Case study II. *Psychotherapy: Theory, Research, & Practice, 45,* 298–315. http://dx.doi.org/10.1037/a0013306

Holtforth, M. G., & Castonguay, L. G. (2005). Relationship and techniques in cognitive–behavioral therapy—A motivational approach. *Psychotherapy: Theory, Research, Practice, Training, 42,* 443–445. http://dx.doi.org/10.1037/0033-3204.42.4.443

Hölzel, B. K., Carmody, J., Vangel, M., Congleton, C., Yerramsetti, S. M., Gard, T., & Lazar, S. W. (2011). Mindfulness practice leads to increases in regional brain gray matter density. *Psychiatry Research: Neuroimaging, 191,* 36–43. http://dx.doi.org/10.1016/j.pscychresns.2010.08.006

Hopenwasser, K. (2008). Being in rhythm: Dissociative attunement in therapeutic process. *Journal of Trauma & Dissociation, 9,* 349–367. http://dx.doi.org/10.1080/15299730802139212

Hycner, R. (1993). *Between person and person: Toward a dialogical psychotherapy.* New York, NY: Gestalt Journal Press.

Hycner, R., & Jacobs, L. (1995). *The healing relationship in gestalt therapy: A dialogical/self psychology approach.* New York, NY: Gestalt Journal Press.

Iacoboni, M. (2009a). Imitation, empathy, and mirror neurons. *Annual Review of Psychology, 60,* 653–670. http://dx.doi.org/10.1146/annurev.psych.60.110707.163604

Iacoboni, M. (2009b). *Mirroring people: The science of empathy and how we connect with others.* New York, NY: Picador.

Iacoboni, M., Molnar-Szakacs, I., Gallese, V., Buccino, G., Mazziotta, J. C., & Rizzolatti, G. (2005). Grasping the intentions of others with one's own mirror neuron system. *PLoS Biology, 3,* e79. http://dx.doi.org/10.1371/journal.pbio.0030079

Imel, Z. E., Barco, J. S., Brown, H. J., Baucom, B. R., Baer, J. S., Kircher, J. C., & Atkins, D. C. (2014). The association of therapist empathy and synchrony in vocally encoded arousal. *Journal of Counseling Psychology, 61,* 146–153. http://dx.doi.org/10.1037/a0034943

Isa, T., & Sasaki, S. (2002). Brainstem control of head movements during orienting; organization of the premotor circuits. *Progress in Neurobiology, 66,* 205–241. http://dx.doi.org/10.1016/S0301-0082(02)00006-0

Jacobi, T. (2012, September 15). *Healthy fall foods that ground you.* Retrieved from http://www.mindbodygreen.com/0-6146/Healthy-Fall-Foods-That-Ground-You.html

Jordan, S. (2008). *Practicing presence: Focusing, Buddhist understanding and core process psychotherapy.* Retrieved from http://www.focusing.org.uk/practising_presence.html

Kabat-Zinn, J. (1990). *Full catastrophe living: Using the wisdom of your body and mind to face stress, pain, and illness.* New York, NY: Dell.

Kabat-Zinn, J., & Kabat-Zinn, M. (1998). *Everyday blessings: The inner work of mindful parenting.* New York, NY: Hachette Books.

Kanter, J. W., Rusch, L. C., Landes, S. J., Holman, G. I., Whiteside, U., & Sedivy, S. K. (2009). The use and nature of present-focused interventions in cognitive and behavioral therapies for depression. *Psychotherapy: Theory, Research, Practice, Training, 46,* 220–232. http://dx.doi.org/10.1037/a0016083

Kasper, L., Hill, C. E., & Kivlighan, D. (2008). Therapist immediacy in brief psychotherapy therapy: Case study I. *Psychotherapy: Theory, Research, Practice, Training, 45,* 281–287. http://dx.doi.org/10.1037/a0013305

Kirschner, S., & Tomasello, M. (2010). Joint music making promotes prosocial behavior in 4-year-old children. *Evolution and Human Behavior, 31,* 354–364. http://dx.doi.org/10.1016/j.evolhumbehav.2010.04.004

Klimecki, O., & Singer, T. (2012). Empathic distress fatigue rather than compassion fatigue? Integrating findings from empathy research in psychology and neuroscience. In B. Oakley, A. Knafo, G. Madhavan, & D. S. Wilson (Eds.), *Pathological altruism* (pp. 368–383). New York, NY: Oxford Press.

Knox, S., & Hill, C. E. (2003). Therapist self-disclosure: Research-based suggestions for practitioners. *Journal of Clinical Psychology, 59,* 529–539. http://dx.doi.org/10.1002/jclp.10157

Kokal, I., Engel, A., Kirschner, S., & Keysers, C. (2011). Synchronized drumming enhances activity in the caudate and facilitates prosocial commitment—if the rhythm comes easily. *PLoS ONE, 6*(11), e27272. http://dx.doi.org/10.1371/journal.pone.0027272

Koole, S. L., & Tschacher, W. (2016). Synchrony in psychotherapy: A review and an integrative framework for the therapeutic alliance. *Frontiers in Psychology, 7*(862), 862.

Krasner, M. S., Epstein, R. M., Beckman, H., Suchman, A. L., Chapman, B., Mooney, C. J., & Quill, T. E. (2009). Association of an educational program in mindful communication with burnout, empathy, and attitudes among primary care physicians. *JAMA, 302,* 1284–1293. http://dx.doi.org/10.1001/jama.2009.1384

Kristeller, J. L., & Quillian-Wolever, R. (2011). Mindfulness-based eating awareness training for treating binge eating disorder: The conceptual foundation. *Eating Disorders, 19,* 49–61.

Laukka, P., Linnman, C., Åhs, F., Pissiota, A., Frans, Ö., Faria, V., . . . Furmark, T. (2008). In a nervous voice: Acoustic analysis and perception of anxiety in social phobics' speech. *Journal of Nonverbal Behavior, 32,* 195–214. http://dx.doi.org/10.1007/s10919-008-0055-9

Lauwers, R. (2015). *The paradox of focus in therapeutic presence: Trust the back roads.* Unpublished manuscript.

Lazar, S. W., Kerr, C. E., Wasserman, R. H., Gray, J. R., Greve, D. N., Treadway, M. T., . . . Fischl, B. (2005). Meditation experience is associated with increased cortical thickness. *NeuroReport, 16*, 1893–1897. http://dx.doi.org/10.1097/01.wnr.0000186598.66243.19

Leahy, R. L. (2003). *Cognitive therapy techniques: A practitioner's guide.* New York, NY: Guilford Press.

Leigh, R., Oishi, K., Hsu, J., Lindquist, M., Gottesman, R. F., Jarso, S., . . . Hillis, A. E. (2013). Acute lesions that impair affective empathy. *Brain: A Journal of Neurology, 136*, 2539–2549. http://dx.doi.org/10.1093/brain/awt177

Lejuez, C. W., Hopko, D. R., Levine, S., Gholkar, R., & Collins, L. M. (2005). The therapeutic alliance in behavior therapy. *Psychotherapy: Theory, Research, Practice, Training, 42*, 456–468. http://dx.doi.org/10.1037/0033-3204.42.4.456

Levey, J., & Levey, M. (2015). *Mindfulness, meditation, and mind fitness.* San Francisco, CA: Conari Press.

Lévinas, E. (1985). *Ethics and infinity: Conversations with Philippe Nemo* (R. A. Cohen, Trans.). Pittsburgh, PA: Duquesne University Press.

Lieberman, M. D., Eisenberger, N. I., Crockett, M. J., Tom, S. M., Pfeifer, J. H., & Way, B. M. (2007). Putting feelings into words: Affect labeling disrupts amygdala activity in response to affective stimuli. *Psychological Science, 18*, 421–428. http://dx.doi.org/10.1111/j.1467-9280.2007.01916.x

Lietaer, G. (1993). Authenticity, congruence, and transparency. In D. Brazier (Ed.), *Beyond Carl Rogers* (pp. 17–46). London, England: Constable.

Lindenberger, U., Li, S. C., Gruber, W., & Müller, V. (2009). Brains swinging in concert: Cortical phase synchronization while playing guitar. *BMC Neuroscience, 10*, 22. http://dx.doi.org/10.1186/1471-2202-10-22

Linehan, M. M. (1993a). *Cognitive behavioral treatment for borderline personality disorder.* New York, NY: Guilford Press.

Linehan, M. M. (1993b). *Skills training manual for treating borderline personality disorder.* New York, NY: Guilford Press.

Llobera, J., Charbonnier, C., Chagué, S., Preissmann, D., Antonietti, J. P., Ansermet, F., & Magistretti, P. J. (2016). The subjective sensation of synchrony: An experimental study. *PLoS ONE, 11*(2), e0147008. http://dx.doi.org/10.1371/journal.pone.0147008

Lutz, A., Greischar, L. L., Rawlings, N. B., Ricard, M., & Davidson, R. J. (2004). Long-term meditators self-induce high-amplitude gamma synchrony during mental practice. *Proceedings of the National Academy of Sciences, USA, 101*, 16369–16373. http://dx.doi.org/10.1073/pnas.0407401101

Lutz, A., Jha, A. P., Dunne, J. D., & Saron, C. D. (2015). Investigating the phenomenological matrix of mindfulness-related practices from a neurocognitive perspective. *American Psychologist, 70*, 632–658. http://dx.doi.org/10.1037/a0039585

Lutz, A., Slagter, H. A., Dunne, J. D., & Davidson, R. J. (2008). Attention regulation and monitoring in meditation. *Trends in Cognitive Sciences, 12*(4), 163–169. http://dx.doi.org/10.1016/j.tics.2008.01.005

MacDonald, F. (2016, May 20). *Bright light at night time can seriously mess with your metabolism, study finds*. Retrieved from http://www.sciencealert.com/checking-your-phone-at-night-could-be-messing-with-your-metabolism

Mander, J., Kröger, P., Heidenreich, T., Flückiger, C., Lutz, W., Bents, H., & Barnow, S. (2015). The Process-Outcome Mindfulness Effects in Trainees (PrOMET) study: Protocol of a pragmatic randomized controlled trial. *BMC Psychology, 3*(1), 25. http://dx.doi.org/10.1186/s40359-015-0082-3

Marci, C. D., Ham, J., Moran, E., & Orr, S. P. (2007). Physiologic correlates of perceived therapist empathy and social-emotional process during psychotherapy. *Journal of Nervous and Mental Disease, 195*, 103–111. http://dx.doi.org/10.1097/01.nmd.0000253731.71025.fc

Marci, C. D., & Orr, S. P. (2006). The effect of emotional distance on psychophysiologic concordance and perceived empathy between patient and interviewer. *Applied Psychophysiology and Biofeedback, 31*, 115–128. http://dx.doi.org/10.1007/s10484-006-9008-4

Marlatt, G. A., Bowen, S., Chawla, N., & Witkiewitz, K. (2008). Mindfulness-based relapse prevention for substance abuse: Therapist training and therapeutic relationships. In S. F. Hick & T. Bien (Eds.), *Mindfulness and the therapeutic relationship* (pp. 107–121). New York, NY: Guilford Press.

Marlatt, G. A., & Miller, L. D. (2009, April). *Mindfulness-based relapse prevention*. Symposium conducted at the Faces Conference, San Diego, CA.

Marsh, K. L., Richardson, M. J., & Schmidt, R. C. (2009). Social connection through joint action and interpersonal coordination. *Topics in Cognitive Science, 1*, 320–339. http://dx.doi.org/10.1111/j.1756-8765.2009.01022.x

Martel, M.-E., Gagnon, J., Bourgault, M., & Dionne, F. (2016, June). *On being present in therapy: Validation of a French translation of the Therapeutic Presence Inventory*. Poster presented at the ACBS World Conference, Seattle, WA.

Matsumoto, D. (1989). Cultural influences on the perception of emotion. *Journal of Cross-Cultural Psychology, 20*, 92–105. http://dx.doi.org/10.1177/0022022189201006

May, R. (1958). Contributions to existential therapy. In R. May, E. Angel, & H. Ellenberger (Eds.), *Existence: A new dimension in psychiatry and psychology* (pp. 37–91). New York, NY: Basic Books. http://dx.doi.org/10.1037/11321-002

May, R. (1983). *The discovery of being: Writings in existential psychology*. New York, NY: W. W. Norton.

Mayes, C. (1998). The use of contemplative practices in teacher education. *Encounter: Education for Meaning and Social Justice, 11*(3), 17–31.

McDonough-Means, S. I., Kreitzer, M. J., & Bell, I. R. (2004). Fostering a healing presence and investigating its mediators. *Journal of Alternative and Complementary Medicine, 10*(Suppl. 1), S25–S41.

McFarland, D. H. (2001). Respiratory markers of conversational interaction. *Journal of Speech, Language, and Hearing Research, 44*, 128–143. http://dx.doi.org/10.1044/1092-4388(2001/012)

McGilchrist, I. (2010). Reciprocal organization of the cerebral hemispheres. *Dialogues in Clinical Neuroscience, 12*, 503–515.

McKay, M., Brantley, J., & Wood, J. (2007). *The dialectical behavior therapy skills workbook: Practical DBT exercises for learning mindfulness, interpersonal effectiveness, emotion regulation, and distress tolerance.* Oakland, CA: New Harbinger.

Mitchell, S. (2000). *Relationality: From attachment to intersubjectivity.* Hillsdale, NJ: Analytic Press.

Mitkidis, P., McGraw, J. J., Roepstorff, A., & Wallot, S. (2015). Building trust: Heart rate synchrony and arousal during joint action increased by public goods game. *Physiology & Behavior, 149*, 101–106. http://dx.doi.org/10.1016/j.physbeh.2015.05.033

Moore, A., & Malinowski, P. (2009). Meditation, mindfulness and cognitive flexibility. *Consciousness and Cognition, 18*(1), 176–186. http://dx.doi.org/10.1016/j.concog.2008.12.008

Moore, M. (2012, June 5). *Food energetics: Traditional Chinese Medicine's best kept secret.* Retrieved from http://www.mindbodygreen.com/0-5048/Food-Energetics-Traditional-Chinese-Medicines-Best-Kept-Secret.html

Mutschler, I., Reinbold, C., Wankerl, J., Seifritz, E., & Ball, T. (2013). Structural basis of empathy and the domain general region in the anterior insular cortex. *Frontiers in Human Neuroscience, 7*(177), 177.

Nangia, D., & Malhotra, R. (2012). Yoga, cognition, and mental health. *Journal of the Indian Academy of Applied Psychology, 38*, 262–269.

National Sleep Foundation. (2015). *Sleep disorder statistics.* Retrieved from http://www.statisticbrain.com/sleeping-disorder-statistics

Neff, K. (2011). *Self-compassion: The proven power of being kind to yourself.* New York, NY: HarperCollins.

Neff, K. D., Rude, S. S., & Kirkpatrick, D. (2007). An examination of self-compassion in relation to positive psychological functioning and personality traits. *Journal of Research in Personality, 41*, 908–916. http://dx.doi.org/10.1016/j.jrp.2006.08.002

Niedenthal, P. M. (2007). Embodying emotion. *Science, 316*, 1002–1005. http://dx.doi.org/10.1126/science.1136930

Norcross, J. C. (2011). *Psychotherapy relationships that work: Evidence based responsiveness* (2nd ed.). New York, NY: Oxford University Press. http://dx.doi.org/10.1093/acprof:oso/9780199737208.001.0001

Nuttall, J. (2000). Modes of therapeutic relationship in Kleinian psychotherapy. *British Journal of Psychotherapy, 17*(1), 17–36. http://dx.doi.org/10.1111/j.1752-0118.2000.tb00554.x

Oberman, L. M., Winkielman, P., & Ramachandran, V. S. (2007). Face to face: Blocking facial mimicry can selectively impair recognition of emotional expressions. *Social Neuroscience, 2*, 167–178. http://dx.doi.org/10.1080/17470910701391943

Ochsner, K. N., Bunge, S. A., Gross, J. J., & Gabrieli, J. D. E. (2002). Rethinking feelings: An fMRI study of the cognitive regulation of emotion. *Journal of Cognitive Neuroscience, 14*, 1215–1229. http://dx.doi.org/10.1162/089892902760807212

Oschman, J. L., Chevalier, G., & Brown, R. (2015). The effects of grounding (earthing) on inflammation, the immune response, wound healing, and prevention and treatment of chronic inflammatory and autoimmune diseases. *Journal of Inflammation Research, 8*, 83–96. http://dx.doi.org/10.2147/JIR.S69656

Ostaseski, F. (2012). *Five precepts*. Retrieved from http://www.mettainstitute.org/ProgramResources/MCS-2012/FiveServicePrecepts.pdf

Osterman, P., & Schwartz-Barcott, D. (1996). Presence: Four ways of being there. *Nursing Forum, 31*(2), 23–30. http://dx.doi.org/10.1111/j.1744-6198.1996.tb00490.x

Paladino, M. P., Mazzurega, M., Pavani, F., & Schubert, T. W. (2010). Synchronous multisensory stimulation blurs self-other boundaries. *Psychological Science, 21*, 1202–1207. http://dx.doi.org/10.1177/0956797610379234

Palmer, P. J. (1999). *Let your life speak*. San Francisco, CA: Jossey-Bass.

Parker, S. C., Nelson, B. W., Epel, E. S., & Siegel, D. J. (2015). The science of presence: A central mediator of the interpersonal benefits of mindfulness. In K. W. Brown, J. D. Creswell, & R. M. Ryan (Eds.), *Handbook of mindfulness: Theory, research, and practice* (pp. 225–244). New York, NY: Guilford Press.

Pascual-Leone, A., Nguyet, D., Cohen, L. G., Brasil-Neto, J. P., Cammarota, A., & Hallett, M. (1995). Modulation of muscle responses evoked by transcranial magnetic stimulation during the acquisition of new fine motor skills. *Journal of Neurophysiology, 74*, 1037–1045.

Perls, F. S. (1969). *Gestalt therapy verbatim*. Lafayette, CA: Real People Press.

Perls, F. S. (1970). Four lectures. In J. Fagan & I. L. Shepherd (Eds.), *Gestalt therapy now: Theory, techniques, and applications* (pp. 14–38). New York, NY: Harper Colophon.

Phillips, J. (2000). *God is at eye level: Photography as a healing art*. Wheaton, IL: The Theosophical Publishing House.

Porges, S. W. (1995). Orienting in a defensive world: Mammalian modifications of our evolutionary heritage. A polyvagal theory. *Psychophysiology, 32*, 301–318. http://dx.doi.org/10.1111/j.1469-8986.1995.tb01213.x

Porges, S. W. (1998). Love: An emergent property of the mammalian autonomic nervous system. *Psychoneuroendocrinology, 23*, 837–861. http://dx.doi.org/10.1016/S0306-4530(98)00057-2

Porges, S. W. (2003). Social engagement and attachment: A phylogenetic perspective. *Annals of the New York Academy of Sciences, 1008*, 31–47. http://dx.doi.org/10.1196/annals.1301.004

Porges, S. W. (2009). Reciprocal influences between body and brain in the perception and expression of affect: A polyvagal perspective. In D. Fosha, D. J. Siegel, & M. F. Solomon (Eds.), *The healing power of emotion: Affect neuroscience, development, and clinical practice*. New York, NY: W. W. Norton.

Porges, S. W. (2011). *The polyvagal theory: Neurophysiological foundations of emotions, attachment, communication, and self-regulation*. New York, NY: W. W. Norton.

Porges, S. W. (2015). Making the world safe for our children: Down-regulating defense and up-regulating social engagement to 'optimise' the human experience. *Children Australia, 40,* 114–123. http://dx.doi.org/10.1017/cha.2015.12

Porges, S., & Carter, S. (2014, June). *The polyvagal theory: The physiology of love and social behavior and clinical applications.* Lecture conducted at Leading Edge Seminars, Toronto, Ontario, Canada.

Pos, A., Geller, S., & Oghene, J. (2011, June). *Therapist presence, empathy, and the working alliance in experiential treatment for depression.* Paper presented at the meeting of the Society for Psychotherapy Research, Bern, Switzerland.

Powers, R. (1999). *Dangerous water: A biography of the boy who became Mark Twain.* Cambridge, MA: Da Capo Press.

Praszkier, R. (2016). Empathy, mirror neurons and SYNC. *Mind & Society, 15,* 1–25.

Purcell-Lee, C. R. (1999, June). *Some implications of the work of Martin Buber of psychotherapy.* Paper presented at the annual meeting of the Society for Psychotherapy Research, Braga, Portugal.

Quillman, T. (2012). Neuroscience and therapist self-disclosure: Deepening right brain to right brain communication between therapist and patient. *Clinical Social Work Journal, 40,* 1–9. http://dx.doi.org/10.1007/s10615-011-0315-8

Raab, K. (2014). Mindfulness, self-compassion, and empathy among health care professionals: A review of the literature. *Journal of Health Care Chaplaincy, 20,* 95–108. http://dx.doi.org/10.1080/08854726.2014.913876

Race, K. (2013). *Mindful parenting: Simple and powerful solutions for raising creative, engaged, happy kids in today's hectic world.* New York, NY: Macmillan.

Rainville, P., Bechara, A., Naqvi, N., & Damasio, A. R. (2006). Basic emotions are associated with distinct patterns of cardiorespiratory activity. *International Journal of Psychophysiology, 61,* 5–18. http://dx.doi.org/10.1016/j.ijpsycho.2005.10.024

Rakel, D. P., Hoeft, T. J., Barrett, B. P., Chewning, B. A., Craig, B. M., & Niu, M. (2009). Practitioner empathy and the duration of the common cold. *Family Medicine, 41,* 494–501.

Ramseyer, F., & Tschacher, W. (2011). Nonverbal synchrony in psychotherapy: Coordinated body movement reflects relationship quality and outcome. *Journal of Consulting and Clinical Psychology, 79,* 284–295. http://dx.doi.org/10.1037/a0023419

Ramseyer, F., & Tschacher, W. (2014). Nonverbal synchrony of head- and body-movement in psychotherapy: Different signals have different associations with outcome. *Frontiers in Psychology, 5*(979), 979.

Reed, R. G., Barnard, K., & Butler, E. A. (2015). Distinguishing emotional coregulation from codysregulation: An investigation of emotional dynamics and body weight in romantic couples. *Emotion, 15,* 45–60. http://dx.doi.org/10.1037/a0038561

Reik, T. (1948). *Listening with the third ear.* New York, NY: Farrar Straus.

Rice, L. N., & Kerr, G. (1986). Measures of client and therapist vocal quality. In L. Greenberg & W. Pinsoff (Eds.), *The psychotherapeutic process: A research handbook* (pp. 73–105). New York, NY: Guilford Press.

Richardson, M. J., Marsh, K. L., Isenhower, R. W., Goodman, J. R. L., & Schmidt, R. C. (2007). Rocking together: Dynamics of intentional and unintentional interpersonal coordination. *Human Movement Science, 26,* 867–891. http://dx.doi.org/10.1016/j.humov.2007.07.002

Rinpoche, S. (1992). *The Tibetan book of living and dying.* San Francisco, CA: Harper Collins.

Robbins, S. B., & Jolkovski, M. P. (1987). Managing countertransference feelings: An interactional model using awareness of feelings and theoretical framework. *Journal of Counseling Psychology, 34,* 276–282. http://dx.doi.org/10.1037/0022-0167.34.3.276

Rodgers, C. R., & Raider-Roth, M. B. (2006). Presence in teaching. *Teachers and Teaching: Theory and Practice, 12,* 265–287. http://dx.doi.org/10.1080/13450600500467548

Rogers, C. R. (1957). The necessary and sufficient conditions of therapeutic personality change. *Journal of Consulting Psychology, 21,* 95–103. http://dx.doi.org/10.1037/h0045357

Rogers, C. R. (1961). *On becoming a person.* Boston, MA: Houghton Mifflin.

Rogers, C. R. (1980). *A way of being.* Boston, MA: Houghton Mifflin.

Romanelli, A., Tishby, O., & Moran, G. (2015). *"Coming home to myself": A qualitative analysis of therapists' reports on changes in therapeutic presence following training in theatrical improvisation skills.* Unpublished manuscript.

Rosen, I. M., Gimotty, P. A., Shea, J. A., & Bellini, L. M. (2006). Evolution of sleep quantity, sleep deprivation, mood disturbances, empathy, and burnout among interns. *Academic Medicine, 81,* 82–85. http://dx.doi.org/10.1097/00001888-200601000-00020

Rotenstreich, N. (1967). The philosophy of Martin Buber. In P. A. Schlipp & M. S. Friedman (Eds.), *The library of living philosophers* (Vol. 12, pp. 97–132). Chicago, IL: Open Court.

Rozière, C. (2016). *The therapeutic presence during an osteopathic treatment.* Unpublished manuscript, Ecole Supérieure d'Ostéopathie, Paris, France.

Rueda, M. R., Posner, M. I., & Rothbart, M. K. (2005). The development of executive attention: Contributions to the emergence of self-regulation. *Developmental Neuropsychology, 28,* 573–594. http://dx.doi.org/10.1207/s15326942dn2802_2

Rumi, J. A. (1995). *The essential Rumi* (C. Barks, Trans.). New York, NY: HarperCollins.

Rushton, C. H., Sellers, D. E., Heller, K. S., Spring, S., Dossey, B. M., & Halifax, J. (2009). Impact of a contemplative end-of-life training program: Being with dying. *Palliative & Supportive Care, 7,* 405–414. http://dx.doi.org/10.1017/S1478951509990411

Safran, J. D., Crocker, P., McMain, S., & Murray, P. (1990, June). *The therapeutic alliance rupture resolution and nonresolution events.* Paper presented at the annual meeting of the Society for Psychotherapy Research, Berkeley, CA.

Safran, J. D., Muran, J. C., Samstag, L. W., & Stevens, C. (2002). Repairing alliance ruptures. In J. C. Norcross (Ed.), *Psychotherapy relationships that work.* New York, NY: Oxford University Press.

Salzberg, S. (1999). *A heart as wide as the world: Stories on the path of lovingkindness.* Boston, MA: Shambhala.

Salzberg, S. (2011). *Real happiness: The power of meditation: A 28-day program.* New York, NY: Workman.

Sänger, J., Müller, V., & Lindenberger, U. (2012). Intra- and interbrain synchronization and network properties when playing guitar in duets. *Frontiers in Human Neuroscience, 6*(312), 312.

Santorelli, S. (1999). *Heal thy self: Lessons on mindfulness in medicine.* New York, NY: Bell Tower.

Scherer, K. R., Johnstone, T., & Klasmeyer, G. (2003). Vocal expression of emotion. In R. J. Davidson, H. Goldsmith, & K. R. Scherer (Eds.), *Handbook of the affective sciences* (pp. 433–456). New York, NY: Oxford University Press.

Schmid, P. F. (2001). Authenticity: The person as his or her own author. In G. Wyatt (Ed.), *Rogers' therapeutic conditions: Evolution, theory and practice* (Vol. 1, pp. 213–228). Herefordshire, UK: PCCS Books.

Schmid, P. F. (2002). Presence: Im-media-te co-experiencing and co-responding: Phenomenological, dialogical and ethical perspectives on contact and perception in person-centred therapy and beyond. In G. Wyatt & P. Sanders (Eds.), *Rogers' Therapeutic Conditions: Evolution, theory and practice: Vol. 4. Contact and perception* (pp. 182–203). Ross-on-Wye, England: PCCS Books.

Schneider, K. (1994). Existential processes. In L. S. Greenberg, J. C. Watson, & G. Lietaer (Eds.), *Handbook of experiential psychotherapy* (pp. 103–120). New York, NY: Guilford Press.

Schneider, K., & Krug, O. T. (2009). *Existential–humanistic therapy.* Washington, DC: American Psychological Association.

Schore, A. N. (2003). *Affect dysregulation and disorders of the self.* New York, NY: W. W. Norton.

Schore, A. N. (2009). Right-brain affect regulation: An essential mechanism of development, trauma, dissociation, and psychotherapy. In D. Fosha, D. Siegel, & M. Solomon (Eds.), *The healing power of emotion: Affective neuroscience, development & clinical practice* (pp. 112–144). New York, NY: W. W. Norton.

Schore, A. N. (2012). *The science and art of psychotherapy.* New York, NY: W. W. Norton.

Schucman, H. (1976). *A course in miracles.* New York, NY: Viking.

Schwarz, N., Snir, S., & Regev, D. (2016). *The therapeutic presence of the art therapist.* Manuscript submitted for publication.

Segal, Z. V., Williams, J. M. G., & Teasdale, J. D. (2002). *Mindfulness-based cognitive therapy for depression.* New York, NY: Guilford Press.

Segrera, A. (2000, June). *Necessary and sufficient conditions.* Paper presented at ICCCEP Conference, Chicago, IL.

Sejnowski, T. J., & Tesauro, G. (1989). The Hebb rule for synaptic plasticity: Algorithms and implementations. In J. O. Byrne & W. O. Berry (Eds.), *Neural models of plasticity* (pp. 94–103). New York, NY: Academic Press. http://dx.doi.org/10.1016/B978-0-12-148955-7.50010-2

Shanafelt, T. D., Boone, S., Tan, L., Dyrbye, L. N., Sotile, W., Satele, D., . . . Oreskovich, M. R. (2012). Burnout and satisfaction with work-life balance among US physicians relative to the general US population. *Archives of Internal Medicine, 172,* 1377–1385. http://dx.doi.org/10.1001/archinternmed.2012.3199

Shapiro, S. L., & Carlson, L. E. (2009). *The art and science of mindfulness: Integrating mindfulness into psychology and the helping professions.* Washington, DC: American Psychological Association. http://dx.doi.org/10.1037/11885-000

Siegel, D. J. (2007). *The mindful brain: Reflection and attunement in the cultivation of well-being.* New York, NY: W. W. Norton.

Siegel, D. J. (2010). *The mindful therapist: A clinician's guide to mindsight and neural integration.* New York, NY: W. W. Norton.

Siegel, D. J. (2011). *Mindsight: The new science of personal transformation.* New York, NY: Bantam Books.

Siegel, D. J. (2013). *Brainstorm: The power and purpose of the teenage brain.* New York, NY: Penguin.

Siegel, D. J., & Bryson, T. P. (2012). *The whole brain child: 12 revolutionary strategies to nurture your child's developing mind.* New York, NY: Bantam Books.

Silsbee, D. (2008). *Presence-based coaching: Cultivating self-generative leaders through mind, body, and heart.* San Francisco, CA: Jossey-Bass.

Solloway, S. (2000). Contemplative practitioners: Presence or the project of thinking gaze differently. *Encounter: Education for Meaning and Social Justice, 13*(3), 30–42.

Stellar, J. E., Cohen, A., Oveis, C., & Keltner, D. (2015). Affective and physiological responses to the suffering of others: Compassion and vagal activity. *Journal of Personality and Social Psychology, 108,* 572–585. http://dx.doi.org/10.1037/pspi0000010

Stern, D. (1985). *The interpersonal world of the infant.* New York, NY: Basic Books.

Stern, D. (2004). *The present moment in psychotherapy and everyday life.* New York, NY: W. W. Norton.

Stiffleman, S. (2015). *Parenting with presence: Practices for raising conscious, confident, caring kids.* Novato, CA: New World Library.

Surrey, J. L., & Kramer, G. (2013). Relational mindfulness. In G. K. Germer, R. D. Siegel, & P. R. Fulton (Eds.), *Mindfulness and psychotherapy* (2nd ed., pp. 94–111). New York, NY: Guilford Press.

Sweet, M., & Johnson, C. (1990). Enhancing empathy: The interpersonal implications of a Buddhist Meditation Technique. *Psychotherapy: Theory, Research, Practice, Training, 27*, 19–29. http://dx.doi.org/10.1037/0033-3204.27.1.19

Sze, J. A., Gyurak, A., Yuan, J. W., & Levenson, R. W. (2010). Coherence between emotional experience and physiology: Does body awareness training have an impact? *Emotion, 10*, 803–814. http://dx.doi.org/10.1037/a0020146

Thompson, W. F., & Schlaug, G. (2015). Music can heal the brain. *Scientific American, 26*(2), 32–39.

Thomson, R. F. (2000). Zazen and psychotherapeutic presence. *American Journal of Psychotherapy, 54*, 531–548.

Tracy, J. L., & Matsumoto, D. (2008). The spontaneous expression of pride and shame: Evidence for biologically innate nonverbal displays. *Proceedings of the National Academy of Sciences, USA, 105*, 11655–11660. http://dx.doi.org/10.1073/pnas.0802686105

Tschacher, W., & Bergomi, C. (2011). *The implications of embodiment: Cognition and communication.* Exeter, England: Imprint Academic.

Valdesolo, P., & DeSteno, D. (2011). Synchrony and the social tuning of compassion. *Emotion, 11*, 262–266. http://dx.doi.org/10.1037/a0021302

Valente, V., & Marotta, A. (2005). The impact of yoga on the professional and personal life of the psychotherapist. *Contemporary Family Therapy, 27*, 65–80. http://dx.doi.org/10.1007/s10591-004-1971-4

Valentine, E., & Sweet, P. (1999). Meditation and attention: A comparison of the effects of concentrative and mindfulness meditation on sustained attention. *Mental Health, Religion & Culture, 2*, 59–70. http://dx.doi.org/10.1080/13674679908406332

Van der Kolk, B. (2014). *The body keeps the score: Brain, mind, and body in the healing of trauma.* New York, NY: Penguin.

van Dernoot Lipsky, L. (2009). *Trauma stewardship: An everyday guide to caring for self while caring for others.* San Francisco, CA: Berret-Koehler.

Vlemincx, E., Abelson, J. L., Lehrer, P. M., Davenport, P. W., Van Diest, I., & Van den Bergh, O. (2013). Respiratory variability and sighing: A psychophysiological reset model. *Biological Psychology, 93*, 24–32. http://dx.doi.org/10.1016/j.biopsycho.2012.12.001

Vlemincx, E., Van Diest, I., & Van den Bergh, O. (2015). Emotion, sighing, and respiratory variability. *Psychophysiology, 52*, 657–666. http://dx.doi.org/10.1111/psyp.12396

Waddington, L. (2002). The therapy relationship in cognitive therapy: A review. *Behavioural and Cognitive Psychotherapy, 30*, 179–192. http://dx.doi.org/10.1017/S1352465802002059

Walsch, N. D. (1996). *Conversations with God: An uncommon dialogue, book 1*. New York, NY: G. P. Putnam's Sons.

Warner, R. M. (1996). Coordinated cycles in behavior and physiology during face-to-face social interactions. In J. H. Watt & C. A. VanLear (Eds.), *Cycles and dynamic patterns in communication processes* (pp. 327–352). Newbury Park, CA: Sage.

Watson, J. C. (2007). Facilitating empathy. *European Psychotherapy, 7*, 61–76.

Watson, J. C., Greenberg, L. S., & Lietaer, G. (1998). The experiential paradigm unfolding: Relationship and experiencing in therapy. In L. S. Greenberg, J. C. Watson, & G. Lietaer (Eds.), *Handbook of experiential psychotherapy* (pp. 3–27). New York, NY: Guilford Press.

Watts, A. W. (2011). *The wisdom of insecurity: A message for an age of anxiety*. New York, NY: Vintage Books.

Watts, J., Cockcroft, K., & Duncan, N. (2009). *Developmental psychology*. Cape Town, South Africa: UCT Press.

Welwood, J. (1996). Reflection and presence: The dialectic of self-knowledge. *Journal of Transpersonal Psychology, 28*, 107–128.

Welwood, J. (2000). *Toward a psychology of awakening: Buddhism, psychotherapy, and the path of personal and spiritual transformation*. Boston, MA: Shambhala.

Wiens, S. (2005). Interoception in emotional experience. *Current Opinion in Neurology, 18*, 442–447. http://dx.doi.org/10.1097/01.wco.0000168079.92106.99

Wiklund Gustin, L., & Wagner, L. (2013). The butterfly effect of caring—clinical nursing teachers' understanding of self-compassion as a source to compassionate care. *Scandinavian Journal of Caring Sciences, 27*, 175–183. http://dx.doi.org/10.1111/j.1471-6712.2012.01033.x

Williams, L. E., Bargh, J. A., Nocera, C. C., & Gray, J. R. (2009). The unconscious regulation of emotion: Nonconscious reappraisal goals modulate emotional reactivity. *Emotion, 9*, 847–854. http://dx.doi.org/10.1037/a0017745

Wiltermuth, S. S., & Heath, C. (2009). Synchrony and cooperation. *Psychological Science, 20*, 1–5.

Winkelman, M. (2003). Complementary therapy for addiction: "Drumming out drugs." *American Journal of Public Health, 93*, 647–651. http://dx.doi.org/10.2105/AJPH.93.4.647

Winnicott, D. W. (1960). The theory of the parent-infant relationship. *The International Journal of Psychoanalysis, 41*, 585–595.

Winnicott, D. W. (1969). The use of an object. *The International Journal of Psychoanalysis, 50*, 711–716.

Wyatt, G. (2000, June). *Presence: Bringing together the core conditions*. Paper presented at ICCCEP Conference, Chicago, IL.

Yang, C., Barrós-Loscertales, A., Pinazo, D., Ventura-Campos, N., Borchardt, V., Bustamante, J.-C., . . . Walter, M. (2016). State and training effects of mindfulness meditation on brain networks reflect neuronal mechanisms of its antidepressant effect. *Neural Plasticity*, (9504642). Advance online publication.

Yontef, G. (2005). Gestalt therapy theory of change. In A. L. Woldt & S. M. Toman (Eds.), *Gestalt therapy: History, theory, and practice* (pp. 81–100). Thousand Oaks, CA: Sage. http://dx.doi.org/10.4135/9781452225661.n5

Yu, N. (2009). *The Chinese HEART in a cognitive perspective: Culture, body, and language.* Berlin, Germany: Mouton de Gruyter. http://dx.doi.org/10.1515/9783110213348

Zuckerman, M., Larrance, D. T., Spiegel, N. H., & Klorman, R. (1981). Controlling nonverbal displays: Facial expressions and tone of voice. *Journal of Experimental Social Psychology, 17,* 506–524. http://dx.doi.org/10.1016/0022-1031(81)90037-8

Zylowska, L. (2012). *The mindfulness prescription for adult ADHD: An 8-step program for strengthening attention, managing emotions, and achieving your goals.* Boston, MA: Trumpeter Books.

# INDEX

# ABOUT THE AUTHOR

**Shari M. Geller, PhD,** is an author, clinical psychologist, and supervisor with a commitment to mindfulness practices and a passion for rhythm and drumming. Dr. Geller has been practicing mindfulness since 1990 and weaves Buddhist philosophy and rhythm-based work into her life and clinical practice. She has been involved in researching, writing, and training in therapeutic presence as a foundational approach to optimizing health care and therapeutic relationships. Dr. Geller coauthored (with Leslie Greenberg) the book *Therapeutic Presence: A Mindful Approach to Effective Therapy*. She has released a companion CD on cultivating presence, with guided practices using the healing power of music and the health benefits of mindfulness. In collaboration with the American Psychological Association she has also released a training video for therapeutic presence. Dr. Geller has a clinical and supervisory practice in Toronto and Grey-Bruce County. Her training with teachers and neuroscientists, along with her personal practice, inspired her to integrate the benefits of mindfulness, group drumming, and emotion-focused awareness into one comprehensive program, Therapeutic Rhythm and Mindfulness (TRM), to cultivate presence. Dr. Geller serves on the teaching faculty in health psychology at York University and for the Applied Mindfulness Meditation program at the University of Toronto, and she is adjunct professor in the Faculty of Music at the University of Toronto, in association with Music and Health Research Collaboratory. She is the codirector of the Centre for MindBody Health, offering mindfulness and compassion-based treatment and professional training.